*To Clare
my far.*

# KIPHUTH OF YALE
## A SWIMMING DYNASTY

*Love
Pop*

# KIPHUTH OF YALE
## A SWIMMING DYNASTY

Peter E. Kennedy, Ph.D

Kiphuth of Yale
A Swimming Dynasty
ISBN# 978-0-692-66097-3

Copyright © 2017 by Peter E. Kennedy, Ph.D.

All rights reserved
Printed in the United States of America
First Edition

*Cover photo (pool image): Mark Zurolo, Yale '01 MFA*

*To my wife of 51 years, Barbara,
who supported me through this labor of love.*

*To my daughter Leigh Ann Kennedy, J.D., who sat patiently beside me
as my editor and advisor.*

*To all of the swimmers I was privileged to compete with and against;
to all the swimmers I was privileged to coach; and to all the coaches
I was privileged to call my colleagues.*

# Contents

*Preface* .................................................................... *ix*
*Acknowledgments* ................................................. *xiii*

**The Man and His Image** ................................................ 1

**The Culture of His Youth: 1890-1914** ......................... 13

**From Tonawanda to New Haven** ................................ 15

**Collegiate and AAU Swimming at the Turn of the Twentieth Century** ........................................................ 19

**Kiphuth to the Helm** ..................................................... 23
    *The Road to Professionalism* ...................................28

**Kiphuth Among the Puritans** ..................................... 31

**The World, Yale, and Kiphuth: 1914-1918** ............... 33

**Kiphuth's Dry Land Program** ..................................... 37

**Building Yale's Legacy** ................................................. 43
    *The World, Yale, and Kiphuth: 1918-1929* .............43
    *Kiphuth's 1919-1929 Seasons* ..................................45

**The Yale Swimming Carnival** .................................... 51

**The Beloved Gymnasium** ............................................ 53

**The World, Yale, Kiphuth, and the Great Depression** ................ 59
    *Kiphuth in the 1930s* ...............................................60

**Kiphuth's Philosophy of Athletics** ............................ 67

**Man of Taste, Man of Letters** .................................... 73

**The World, Yale, and Kiphuth: 1941-1950** ............... 79
    *Personal Tragedy Strikes* .........................................80
    *An Epoch of Victory* .................................................82

The Panamanian – Alan Ford ................................................. 83
  Kiphuth's Post War Years ....................................................... 85

**Yale's Finest Team – The Class of 1953** ........................................ 87

**Kiphuth International** ........................................................ 101
  International Recognition ..................................................... 101
  Japan Re-enters the World Scene ............................................... 113

**The Olympic Experience** ...................................................... 129
  1928 Olympics: Amsterdam, The Netherlands ..................................... 129
  1932 Olympics: Los Angeles, California, U.S.A. ................................ 130
  1936 Olympics: Berlin, Germany ................................................ 131
  1940 and 1944 Olympics become 1948 Olympics:
    London, England ............................................................. 135
  1952 Olympics: Helsinki, Finland .............................................. 136
  1956 Olympics: Melbourne, Australia ........................................... 137
  1960 Olympics: Rome, Italy .................................................... 137

**An Analytical Mind** .......................................................... 139

**Kiphuth's Irish Staff** ....................................................... 145
  Harry Burke ................................................................... 145
  Phil Moriarty ................................................................. 147
  Bobbie Higgins Dawson ......................................................... 148

**Kiphuth and *Swimming World Magazine*** ....................................... 153

**The Swimmers Speak** .......................................................... 157

**Man of Criticism** ............................................................ 163

**Farewell to Team Yale: 1954-1959** ............................................ 169

**The Final Yale Years** ........................................................ 173
  Kiphuth's Navy ROTC Team: 1959-1960 ........................................... 173

**The End of an Era** ........................................................... 177

**Afterward: My Journey to the Castle within the
Kingdom (Bob and Me)** ......................................................... 181

# Preface

To write a book about Robert John Herman Kiphuth has been a dream of mine for many years. Part of the origins of that dream can be traced back to 1973, with the publication of my doctoral dissertation on Kiphuth, completed at The Ohio State University. Two members of my doctoral committee were former OSU swim coach Dr. Bruce Bartels and former OSU professor and diver Dr. Donald Harper, both men who knew Kiphuth personally.

Kiphuth's contributions to swimming and to humanity were almost limitless. The number of people whose lives he influenced is impossible to ascertain. Therefore, the biggest challenge I faced in writing this biography was setting its parameters. I could only hope to follow the most important avenues of his life. In Kiphuth's case those avenues were wide and varied. The book, as it stands, is a true account of the life of one of the most extraordinary people in the history of Yale University, collegiate swimming, and international swimming.

In researching Kiphuth's life, I was challenged at every step. He was incredibly active throughout his life and his actions touched many people and institutions.

Moreover, the journey through the pathways of Kiphuth's life instilled in me a new appreciation for not only the performing arts, but also the fine arts, of the first half of the 20th century. In addition, the search revealed the dynamic history and evolution of collegiate and international swimming, disclosing as well certain niche elements of American history.

For example, the Tonawanda City Directory reawakened in me an enthusiasm about the history of the Erie Canal and the subsequent migration to the Niagara frontier. The *YMCA 1000 Strong* document re-emphasized the powerful influence the YMCA organization had on the youth of yesteryear. Research on the Twentieth Century Club aroused an interest in the development of the women's clubs and activities of women at the turn of the century. A review of George Wilson Pierson's two-volume work, *Yale College 1871-1937*, Brooks Mather Kelley's *Yale: A History* and Yale's *Presidential Reports* revealed an intriguing look at the university's past. What I felt was an extensive personal knowledge of the history of competitive swimming seemed insignificant in relation to the knowledge gained from a comprehensive study of William Deegan's *Yale Swimming 1899–1948*, the Robert Nelson Corwin Papers (Yale University Library Manuscripts and Archives), the *Yale Swimming News Letter*, the *New York Times*, the *Yale Daily News* from 1900-1967, the *Intercollegiate Swimming Guide* during the same period, and personal interviews with Kiphuth's former professional associates such as Karl Michael, Phil Moriarty, Harry Burke, Gordon Chalmers, and Ed Kennedy.

Gwyneth Brown, wife of sport sculptor Joseph Brown, added a female perspective and a further in-depth analysis of Kiphuth's love of dance. Olga Maynard, *American Modern Dancers-The Pioneers*, and Walter Terry, *The Dance in America*, became major sources for educating the uneducated about the early pioneers of American dance. I found I had to either read or reread the history of the arts in order to stay abreast of Kiphuth's artistic tastes. I took a refresher course by reading Frederic A. Conningham's *Currier and Ives Prints: An Illustrated Checklist* (1930) and by reviewing the New York: Gallery of Modern Arts' *George Bellows; Paintings, Drawings, Lithographs* (1966).

Testimony by Meta Gangwish, Kiphuth's sister, and by DeLaney Kiphuth, the subject's son, provided me with insight into the more personal aspects of Kiphuth's life. Personal remembrances of Kiphuth, as well as letters we exchanged, allowed me a greater flexibility of introspection, especially during interviews.

Kiphuth's own writings unveiled the details of his professional interests. More importantly, his writings in the *Yale Daily News* and various quotations attributed to him in the *Boston Transcript*, the *Hawaii Advertiser*, the *New York Times*, *Amateur Athlete*, the *Literary Digest*, and others, supported the oral testimony of colleagues with respect to his philosophy of physical education and athletics.

Additional information resulted from the examination of past and present sources on swimming such as Ralph Thomas's *Swimming* (1904), Richard Francis Nelligan's *The Art of Swimming* (1906), François Oppenheim's *The History of Swimming* (1971), as well as reports by Yale University swimming managers and various Yale scrapbooks.

Time passes quickly, family comes first, and the opportunity to write this book seemed most improbable until Tim Jecko, a former Yale swimmer and 1956 Olympian, contacted me in 2000 about his interest in writing a book on Kiphuth. I had trained with Tim prior to the 1956 Detroit Olympic Trials.

Tim, a graduate of Yale's Drama School, had gone on to become a Broadway actor. According to the Washington Post, he performed "in *Annie* and *Woman of the Year* with Raquel Welch...appeared in prime-time and daytime television programs," and later became deputy director of performing arts for the Smithsonian Institution. At the Smithsonian he "developed national and international performances, including U.S. entries in the cultural festival of the 1968 Olympic Games in Mexico City."

He was diagnosed with Lou Gehrig's disease in June of 2003, and died on January 11, 2005. Prior to Tim's death, he, John Hanley, a former Springfield College swimmer and UCLA professor, and Olympian Jeff Farrell had put together an incredible 34-page book proposal: *Kiphuth: A Mighty Fortress*. Unfortunately, the years passed too swiftly and no publisher was found. With the subsequent death of Hanley, the project was stalled.

In 2010, I reconnected with Olympian Jeff Farrell and joined an on-line forum for discussing Yale swimming lore, where I was again inspired to take up this writing project.

# Acknowledgments

I would like to acknowledge and extend my heartfelt gratitude to the following individuals:

Sean Kennedy (my son), M.A., Boston College, who inspired me to be less technical and instead tell the story, and for his assistance with the final layout of this book.

Amanda Byler (my granddaughter) B.J., University of Missouri School of Journalism, and social media intern at the University of Louisville athletic department, who provided editorial advice.

Joshua Poe (my grandson), Regina High School (Iowa City, IA) class of 2020, who designed the front cover.

Dave Ross, University of Iowa swimmer, class of 1984, for his advice, encouragement, and for designing the back cover collage.

Sandy Thatcher, Princeton class of 1965, to whom I will be eternally grateful for his honest critique of the original manuscript.

Julie Checkoway, author of *The Three Year Swim Club*. My conversations and e-mails with Julie reinforced my belief that both the written and oral history of swimming have been neglected.

Jeff Farrell, NROTC Yale team and Olympic gold medalist, for his encouragement and for providing material pertinent to the writing of the book.

Tim Jecko, Olympian, Yale class of 1959 and John Hanley, former British Olympic swimmer and UCLA professor of psychiatry and biobehavioral sciences, for their informative 32 page book proposal.

The following Kiphuth swimmers who provided invaluable contributions and insights: John McGill, Syracuse University and NROTC Yale team; Peter Parsons, Yale class of 1960 and author; Jimmy McLane, Olympic gold medalist and Yale class of 1953; Don Sheff, Yale class of 1953; and Rex Aubrey, Australian Olympic swimmer and Yale class of 1957. A special thank you to the Yale swimmers, too numerous to mention, who shared their warm memories of Bob.

George Breen, Olympic bronze medalist 1956 and 1960, world record holder, Cortland State University and Indiana University, for his personal recollections.

John Lapides, Yale class of 1972 and past president of the Yale Swimming and Diving Association from 1982 to 2011, for sharing the Hawaii scrap books and for his introduction to Michael Lotstein.

Michael Lotstein, Head of University Archives, Yale University, for his invaluable contributions and support.

Bruce Wigo, International Swimming Hall of Fame, for his assistance, advice, and encouragement.

Annie Grevers at *Swimming World* magazine for her assistance and support.

Nicholas Jallat, Messiah College (Pa.), Yale sports publicity intern, for his interest in and research for this project.

Tru Art Color Graphics, Iowa City, Iowa, for assistance with the layout of this book.

ROBERT J H KIPHUTH

## The Man and His Image

In 1914, Yale University hired a mite of a man, physically only five feet, five inches tall, with, as Cecil Colwin described him, a "bullet head, bull shoulders and booming baritone voice," as an instructor in physical education. Robert John Herman Kiphuth, a dynamic, self-educated intellectual, capable of exploiting his charisma, over time played a key and unique role in sports administration, coordination, and politics.

He was the pioneer who opened the doors of administrative and political arenas to the swimming coach. He accomplished this by utilizing the prestige of his position at Yale, his administrative ability, and his cultural and intellectual capacities to create a highly respected personal image. As a result, he redefined the concept that a swimming coach was a "dressing-gown-clad 'baths-bum,'" a mere trainer that should be seen and not heard by the administrative elements in swimming. Instead, he presented the new image of a modern, well-dressed, and knowledgeable coach to the sports world.

With Yale as his revered mother and the Gothic Payne Whitney Gymnasium his cathedral, Robert J. H. Kiphuth was not only a cultured intellectual man of charm, but also a human dynamo of activity who demanded respect and loyalty for Mother Yale. Protocol was a major precept of his very being, but he loved the informality of social intercourse within the Gymnasium. To some he was a tyrant, to others an esteemed god, and yet to most, and to those who knew and understood him best, he was just "Bob." Nonetheless, as Cecil Colwin stated, "on a campus of world famous scholars and sportsmen he was 'Mr. Yale.'"

He created a unique and colorful dynasty. But then again, the man himself was unique and colorful. His span of activity at Yale was 53 years, but his impact was world-wide, influencing generations yet unborn. Though, fundamentally, he slaved for Mother Yale, the world was his domain.

His tenure at Yale, from 1914 until his death in 1967, included duties as instructor of physical education, swimming coach, director of the Payne Whitney Gymnasium, director of athletics, and, in retirement, lecturer in physical education. During these years he acquired a reputation as philosopher, art connoisseur, scholar, and teacher.

The Rev. Sidney Lovett, renowned Yale chaplain, stated that Kiphuth was a "carnivorous reader," capable of holding his own with faculty "especially in literature and art." Both Lovett and art professor Deane Keller (responsible for the identification, return, and restoration of stolen Italian art during World War II) agreed that, as a result, Kiphuth was one of "the best known, most respected, and most loved 'professors' on campus."

Kiphuth's passion for the arts was in no way limited to book knowledge. He was a voracious consumer of the popular arts and culture of the time, from theatre and dance to film and the fine arts.

Kiphuth augmented this cultural expertise with impeccable manners and a perceptive taste for fashion. Fully aware of the status of his position, his personal dignity and uncompromising respect for Mother Yale dictated the decorum, propriety, and etiquette of both his behavior and mode of dress. Although inherently attentive to the formality of social dress, Kiphuth allowed himself the pleasure of the latest campus fashions. As John Knowles mentioned in the *Saturday Evening Post* "[although] he attired himself like a Wall Street Banker...sometimes (he) dressed like an Ivy League student, with bright bow tie, buckskin shoes, tweed jacket, and grey flannel slacks." According to Betty Philcox, the first woman president of an AAU association and a National AAU official, "Kiphuth was always fashionably dressed, meticulously polite, and a perfect gentleman at all times."

Kiphuth combined his broad cultural interests with an active social life. He possessed a tremendous enthusiasm for everyone and everything. He was not a dilettante but an enthusiast and student in everything he did. The generation gap never existed for him because he cultivated the latest campus fads in dress, entertainment, intellectual, and social habits. Each Sunday afternoon, prior to his wife's death in 1941, he and Louise entertained numerous swimmers and other guests with food and conversation.

Dr. Roswell Gallagher, credited for shaping the field of adolescent medicine into a recognized discipline, recalled Kiphuth's "inexhaustible supply of enthusiasm, his wide variety of interests, his sincere enjoyment of people, how unselfish he was about his time." Due to his disdain for the "front office block," his door was always open. Kiphuth's former assistant and later the coach at Dartmouth, Karl Michael, said that Kiphuth was a person with a genuine interest in youth, without a selfish motive, and a man doing it "out of the love of his own heart."

A journey across campus with Kiphuth at the helm was a memorable excursion. The postman, the policeman, the shoe shine boy, a passing derelict, a beautiful woman, the Ivy-suited or unkempt student, the professor of history, art, or philosophy, the riotous or vanquished child, the stray animal, the singing bird, or the returning alumni, never escaped the piercing analysis of a Kiphuth dictum. Mixed amid the warm greetings and humorous exchanges were prolific observations and dialogs about life, people, and the American system. Wherever he went, people knew him and he knew them. Lunches, dinners, and late evening snacks found him exchanging warm greetings, witticisms, and gossip with countermen, waitresses, or managers. He possessed an honest curiosity in all things and all people. Charles Loftus, Yale's highly regarded sports information director, proclaimed Kiphuth was, "Yale's version of the lovable Mr. Chips." A conversation with Kiphuth was a vivid and unforgettable experience. The words and expressions flowed fluently while his facial commentary enlivened the moment with lasting significance. The raised eyebrow, the dilated eyes, the lolling chin, the disgust or the humor, the questioning or the answering were all part of his charismatic persona.

He could converse in the language of kings or serfs. With one brief utterance he could charm the ladies or disarm the men. With a gracious flow of words he captivated one for life. His style was a unique combination of intelligence, alterability of topic, and variations of tempo, mingled with expressive innuendos.

Although a bona fide conversationalist, he had a most attentive ear. Curiosity dictated the probing manner of his ways. If one's interest differed from his own, he questioned incessantly. The interest was another's, but he wanted to share the experience.

As Kiphuth concentrated deeply while in conversation, one could not help but observe the absent-minded massaging of his hands. Unbeknown to most, Kiphuth suffered from severe arthritis, something he never mentioned or allowed to limit his activities.

Kiphuth's charm and grace made him easily approachable to student, colleague, or employee outside of the working relationship. Initially, though, the magnitude of his very presence could overpower anyone unfamiliar with the fact that once Kiphuth passed through the portals of the Payne Whitney, this was his castle and he was king. His very manner demanded that his staff exhibit ordinary common sense and adhere to the basic rules of protocol. Incompetence and laziness were cardinal sins. South African swimming coach and historian Cecil Colwin portrayed Kiphuth as "perpetual motion personified," a man who "took only four hours sleep every night." He further described Kiphuth as "a pocket battleship of a man" who packed "a lot of power into everything he thought did or said."

Often times, the slow-to-learn, or those choosing not to remember, felt the sting of a Kiptonian edict. Yet, on many occasions, Kiphuth chose to make his point by requesting someone else have an employee report to his office. According to legend, he pretended to be in deep concentration over a book he was reading while the offending party fidgeted and waited. The protocol of the day required that one not interrupt but wait for acknowledgment. An hour or more could pass before Kiphuth would utter "yes?" No further word was needed; the employee knew Kiphuth was aware of his shortcoming.

On one occasion, former employee Dick Steadman laughingly recalled a similar experience. Reporting to the fifth floor office, he found Kiphuth seemingly absorbed in a book. Not being acknowledged, Steadman selected a book from the shelf and, as Kiphuth read, Steadman read. After about an hour and a half, Kiphuth finally said, "Well, what is it?" Both had won their point.

The gym staff, as well as swimmers, often joked about the legendary Kiphuth key ring. This ring held dozens of keys through which he juggled and fiddled his way until he found the right one. Mostly untagged, they were unidentifiable except to him. Though the gym staff believed most were obsolete, Kiphuth would not throw any away, for these were the keys to his Kingdom.

Kiphuth's two modes of transportation were his English bicycle and his Jaguar. Ignoring the common rules of courtesy, he rode both with reckless abandonment and total disdain, ignoring pedestrian and vehicle alike. Indeed it was a sight to see the bespectacled Kiphuth advancing on his journey to the gym by maneuvering his bicycle between anyone and anything remotely in his way, gesturing on occasion with his arm as if conducting the Philharmonic Orchestra or singing a verse from a recent Broadway musical. There existed no doubt as to his ability to enjoy the simple pleasures of life. On bicycle or in car, he would test the limits of New Haven traffic laws before finally cruising up onto the wide sidewalk in front of the gym, ready for work.

Former Yale football coach Carmen Cozza recalled riding with Kiphuth in the Jaguar. "Kiphuth was known to be a speed demon. Although he was in total control, riding with him was always hair-raising. I rode with him once and that was enough!" Joe Koletsky, class of 1959, drove with Kiphuth on his return trip from the nationals and recalled how Kiphuth "destroyed a poor chicken trying to cross the road," after which Kiphuth "ranted and railed for miles about how much the repairs to his front grill would cost." Navy swimmer John McGill remembered a return trip from an exhibition at Kiphuth's granddaughter's summer camp in Maine. Kiphuth requested that McGill drive. From the moment McGill took the

> **Sight Set on the Finish**
>
> *I fondly remember two 21-hour, non-stop trips from New Haven to Indianapolis to the Outdoor AAU nationals in 1953 and 1954. As I tried to stay calm in the front seat, Kiphuth ignored all speed limits posted on the Merritt Parkway, the George Washington Bridge, the New Jersey Turnpike, the Pennsylvania Turnpike, and even on the narrow bridge crossing into West Virginia, and the ensuing two lane roads to Indianapolis.*
>
> *My revenge came in the summer of 1958. Prior to the team's departure to the Indianapolis Broad Ripple pool, Kiphuth handed me the keys to a Yale station wagon, as I was now one of the older competitors. The return trip turned into a challenge for the swimmers in my vehicle. Could we dare to race the master to the finish line? Adopting all of Kiphuth's methods of "gas, pee, and eat" almost simultaneously, victory was ours! Kiphuth, in line with his competitive nature, never seemed to recall this episode.*

wheel, Kiphuth "egged him on unmercifully to drive faster." But McGill "refused to take the bait."

Kiphuth was a doer, not a procrastinator. The time was now. Later was too late. The event, the person, or the performance was the prime consideration. Everything else was secondary. Distance, time, price, and availability of tickets were all inconsequential. He loved people and performances, but he loved best the performing people. He was as equally at home in the arena of the performing arts as he was in the arena of sport. Louis Armstrong, Ethel Merman, Rex Harrison, and other artists commanded the same attention and analysis as Olympic figure-skater Dick Button, boxer Joe Lewis, or runner Wes Santee.

One time in the 1950s, when Santee was the premier miler, George Kellog, the admissions director at Hotchkiss Preparatory School, mentioned that he would love to see Santee run. Kiphuth reacted with information that Santee was running that weekend in Dayton, Ohio. In a few moments, a car was seen speeding through the Connecticut countryside with Kiphuth at the wheel, his son DeLaney and Kellog as passengers. They arrived in time to see the Santee mile, then directly returned to Hotchkiss.

On another occasion, Kiphuth and his assistant Phil Moriarty and coach-in-residence Peter Daland were discussing the upcoming Ohio State vs. Michigan dual swimming meet. At Kiphuth's insistence, they departed late Friday afternoon arriving in Columbus with just enough time to enjoy Ohio State coach Mike Peppe's offer of a steam bath, shower, and a place to rest prior to the commencement of the scheduled meet. Promptly at the conclusion of the meet, they paid their respects to Peppe and Michigan coach Matt Mann and departed for New Haven with Kiphuth at the wheel.

Athletic events and athletes outside of swimming were an important part of Kiphuth's life. Yale football, baseball, hockey, crew, fencing, and track commanded a great deal of his time. He often followed the track team and other sports to away events. Caldwell B. Esselstyn, Jr., M.D., a member of Yale's 1956 Olympic Gold Medal crew team remembered seeing Kiphuth at the Olympic crew race in Australia. "With the Australian loss the crowd was hushed and one familiar voice rang out, 'Es!' It was Bob Kiphuth…who had taken the train from Melbourne to Ballarat to see the race."

Among the more notable athletes who captured his attention were: track and field stars Wes Santee, Jesse Owens, Paavo Nurmi, Bob Mathias, Billy Mills, Emil Zatopek, and Parry O'Brien; gymnast Takashi Ono and Vera Caslavsko; figure skaters Dick Button and Hayes Jenkins; sculler Vyacheslav Ivanov; boxers Jack Dempsey, Gene Tunney, Joe Louis, and in his opinion the best of them all – Sugar Ray Robinson. Kiphuth sat among the thousands who witnessed the second Louis-Schmeling fight at Yankee Stadium. During the summer of 1956, Kiphuth invited the Olympic hopefuls training under him at Yale to view the Olympic track trials on television. He knew all the athletes, their times, and their weaknesses and strengths. Although he attended many team events, the true intrigue that captured his imagination was the panorama of man against man, and man against himself.

After his wife's death in 1941, he moved on campus as a Professor in Residence at Timothy Dwight College (TDC) at Yale. Here, in his new quarters, Kiphuth conducted an open door policy. He thrived on the hectic and frantic activity surrounding football weekends. With the passing of his wife Louise, his daughter-in-law Janet became his hostess. Alumni, friends, and guests were all warmly welcomed by Kiphuth and Janet. All were welcome to share in the cultural environment of his apartment. His living quarters consisted of a large living room, a small kitchen, two bedrooms, and book shelves lined with thousands of volumes. The living room became a display case for his interest in Japanese culture. Although one could find both Asian and classical selections, musical comedies dominated the record collection. It meant a great deal to him to have people visit and appreciate his various collections.

The Kiphuth center of activity had a constant flow of both foreign and domestic guests. His company ranged from dignitaries and fellow professionals to graduate and undergraduate students. There was a constant influx of world-wide guests-in-residence who enjoyed the warmth of a room in his apartment. All were allowed to live their own lives with one exception, that each morning Kiphuth mustered everyone from their beds in order to join him for 7:30 a.m. breakfast in the TDC dining hall. No matter how late one had burned the candle, it was understood that everyone would break bread and share in dialogue with their host.

In addition, the dining pleasures of Yale's famous eating establishment – Mory's – with its picturesque reminders of earlier college days, was often part of the experience. It was here that Kiphuth could be found indulging in a late night snack of lightly-toasted saltine crackers.

Gwyneth King Brown, a friend of Kiphuth's and the wife of sculptor and Princeton boxing coach Joseph Brown, humorously recalled, "Bob frequently and generously offered the use of his guest room but sometimes mixed up the dates; at times we would awake about 2 a.m. with a knock on the door by a confused guest who tiptoed around then ended the night on the living room couch. We never mentioned these incidents to Bob and perhaps no one else did."

Prior to Kiphuth's heart attack in 1949, every afternoon between noon and two o'clock Kiphuth's staff was expected to participate in a tournament of handball. His rules allowed no fouls and no "lets." Anything went. A little pushing and a little shoving were all part of the game. It was survival of the fittest. Kiphuth did not allow his arthritic hand to deter him from being an extremely competitive player. He would spend at least a half-hour soaking the hand and taping every finger nail prior to the game. Spry on his feet and energetically covering the court, he threatened his opponent by spreading his arms and charging both the ball and the man.

Carmen Cozza, Yale's football coach for 32 years, wrote: "Bob liked handball which was a sport I enjoyed playing. This gave me an in with him. He was a man I will never forget." Cozza went on to say: "He was a legend; he *was* Yale athletics! My wife and I stayed in his apartment when we first arrived and I couldn't believe the number of books he had accumulated. His secretary Bobbie told me he bought a dozen or more books a month which could explain how he knew something about every subject. He was a born leader and mentor and I admired him greatly. My only regret is I did not know him longer."

Along with being a fierce competitor himself, Kiphuth pictured Yale as a realm for pure athletic competition. From March 1946 until his heart attack, he took on additional duties as Director of Athletics and was responsible for 16 varsity sports, 10 junior varsity, and 16 freshman teams. A consensus among staff was best summarized by Yale track coach Geigengack, "Bob was a grand plan man who had a grasp of the total athletic picture. As a result, he developed a strong relationship with his coaching staff and was able to direct the University with sound policies of amateurism and athletics." Although astute in his selection of staff appointments and coaches, Kiphuth's "flaw was his disregard for detail." Aside from the building of the PW, Kiphuth rarely found time to attend to details. He focused on the big picture, leaving the minutia to others.

The more noted coaching appointments were Geigengack (track), Howard Hobson (basketball), Adam Walz (crew), and Howie O'Dell (football). In hiring assistant swim coaches Kiphuth often gave preference to recent graduates of the local high schools.

In spite of personal or professional differences, Kiphuth earned both respect and praise from foe and friend alike. A repertoire of coaches described him in the following manner: "A very strong man who could not be talked back to, and yet was very soft-spoken, obliging, hospitable, and a tremendous host," a man with a "magnetic" personality and the "ability to lead," "a person never too busy to help anyone in spite of circumstances or affiliation," "a tough customer, almost domineering" since he was "in it for all he was worth." Kiphuth made swimming "a respected sport in the eyes of the academic world and he always did nice things for people when things happened against Yale, not only for Yale." Because of "his generosity in terms of finances and time, at no income to himself, he kept America in the international picture." Kiphuth had "world-wide contacts, tradition, culture, and charisma."

In his story "Yale Churns On at the Water Works" (January 23, 1956), *Sports Illustrated* writer Alfred Wright correctly labeled Kiphuth as "the scholar and teacher" of the art of swimming, not the innovator of stroke or technique. In a 1956 interview with Wright, Cornell University swim coach Gordon Little said "Kiphuth is the greatest conditioner of athletes in the world today."

West Point swim coach Jack Ryan recalled that in 1966 when Army defeated Yale, Kiphuth, in recognition of Army's performance, sent him a key ring with the Yale crest and the final score of the meet. In 1936, Matt Mann cited Kiphuth as a coach who "has raised the standards of American swimming…[and stands for] what is right in athletics and good sportsmanship." He stated American swimming benefited from Kiphuth's "financial ability to take the time off necessary to coach an overseas American team." Internationally, Australian coach Forbes

Carlile, paraphrasing from Shakespeare's *Julius Caesar*, described Kiphuth's image best. He wrote, "Bob's image was so great that he strode the narrow world as a Colossus among coaches." But, perhaps one of the greatest tributes paid to him was when Dr. Willard P. Ashbrook, a former swimming official and renowned professor of physical education at The Ohio State University, stated that Kiphuth "epitomizes the Greek concept of physical education, blending the man of action with the man of wisdom."

Upon Kiphuth's retirement in June 1959, sports writer Red Smith of the *New York Herald Tribune* wrote: "Chances are every college has its own approximation of the fictional Mr. Chips, the beloved old schoolmaster in James Hilton's novel, whose influence stamped generations of undergraduates. In the academic life of Yale, it must have been the late William Lyon Phelps. In the somewhat broader existence of the University as a whole, it has to be Robert John Herman Kiphuth."

Smith's sentiments were echoed by Yale's president Kingman Brewster: "To Bob Kiphuth, athletics were an integral part of learning, and all learning was an exercise in self-fulfillment and self-discipline. He was as demanding of intellect and character as he was of physical perfection. Generations of students and colleagues at Yale and throughout the world have outdone themselves because of the values he inspired and the standards he set."

During his career, over 20,000 swimmers came under his direction. All his charges respected his ideal that the road to success involved work and dedication. His initial presence was overpowering. Swimmers (his flock) listened intently to his dicta on the importance of education and the finite nature of athletic accomplishment. As an example, in 1952, he counseled Frank Chamberlain to remain at Yale, even if it meant giving up swimming, in order to complete his studies. Inspired by Kiphuth's concern for his future, Chamberlain not only remained at Yale, but continued to compete. As a result, Frank qualified for the 1952 Olympic Team, and graduated with his class of 1953. Sympathy for youth was one of Kiphuth's outstanding qualities, and each and every swimmer soon learned to address him simply as Bob. To his athletes, he was a friend, counselor, and away-from-home father, who was available day or night.

Caring for his swimmers only touched the surface of Kiphuth's involvement at Yale. He was an active member of Yale's Alpha Delta Phi, St. Elmo Society, Torch Society, and the Elizabethan Club. Friends since 1929, Kiphuth and Deane Keller belonged to a small group of confederates known as the "Pyknics", a Greek word meaning short and wide.

This Yale group of short, stocky, and muscular men assembled each Tuesday for lunch and chatter at the Graduate Club from 1945 until 1953. Among the more notable and faithful of the constituency were Clem Fry (psychiatry professor and collector of medical art); Dr. Ashley Oughterson (surgeon and editor of *Medical Effects of the Atomic Bomb in Japan*); Edward Boucher (professor of law and esteemed authority on international law); and Eugene Davidson (editor of the Yale Press and author of *The Trial of the Germans-Nuremburg 1945-1946*). Even though the luncheon discussions rambled from the humorous to the serious, the exchange among members was lasting and pertinent. Kiphuth listened, learned, and vocalized to the enjoyment of all.

Beyond his social realm, Kiphuth became renowned outside his Kingdom at Yale. In 1958, he was the recipient of the Amateur Athletic Union Swimming Award, which, according to AAU literature, is "conferred annually upon an individual or organization making the outstanding contribution in the fields of aquatics and lifesaving." Kiphuth had actually been the creator of that very award four years earlier. He had the idea, and recruited Bruce Hopping, who had started a foundation, Kalos Kagathos, to put athletic fitness on a pedestal. Hopping was also a swim coach, and he was immediately receptive to the idea of having his foundation endow the award.

In 1963, President John F. Kennedy nominated Kiphuth for a Freedom medal, an honor for distinguished civilian service in peacetime. Due to the assassination of President Kennedy, the 31 honorees (later 33 with the addition of President Kennedy and Pope John XXIII) received their Freedom medals from President Lyndon Johnson in a ceremony at the White House on December 6, 1963. Kiphuth's award medal read: "Teacher and coach, he has inspired generations of athletes with high ideals of achievement and sportsmanship."

In 1960, the Emperor of Japan bestowed upon Kiphuth the honor of the Order of the Sacred Treasure – Third Class. The First Class and Second Class Order of the Sacred Treasure are reserved for heads of state, politicians, diplomats, academics, and military officers. The Order of Third Class, established in 1888, is ranked from first-to-eighth in order of significance of a person's distinguished service to the Japanese people. According to Jiro Niawa of the Japanese Consulate in New York City, Kiphuth received the award because of his appreciation of Japanese culture, his tireless efforts on behalf of Japanese youth, and due to his many contributions to Japanese and American swimming. The Japanese considered him the father of modern-day Japanese swimming.

The respect and love the Japanese had for Kiphuth transcended the competitive venue of sport. Previously, in 1953, Yale President A. Whitney Griswold had accepted from the Japanese Consul General, Hisanaga Shamadzu, a bronze life-sized bust of Kiphuth created by Fumio Asakura, Japan's leading sculptor. It was given "for the time and consideration he has so generously bestowed on the Japanese youth and for his spirit of good sportsmanship he has helped to instill in our people." Despite the grand gesture, the sculpture was stolen from the lobby of the Payne Whitney, never to be found.

Authorities have cited Kiphuth as the person primarily responsible for the emergence of swimming out of the dark ages because of his public image, dual meet record, flair for record attempts, ability to garner headlines, his part in the construction of the Payne Whitney Gymnasium, and his undying effort to promote swimming. He never passed up an opportunity to speak, even at his own expense, anywhere in the world about the sport of swimming. Without a doubt, he established himself as the world's foremost bodybuilding and competitive swimming authority and as an expert on the proper technique for fitness and posture. Scientist and swim coach Cecil Colwin stated that "Kiphuth knew more about the human body in action than any man I've met before or since." His approach was truly revolutionary. Many of his teachings continue to form the core philosophy, knowingly or unknowingly, of present day coaches.

Kiphuth's former protégé, Olympic and University of Southern California coach Peter Daland, remembered Kiphuth as follows:

> Kiphuth put the coach in coat and tie and removed him from the bathrobe image of the past. He possessed more status and polish than his rivals. He was the first great conditioner and the first professional coach in international swimming. He was the instigator of bringing body building, free exercise, and weights into American swimming. He was very intelligent and had tremendous drive. He had a very strong, positive view on most subjects. Yale was the great institution in his life. He really admired the University and it was very important in his thinking. Bob was never in swimming for the money. I don't agree with that policy but I certainly had to admire him for it.

## The Culture of his Youth: 1890-1914

Robert John Herman Kiphuth was born November 17, 1890, in Tonowanda, New York. He was one of six children born to Marie Elizabeth Bennin and John J. Kiphuth. His maternal grandparents were Marie Elizabeth Robert (born in Buffalo, New York, in 1845) and Herman Bennin (born in Mecklinberg, Schwerin, Germany). Fredericke Hillman and Johann Joachim Helmuth Theodore Kiphuth (both born in Stettin, Preussen, Germany) were his paternal grandparents.

His mother was a homemaker and his father was a machinist at one of the industrial plants on the Niagara frontier. He was educated in the local public schools, graduating from Tonawanda High School in 1909.

The 350-mile-long Erie Canal, the first great canal in the United States, with one of the largest ports in America, is a significant factor in local activities for the towns of Tonawanda and North Tonawanda. One can imagine the young boy and his friends watching the teams of men or mules tie up to boats and barges and guide them through the shallow canal in an exercise known as "bow haulage." One can only speculate as to Kiphuth's participation in the July 4th celebrations of "greased pole walking" across the Barge Canal between the two towns.

The lumber industry was the signature employer of local men while the Northern Silk Mills provided employment opportunities for women. During Kiphuth's youth, capitalism still reigned supreme in the town of Tonawanda. However, the rise of social problems, pauperism, unemployment, and labor disputes had given rise to populist trade unions, revolutionaries, and socialists, all seeking their definition of what would constitute labor reform and social justice for the masses. According to MacTaggart's *A Labor History of Buffalo*, there were at least 13 major labor strikes in Buffalo in 1913 alone. The 1700 Street railway workers' strike was the most significant as it impacted not only Buffalo, but the neighboring towns.

The towns' ethnic populations, by the turn of the nineteenth century, consisted predominantly of large Polish, German, Italian, and Austro-Hungarian immigrants or descendants of immigrants. Many came to escape economic hardship or religious, racial, and political persecution.

In spite of the formation of ethnic enclaves within the towns of Tonawanda and North Tonawanda, assimilation occurred within the schools, at sporting events, the YMCA, and various cultural festivities. Thus, Kiphuth was exposed to America's unique experiment – "the Melting Pot."

The North Tonawanda YMCA was a center of the community. Built at the southeast corner of Main and Tremont Streets in 1892 for $75,000, the club served as a multi-purpose structure housing the town and county hall as well as the police station, with apartments on the top floor. The Sweeney Street side of the building housed a small wooden waiting room for passengers to board trolley cars for Niagara Falls or Buffalo.

At the turn of the nineteenth century, Buffalo, known as the Queen City, was the educational and entertainment center of western New York. Many venues such as Shea's Music Hall, the Star, the Criterion, the Grand Opera House, the Metropolitan, the Great Lakes Theatre, and the Auditorium at D'Youville College all presented theater, lectures, concerts, and dance recitals featuring the prominent leaders and stars of that era. For Kiphuth, the trolley car offered easy access to these many opportunities. Moreover, Buffalo, with its large German population, had its own German language newspaper, political groups, and eating establishments, allowing Kiphuth to maintain contact with his heritage.

American vaudeville, with its family-oriented atmosphere of performance, as established by its founder Benjamin Franklin Keith, soon came to Buffalo. This was Kiphuth's introduction to the "soft shoe." His fascination with and dream of an on-stage tap dance performance, hat on head and cane in hand, became part of Yale's after-practice swim lore. However, it was a dream never realized, for as Harry Burke (Kiphuth's future assistant coach at Yale) stated, the short, stocky Kiphuth "did not have the legs for it."

## From Tonawanda to New Haven

As a youth, Kiphuth was not a talented athlete but had a strong competitive drive which enabled him to exhibit skill as a capable swimmer, an aggressive handball player, an effective gymnast, and an enthusiastic dancer. Although he spent most of his leisure hours at the YMCA, he did not ignore his other interests. He enjoyed winters on the Niagara Frontier ice skating on nearby Ellicott Creek, and he pursued his interest in music by playing comic operas on the violin, with accompaniment by his sister, Meta, on the piano. Raised in a strong church-family unit, Kiphuth's character was formed by the virtues of hard work, thrift, and sobriety. He attended family and youth services and later taught Sunday school at the Evangelical Synod of North America (United Church of Christ).

Following his graduation from high school as valedictorian he was employed as a clerk, first by the local power company and then by the hardware store of H. E. Koenig. According to his sister, Meta, during this time he "continued his youthful interest in all phases of 'Y' activities, physical, religion, even music…Spirit-Mind-Body. He was always a leader and eventually was asked, at age 20, in 1910, to become the Physical Director of the Tonawanda Y." For her there was no question that Kiphuth's leadership skills were honed by his administrative duties at the YMCA.

Always eager for self-improvement, Kiphuth was encouraged by his mother to pursue every opportunity available to him. He attended physical education classes at the YMCA Summer School of Physical Education at Silver Bay, New York, in 1911 and Dr. Dudley Sargent's Harvard Summer School of Physical Education in 1912. Sargent, a leader in the movement of exercise and athletics for the general populace, played a significant role in shaping Kiphuth's philosophies of both physical education and athletics. His philosophy was further influenced by other great leaders such as Dr. Edward Hitchcock, and Dr. William G. Anderson.

The lack of cultural stimulation in the Tonawandas, plus a developing interest in assessing the proper perspective for the body in the educational process, led Kiphuth to various nearby Buffalo theatrical productions and eventually to an intense and lifelong interest in dance. As a direct result of this interest in dance, he met his future wife Louise DeLaney, while studying basic ballet technique at the Twentieth Century Club (TCC) in Buffalo during the summers of 1912 through 1914. Louise Delaney was a graduate of the Anderson Normal School of Gymnastics, The Gilbert Normal School of Dance, and the Louis Harvey Chalif Normal School of Dancing, and she conducted classes for the TCC.

The TCC club was founded in November 1884 by Charlotte Mulligan, a teacher, writer, and musician. The club was composed exclusively of prominent women of Buffalo. It was a unique club in that it was the only women's club in America which owned and operated its own building. Facta Probant (*Let Deeds Tell*), engraved on the TCC crest, stands as an epitaph to Ms. Mulligan's purpose of education, literature, and art. By 1904, the club had a dining room, ballroom, music room, gymnasium, and swimming pool. Classes and private lessons were offered in swimming, dance, fencing, badminton, and bridge. From its inception, the doors were open to performances by leading musicians as well as lectures by noted writers, speakers, and international personalities. In a few short years, the club became a vital and important force in Buffalo society.

A significant cultural awakening in Kiphuth was initiated by his relationship with Miss Delaney and his exposure to the distinguished and refined members of the TCC. Miss Delaney redefined his image, taught him gentlemen's etiquette, piqued his interest in the literary giants of that era, exposed him to the *New York Times*' recommended reading list, and introduced him to many of the renowned dancers of that era. Wisely, as if by intuitive design, Kiphuth absorbed the culture exposed before him. As a result, he now had the social graces necessary to blend unencumbered into any class of American society.

> As an example of the prominent social position the club played in Buffalo society, in 1901, the TCC hosted many of the elite visitors to the Pan American Exposition World's Fair held from May 1 to November 2 of that year. These visitors included Vice President and Mrs. Teddy Roosevelt and their daughter, the Chinese Minister Wu Ting Fang, New York Governor and Mrs. Benjamin O'Dell, and most notably Mr. and Mrs. Booker T. Washington. Activities concluded with a dinner for the wives of foreign diplomats and a gala ball for the Corps of Cadets from the United States Military Academy. Building upon these esteemed honors, the club continued its prominent position in Buffalo society.

Louise DeLaney was to be instrumental in Kiphuth's appointment to Yale in 1914, as she was a former student and personal friend of Yale's Director of Physical Education, William G. Anderson. Conceivably because of the developing friendship between Kiphuth and Miss Delaney, but possibly more importantly because she recognized and shaped the dynamic qualities of the man, she wrote to Anderson and arranged an interview. In turn Anderson, impressed with Kiphuth's decorum and their philosophical compatibility, appointed him as an instructor of physical education in the fall of 1914.

Kiphuth returned to Buffalo in the summers of 1915 and 1916, and served as Associate Director of the Normal Course of Dancing at the TCC. He and Louise were married in Chicago on June 6, 1917. It was a common practice for couples from Buffalo to travel to Chicago rather than nearby Niagara Falls to be married. Louise's parents, as listed on her death certificate, were Charles Delaney and F. L. Dole of Buffalo. Although there is some debate about Louise's age at the time of the marriage, the Cook County, Illinois, Marriage Index dated June 6, 1917, listed her age as 42, and her date of birth as about 1875 – 15 years before Kiphuth was born. The passenger list of the Graf Waldersee, departing from Hamburg, Germany, to New York, dated October 4, 1913, confirms her age, with date of birth as March 11, 1875, and place of birth as Buffalo, New York.

After the wedding, the couple immediately returned to New Haven and purchased a home on Cleveland Avenue, a short distance from the newly completed Yale Bowl. A son, DeLaney, was born in March 1918.

The Yale Bowl, designed by Yale graduate Charles A. Ferry, was completed just in time for the Yale-Harvard game on November 21, 1914, with a seating capacity of 70,896 at a cost of $750,000. The *New Haven Register* reported that Presidents Howard Taft and Teddy Roosevelt attended the game, which was won by Harvard 36-0. It was the first bowl-shaped stadium in America, and it inspired the design of such stadiums as the Rose Bowl, Los Angeles Coliseum, and the University of Michigan Stadium. The Yale Bowl is located about 1.5 miles from the main campus. Brown University's Fritz Pollard was the first African-American to play in the Bowl in 1915. Levi Jackson, who this author was privileged to watch play in the Yale Bowl in 1948, was the first African-American to wear the blue and white when he took the field on September 28, 1946.

The Bowl hosted many local high school championship games and even many NFL exhibition games. The New York Giants played all their home games at the Bowl while Yankee Stadium was being renovated during the seasons of 1973 and 1974. The professional players did not appreciate the fact that the architect did not provide locker rooms within the stadium. The players had to dress in the Smilow Field Center and walk the 200 yards to the stadium.

It was in the shadow of this famous athletic arena that the Kiphuths began their life at Yale. Cleveland Avenue was the perfect venue for them to enter Yale society, and for Louise to entertain the dignitaries of the era. Perhaps Kiphuth and Louise, at this point, recognized that their destiny and security rested within the intellectual and cultural offerings at Yale and the nearby city of New York. But in reality, they could not have known the breadth of opportunity Yale held for them. As "fate is the hunter" unforeseen and unpredictable circumstances and events determine the ultimate path of life. Ability in order to function needs opportunity, and Kiphuth's opportunity, unrecognized at the time, arrived in the fall of 1917, when Dr. Anderson appointed him to the directorship of the Carnegie Pool.

# Collegiate and AAU Swimming at the Turn of the Twentieth Century

Intercollegiate swimming was born in 1897 when competitions between the University of Pennsylvania, Yale, and Columbia took place. Prior to this time, Professor Sir Charles Holroyd of Columbia University, labeled as a swimming master, came to various universities and conducted exhibitions of swimming strokes and water polo matches. This usually occurred in collaboration with the National Swimming Association which was founded in 1893 in Philadelphia. Because of the popularity of water polo, conducted under the "no holds barred" rules, the exhibitions became a popular event on the campuses of eastern universities.

The University of Pennsylvania became the leader in intercollegiate swimming with the appointment of former world champion English swimmer George Kistler, whom they rescued from his job in the coal mines of Pennsylvania, as instructor of swimming on April 5, 1897. Kistler took full advantage of the opportunity to be recognized as an aquatic authority. He terminated the services of Sir Holroyd and assumed full responsibility for all productions to take place at Penn's Houston Hall Pool.

In spite of instructing in Penn's 10-by-30-foot pool, Kistler developed the first outstanding collegiate swimmer in Edward Schaeffer. Schaeffer established 37 American records and five world records just prior to the 1900 Olympics. Due to lack of funds, Schaeffer did not compete in the Games of the II Olympiad in 1900 in Paris, France.

In 1904, Kistler, credited as the pioneer of intercollegiate swimming and the inspiration behind the formation of the East Coast Intercollegiate Swimming League, officially, with approval of Penn's Athletic Association, shredded the title of instructor of swimming and began his career as coach of swimming. In 1914, he was rewarded with a new 30-by-100-ft (33 1/3-yard) pool.

Most eastern universities at the time had athletic associations controlled by the undergraduate captain of the team, assisted by a student secretary who arranged schedules, purchased supplies and decided the events to be contested. As a result, many of these collegiate teams competed in only one to seven dual meets yearly, as compared to 14 or more beginning in 1921. It was not uncommon for teams to compete against each other twice, both home and away, in any given year. Freshmen were often restricted from competing at the varsity level at most universities until 1951. Following the lead of team sports, the championship of the Intercollegiate Swimming Association was based solely on head to head competition. The ISA's Individual Championship, despite team scores being tabulated, did not demand as much respect as dual meets until years later. By 1919, the ISA Championship Meet, held at City College of New York's 100-ft. pool, found 100 swimmers representing 12 universities. All competed for individual honors in the six-event program. The program included the 50, 100, and 220-yard freestyle, the plunge for distance, and the 200-yard varsity and freshmen relays.

Perhaps most remarkable was that the growth of collegiate swimming, as well as other collegiate sports, occurred in spite of major opposition from faculty and administrators. However, the early proponents of collegiate physical education programs believed in the necessity of aquatic safety, and agreed that every student should be required to pass a swim test prior to graduation.

To meet this requirement, universities such as Yale, Princeton, Columbia, the City College of New York, and the University of Pennsylvania hired "pool men" who served as custodians. They instructed the general student body in survival swimming, and often, whether requested or not, offered professional expertise to swim team members. However, by the time Kiphuth was hired as coach in 1918, some small New England colleges had followed suit. The first collegiate swim teams consisted of experienced athletes who, for the most part, had competed on YMCA, Jewish Community Center, Boys Club, Athletic Club, and high school swim teams.

Initially, the student-organized athletic associations handled most of the problems. But as the temptation grew to recruit, and even to employ non-university students to participate in sports like football, the desire to play more opponents increased. Travel therefore became more complex and funding became a major issue. Universities began to realize the importance of institutional control. This resulted in faculty and administrative intervention as a means of ensuring the integrity and future of collegiate athletics, with dubious success. As the reins of power shifted from external to university control, coaching began to pass from team captain and secretary into the hands of a professional coach.

For the first two decades of the twentieth century, competitive swimming remained the protégé of eastern universities. This eventually led to the formation of the Intercollegiate Swim Association (ISA) in 1906, and later the Eastern Intercollegiate Swimming League (EISL) in 1935. The evolution of sport finally led to the creation of The Ivy League Football Conference in 1945.

The adoption of the Ivy League Code of Conduct for all sports in 1954 cemented the birth of the Ivy League. The cornerstone for true Ivy identity had been established.

In the early 1900s and before, America experienced the emergence of a national sports culture. Many towns began to sponsor two or three athletic clubs for men's baseball and basketball and women's basketball and softball. At the same time in many of the industrial towns of the northeast there were well-attended Sunday afternoon basketball leagues. The factories sponsored teams for the benefit of former high school players in their employment. The teams competed in local, state, and national competitions for both men and women. Americans from all walks of life began to fully embrace sports. The golden age of sport came to life. The public eagerly followed the exploits of emerging athletic stars such as: Gertrude Ederle and Johnny Weismueller (swimming), Bobby Jones (golf), Babe Ruth and Lou Gehrig (baseball), Jack Dempsey (boxing), Red Grange (football), Bill Tilden and Helen Wills (tennis), and Charlie Paddock and "Babe" Dickenson (track & field).

While these local athletic clubs offered swim competitions for women once a year, many YMCA and Boys Clubs, especially along the eastern corridor, from New York to Maine, offered both youth and adult swim team opportunities for men and boys. Youth teams had mostly volunteer coaches while the adult teams usually operated under the direction of the elected captain. Dual meets, state meets, and even interstate meets were held each year.

At the turn of the 20th century, the rich and influential families of American society controlled all administrative positions within the Amateur Athletic Union (AAU) for national and international swimming and, in turn, the political power that went with it. The objective of the AAU, founded by William Buckingham Curtis in 1888, was to keep American sport free of fraud and corruption. Curtis founded the New York and Chicago Athletic Clubs. These two organizations, along with other similar clubs, played an important role in supporting and conducting athletic events for America's non-collegiate athletes, particularly swimming. However, the doors were so securely locked that no coach, profiting from the talents of another person, could intrude into the realm of power. Professional coaches were barred from the pool decks of international swimming. Only the volunteer, unpaid coach was given recognition.

While Kiphuth burst to the forefront nationally and internationally, there were certainly other coaches who served as early pioneers and made contributions to the evolution of American intercollegiate swimming. These coaches included: Frank Sullivan of Princeton, Ed Kennedy of Columbia, Michael Kennedy of Amherst, Frank Foster and Henry Ortland, Jr. of the Naval Academy, Radford McCormick of the City College of New York, Frank Wall of New York University, Robert Muir of Williams, Matt Mann of Michigan, Thomas Robinson of Northwestern, Dave Armbruster of the University of Iowa, Mike Peppe of The Ohio State University, Ed Manley of the University of Illinois, Joe Steinauer of the University of Wisconsin, Ed McGillivray of the University of Chicago, Niles Thorpe of the University of Minnesota, Bob Royer of the University of Indiana, Larry La Bree of Purdue University, Ernst Bransten of Stanford University, Arthur Eilers of the University of Washington, and Fred Cady of the University of Southern California. A true historian would be well served to study the contributions these men made to American swimming.

In the fall of 1917, an obscure Robert John Herman Kiphuth, unknowingly, and unexpectedly, entered this world of collegiate, national, and international swimming.

# KIPHUTH TO THE HELM

It is unbelievable how a simple request by a student athlete, on a single college campus, rather than national or world events, would play a most significant role in the history of competitive swimming. The event, so minuscule but so very important, would revolutionize the sport of swimming and impact generations unborn.

Yale's competitive swimming program had functioned primarily under the leadership of the team captain and the administrative guidelines of the team manager since its debut in 1897. From 1906 until 1917, pool attendant Max Schwartz contributed his services. He was ably supplemented in an informal capacity one or two days a week, by Ogden M. Reid, President of the *New York Tribune*, a former Yale football player, and former captain of the Yale swimming and water polo teams. Reid had served as Yale's swimming and water polo instructor

while in law school in 1905 and even after he became president of the *Tribune*. As reported by the *New York Times* on January 24, 1907, Reid was instrumental in securing $40,000 from Andrew Carnegie to build the Carnegie Pool on Elm Street (presently Trumbull College). The pool opened in the fall of 1910 and was credited with being the finest swimming pool in the world.

Although necessity is rightfully termed the mother of invention, it is fate which often determines the outcome. In spite of the fact that necessity required the hiring of an instructor of swimming at Yale and the fact that both the alumni and especially the team captain worked endlessly for the hiring of the "prestigious" Matt Mann, fate would determine that the "obscure" Kiphuth would assume the position. The circumstances surrounding this occasion occurred in the following sequence.

During the 1915-16 and 1916-17 seasons, Reid, who was serving as Yale's water polo coach, obtained Mann's services to teach technique to Yale's swim team. Reid and Mann traveled to New Haven two days a week, Saturday and Sunday, during the month of January to instruct Yale's swimming and water polo teams. Mann received the sum of $180, paid by Reid to the Yale Athletic Association, as reimbursement for his travel expenses. Apparently, a strong friendship and mutual respect developed between Reid, a member of the New York Athletic Club (NYAC), and Mann, who at the time was coaching at the NYAC, Brooklyn Poly Prep, Lawrenceville Prep, and the United States Naval Academy. Mann was an English immigrant who in his early years was a well-respected "vagabond" coach. He did not allow geography to interfere with his passion for coaching. He was one of the first United States high school coaches, and his "hunger to win swimming meets was never quenched, [his] energy and enthusiasm were never drowned," according to the International Swimming Hall Fame.

In March of 1917, Professor Robert Nelson Corwin, the chairman of Yale's Board of Athletic Control, received a letter from Andrew Wilson, Jr., a former Yale captain of swimming. Wilson wrote concerning the graduate and undergraduate sentiment of Yale men "in regard to the swimming situation at Yale." He expressed his "warmest personal regards" for Max Schwartz, but he nonetheless pointed out to Corwin that a "step of vital importance to aquatics at Yale (should) be taken at this juncture." Wilson deplored the fact that "hundreds of men have graduated unable to swim for want of a competent instructor at the pool." Wilson attributed Yale's competitive success "to a wealth of material, a beautiful pool and smiling fortune." Having rationalized his motive, he proceeded to enhance Mann's image, pointing out that, in spite of only being able to be at the pool on weekends, Mann "enabled Yale to win the title last year with a mediocre start and only fair material. I mention Mr. Mann to you, at this juncture, because I know him, and have heard him suggested by many thoughtful Yale men for the position."

The campaign to hire Mann as the coach of Yale swimming had begun in earnest. The year 1917 found Max Schwartz besieged by illness and unable to perform his duties. The captain elect Richard Mayer also approached Corwin and requested that Mann be hired as the resident instructor in swimming. Mayer had also spoken to Thomas Dunnell, a member of the Yale Athletic Association. Dunnell followed up that meeting with a letter to Corwin stating that "Max Schwartz is now of practically no use at the pool, as he is liable to be out most of the time on account of sickness, and I am absolutely certain that Mr. Mann would be a big addition to swimming in the University."

On May 5, Yale Commander Carl Schlaet, a former Yale swimming captain, wrote to Corwin and reminded him that he (Schlaet) had spoken to him (Corwin) "about this last year," and that in his opinion Mann "is ideal for the job." He concluded with the statement, "I feel sure you will use your influence to get Mann at Yale permanently."

In response, Corwin wrote Schlaet that "[a] committee is to be appointed for considering it," thanking him for his excellent suggestion, and noting "there are money elements involved." At this point, evidently, no committee was ever formed and the campaign seems to have temporarily ceased. However, an undated memorandum, signed by Mayer and P.C. Walsh, the team manager, which included conditions for employing Mann, can be found among the Robert Nelson Corwin Papers archived at Yale. The next communiqué took place between Mayer and Corwin's secretary, N. P. Elliot. Mayer wrote requesting information as to the failure of the world record relay team to receive major "Y's" (a Yale athletic letter award) and said that he and Walsh, the team manager, were "still very anxious about procuring Mr. Matthew Mann's services as an instructor this year." Mayer concluded that they were determined to "make the sport what it used to be."

What part Mann played in the early proceedings, one can only speculate. It seems safe to assume that Mann was aware of the pressures being exerted on Yale to hire him. Certainly Mayer and others must have approached Mann as to his interest. It is highly unlikely that the colorful Mann remained passive during the initial proceedings. That Mann greatly desired and lobbied for the position, there exists little doubt.

In October, when Schwartz submitted his resignation due to his illness, Dr. William Anderson, Yale's Director of Physical Education, appointed

Kiphuth as Director of the Carnegie Pool with orders "to keep things sanitary."

The next chapter in the Yale swimming saga began on October 5, 1917, when Mann officially entered the negotiations by forwarding a letter to Corwin, pointing out that he had just signed a three-year contract at the Duluth Boat Club. However, the contract was such that he could take a three-to-four month leave of absence during the winter months. If Yale were interested, he offered to begin work on either November 1 or December 1, and work through April 1.

Corwin replied, "[A]s you probably know matters both scholastic and athletic are now in charge of the Commandant of the Yale Training camp (due to World War I). I agree with you as to the importance of swimming…but the decision…rests with him."

Frustrated with the snail's pace with which the halls of academia function, Captain Mayer, with teammates in tow, decided to test the changing of the guard at the Carnegie. In November of 1917, he asked Kiphuth if he would help the swimmers for the time being. The label "pool man" was now obsolete, for the ever-professional Kiphuth had taken command.

After a review of the swimmers' technique and ability to exhibit speed, Kiphuth, in line with his philosophy of a well-conditioned body, recommended attendance at his body building classes as a means of building the stamina necessary for finishing a race. Kiphuth's advice, unchallenged by most of the team, was rejected by Mayer's dogmatic belief in Coach Mann's tenet that "fish do not do body building."

Obviously, Mayer did not allow negotiations to falter because Corwin's correspondence to Mann on December 10 stated that Mayer had kept him informed concerning the negotiations and that, "you agree to coach" the varsity and freshman swimming teams and the water polo team for "three months beginning January 8, 1918, at a salary of $250 per month." The salary was guaranteed by Ogden Reid and was to be paid through the Yale Swimming Association. As Mayer and Walsh put their signatures to the contract they must have been totally exuberant. After nine long months, they had finally tasted victory.

But once again fate intervened and Mann responded to Corwin, "Owing to some big changes in the swimming branch of the [Duluth Boat Club] here, the officials have decided that it is impossible to grant me a three month leave of absence." Mann informed Corwin that he had written full details to Mayer and expressed that he was "with Yale to the last" and if he could afford to break the contract, he "should come anyway." Corwin, undaunted by Mann's response and under pressure from many sources, asked Mann if he could, in accordance with his correspondence with Mayer, coach for "three or four weeks after the beginning of the second term on January 8."

These terms were accepted and Mann was to come to Yale from January 8 until January 26, three full weeks. Mayer had won a partial victory. At least for that period of time, the team would have Mann, "a great seat of the pants psychologist," directing their destiny.

Mann did come to Yale and coached until January 25, 1918. An unsigned and undated memorandum in contractual form was found among the Corwin Papers to the effect that a Robert Zimmerman, from Chicago, would report to Yale to take "up the work which Matthew Mann leaves off Friday, Jan. 25th." Just exactly who Zimmerman was and how he factored into this remains a mystery. Most likely Mayer, a Chicago resident, played an instrumental role in moving negotiations in this direction. No other correspondence mentions him, it appears that he never arrived, and Zimmerman remains simply a typewritten name on an unsigned contract in the pages of Yale's swimming history.

At this point, the conscientious and determined Mayer, in spite of their philosophical divide, took matters into his own hands and approached the personable Kiphuth and asked him "if he would contribute his services in support of the team" for the remainder of the season. Kiphuth with his typical tongue-in-cheek sense of humor replied: "[I] might like a crack at bossing them around."

Those nine words would change the sport of swimming forever.

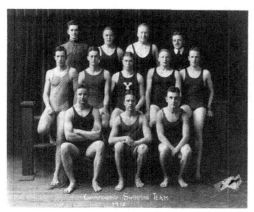

**1917-18 Yale Swim Team**

*Photo of Intercollegiate Champion team members.*

Row 1: C. R. Wagner; L. Prettyman; B. O. Benjamin.

Row 2: E. B. Archbald; J. M. Hincks; R. Mayer (Coach); E. Peterson; J. McHenry.

Row 3: P. C. Walsh (Mgr.); G. Boyce; L. R. Loeb; R. J. H. Kiphuth (H. Coach).

## The Road to Professionalism

Thus, in 1918, Kiphuth began a 42-year career that would lead to international prestige for the sport of swimming, Yale, and himself.

He had inherited a most unenviable position. Both the Yale alumni and the Yale swimmers had thrown their support to Mann. Yale had just won six consecutive dual meet titles and was favored to win a seventh. Moreover, Mann, a great motivator, had just given the team three weeks of his personal care. His departure destroyed the continuity of the program and caused a decline in team spirit. Mann, who even under normal circumstances would not be an easy act to follow, made Kiphuth's foray a most uncertain one.

Kiphuth's debut seems to have remained one of Yale's least publicized coaching appointments. Because of the informality of his acceptance as well as economic considerations, the Board of Athletic Control regarded his internship as strictly voluntary and unofficial. The only recognition appeared in the *Yale Daily News* on April 12, 1918, "The coaching of the swim team was ably carried on by Robert J. H. Kiphuth."

Unsuccessful in their attempt to secure Mann, the 1917-18 team suffered further setbacks when Edmond B. Alexander (50 freestyle) and S.C. Badger (plunge for distance) answered the call to arms. Consequently, Kiphuth inherited a talented team, but one that was reduced in strength. Competition at the time took place mainly during the months of January, February, and March. This left Kiphuth with a very short window to bring the team together after Mann's departure. Wisely, he utilized Mayer's leadership ability and supplemented it with his own gregarious nature to re-establish team unity and spirit. As a result, the team concluded the season with nine wins and one loss, to the New York Athletic Club, a non-collegiate team. Yale also won its seventh straight ISA title by defeating Princeton in home and away meets by identical scores (30 to 23) on March 1 and March 16. Kiphuth, in the *Yale Daily News*, gave full credit to Mayer's leadership ability, divers J. McHenry and B.O. Benjamin, new members John M. Hincks and E. Archbald, and especially to E. Peterson, captain of the water-polo team for his crucial anchor leg in the 200 freestyle relay against Princeton.

At the start of the 1918-19 season, captain John. M. Hincks and manager W. Mallory Chamberlin approached Corwin concerning the appointment of a recognized coach. But after the departure of Mann, Reid had withdrawn his financial support and the Athletic Board was unwilling to finance the venture. Therefore, Corwin rejected their bid but encouraged them to submit a definite proposal. Nonetheless, Kiphuth continued to coach the team despite the lack of "understanding that he should help the swimming team" on the part of the administration, and the lack of remuneration. Kiphuth, along with other gym employees, did receive a stipend of $150 dollars in the spring of 1919 "in recognition of his efforts on behalf of the Swimming Team" from the Yale Athletic Association.

The financial recognition involved reciprocal correspondences between Corwin and George P. Day, Yale University treasurer, and among Corwin and swim team manager, W. Mallory Chamberlin, and Dr. William Anderson, director of the gymnasium. On March 15, 1919, Anderson responded:

> I have just had a talk with Mr. Robert Kiphuth who is in charge of the Pool. He has been the successful coach of the Team and has given much outside time to the individuals who represented the U.S.A. By outside time I mean noon hours and evenings. He receives an inadequate salary from the Gymnasium ($1250.00) is married with a small family [and] consequently feels that he should receive something extra for taking the place of a higher price coach.
>
> I have told Mr. Kiphuth that he would receive careful consideration from you and I also believe he is entitled to extra remuneration. The Swimming Teams make no return to the Department for light, heat, use of building etc. but are on the safe side of the credit balance account.

The account had been opened and Kiphuth had become a paid and recognized coach of Yale swimming. At the start of the 1919-20 season, the initial swim team meeting drew 65 candidates addressed by Kiphuth with the words, "It takes Yale spirit to make Yale teams." In line with his philosophy that education trumps athletics, Kiphuth informed the young aspirants that he would be available throughout the day to coach anyone unable to attend regular practice sessions because of academics.

# Kiphuth Among the Puritans

How could a college, founded for the purpose of the preservation of "orthodox Congregationalism" and dedicated in its early history to classical education and "public prayer morning and evening," take a leadership role in the development of intercollegiate athletics?

Myth and history often collide. Judith Schiff, Chief Research Archivist of Yale Library, claims Yale College was founded when a group of Puritan clergymen met in the fall of 1701 and Congregational Minister and American educator Thomas Clap declared "I give these Books for the founding of Collegiate College." Clap then became president of Yale College from 1740 to 1766. But Brooks Mather Kelley, in his book *Yale: A History*, calls that tale a "charming story much cherished in the mythology of Yale," though he questions the historical facts.

According to Kelley, the older order of student activities consisted of hunting, sailing, swimming, skating, sledding, and hiking to the salt marshes of East Rock and Judges' Cave at West Rock. He continues by saying, "the taste for collegiate sport did not arise until the last quarter of the nineteenth century." Kelley documented that "one of the delights" of a "moralistic Puritan" student body was "informal, unorganized, random football on the New Haven Commons," mixed with clashes between town and gown. This led to student-organized sports, volunteer coaches, and in some cases, alumni financial support.

Yale's golden era of athletic achievement took place between 1870 and 1910. As documented by Kelley, this 40-year period found Yale as "the power in college sports." It was the "great athletic age" of Yale sports teams.

It was the era of Yale's Walter Camp, known as the "Father of American Football." In spite of being an absentee coach (he had a day job with his family's clock business), Yale football had nine consecutive undefeated seasons. His wife, perhaps the first female football coach, unofficial as it was, would observe practices, take detailed notes, and report back to him, allowing Walter to have productive meetings with assistant coaches and team members and prepare the agenda for Saturday's games.

Camp, who competed in intramural swimming races while at Yale, made his contribution to the future of Yale swimming, and the legacy that would be Kiphuth's, when, in 1901, he decreed swimming as a varsity sport.

By the time Kiphuth arrived on the Ivy campus in 1914, not only was the physical landscape changing but also the definition of intercollegiate athletics was being redefined. Students, alumni, and faculty, for different reasons, demanded institutional control and professional coaches for all of the sports teams. Although Yale would never regain the glory of by gone days and yesteryears, Yale swimming, under Kiphuth's direction, moved the university to the forefront of national and international sports recognition, minimizing the 40-year reign of Yale as the power in intercollegiate sport.

# The World, Yale, and Kiphuth: 1914-1918

Not only world events and internal and external politics but also socio-economic circumstances, combined with man's ego, jealousy, and pettiness, all play a significant role in the history of Yale swimming. World War I, the Great Depression, World War II, the construction of the Payne Whitney Gymnasium, the 1950s polio epidemic, Yale's strict January pre-exam six day reading period, and the NCAA and AAU conflicts, all left indelible marks on the sport.

First and foremost, neither man nor swimming performs in a vacuum. Internal and external events play a significant role in the outcome. By 1900, student pressure for extra-curricular activities, controlled by the students with assistance from the alumni, found Yale offering sports such as baseball, football, tennis, golf, track, crew, rugby, yachting, and swimming. Brooks Mather Kelley in his book, *Yale: A History*, stated that by the turn of the 20th Century "where once competition had been in the classroom and the literary society, now it was on the playing field." The college campus now offered a new world of opportunity to a resourceful man, and Kiphuth, being that man, would emerge triumphant.

In the autumn of 1914, Kiphuth's journey from oblivion to world fame was about to unfold. The 24-year-old took up the task of conditioning Yale undergraduates, utilizing his YMCA leadership skills and his barking baritone voice. His rise to power within the Ivy towers was the result of innocuous human events.

Mann arrived in New Haven on January 7, 1918, just five days prior to Yale's two home dual meet victories over City College of New York and University of Pennsylvania. At this point in time, Alexander and Badger joined the war effort and Yale's mandatory pre-exam reading period banned all intercollegiate competitions until February.

There can be no question that the initial meeting between Kiphuth and Mann in January of 1918 established two major points of contention that would impact the present and future relationship between the two. In line with his gregarious personality, Kiphuth made it very clear that he was in charge of the Carnegie Pool and that the physically fit man was his expertise. Although a neophyte to competitive swimming, he was skilled in the art of physical fitness, and recommended the concept of "muscle and mileage." In turn, Mann, in line with his vibrant personality, certainly made it very clear to Kiphuth that competitive excellence was his and his alone and that "muscle" was not part of the equation.

The "gauntlet" had been thrown, the future was about to unfold, and each coach would remain a steadfast proponent of his philosophy. This, combined with the fact that Mann believed Yale would be his destiny, "formed the major professional disagreement" between Mann and Kiphuth, according to Karl Michael, former Kiphuth assistant coach.

> Richard Mayer, the captain of Kiphuth's first Yale team, a faithful follower of Mann's philosophy of loose and flabby muscles, combined with stroke technique, rejected Kiphuth's innovation of dry land exercises and a muscular body. Possibly as a result of this rejection, Mayer had a disappointing performance at the championships in 1918, when he only tied for second in the 50 freestyle and tied for first in the 100 freestyle with times far below his season best.

During the period of these aquatic transitions at Yale, the world's political climate was undergoing radical changes. The Communist Manifesto, originally a 23-page pamphlet published in 1848 by philosophers Karl Marx and Friedrich Engels, was published in German and thirty other languages in 1872. Over the next forty years the Manifesto influenced the world's intellectuals, who envisioned a new world order with them as the "vanguards" of the "dictatorship of the proletariat." The Bloody Sunday Russian revolution on January 22, 1905, and Russia's entry into WWI in 1914, eventually led to the Revolution of 1917 bringing Vladimir Lenin and the Bolsheviks to power in Russia.

The American political scene, stained by the politics of power, found the Republicans nominating the conservative William Howard Taft for a second term, and the progressive Teddy Roosevelt bolting from the Republican Party and forming the "Bull Moose Party," insuring Taft's defeat by Wilson. The Democrats on the other hand nominated Woodrow Wilson in spite of his hostility for the Constitution, his declaration that the Bill of Rights was nonsense, his defense of segregation, and his bigotry in classifying eastern and southern Europeans as "members of the lowest class."

President Woodrow Wilson's policy of non-intervention and his slogan that America would be the "broker of peace" was challenged by the sinking of the British ocean liner, the Lusitania, on May 7, 1915, causing the deaths of 128 Americans. Eventually, Wilson's foreign policy would collapse in the face of international events. The German policy of unrestricted submarine warfare, the subsequent sinking of seven United States merchant ships and the release to the American public of the contents of the Zimmermann Telegram, a diplomatic proposal calling for a military alliance between Germany and Mexico, forced Wilson to ask Congress for a Declaration of War. On April 6, 1917, Congress granted Wilson's request for the United States to enter what was to be termed a "war to end all wars" and the landscape of many collegiate campuses fell under the jurisdiction of a military commandant.

> Although some historians attribute the term "a war to end all wars" to Woodrow Wilson, the true author was British writer H.G. Wells.

German-American loyalty became a major issue of the Wilson Administration. Anti-German hysteria gripped the United States from coast to coast. Both private organizations as well as Wilson's anti-German propaganda machine took front and center attacking German churches, schools, societies, and newspapers. The German community of New Haven faced similar discriminatory practices. The world in apparent turmoil, the future unsure, Kiphuth dutifully complied with the Selective Service Act of 1917 and registered. He was granted an exemption on the basis of: "Physical Trainer ROTC Yale."

Kiphuth proudly announced that "all members of Yale's 1917-18 swim team were also either members of the Yale Naval Reserve Officers' Training Corps or the Army Reserve Officers' Training Corps," a most important fact as the law only allowed 220 students to enroll in ROTC. Throughout its early history and until a faculty vote in 1969 eliminated credit for ROTC courses, Yale ROTC programs played a significant role in America's military history. The names of the fallen, such as Nathan Hale, can be found inscribed on the walls of Woolsey Hall.

With Mann's departure on January 26, 1918, Kiphuth, the unofficial and unpaid volunteer, resumed control and led the team to its seventh straight Intercollegiate Swimming Association dual meet title.

## Kiphuth's Dry Land Program

With respect to competitive swimming, Kiphuth, in 1918, was a greenhorn. But he was a wise and observant greenhorn. Kiphuth adopted most of the old methods, but held firmly to his own belief in the physical and well-conditioned body. He ignored the vast majority of experts who insisted that swimmers must have loose and flabby muscles.

There is evidence that others advocated similar dry land exercises for swimmers. Archibald Sinclair and William Henry, in the 1916 fourth edition of their book *Swimming*, highly recommended gym work. Professor Nelligan who was at Amherst College at the time added three-to-five mile walks and slow runs of 800-yards followed by 15 minutes of chest weights or dumb bell work to his swimming program.

Despite those early pioneers, Ed Kennedy, the Columbia University coach from 1910 until 1955, stated that anyone advocating gymnasium work for their swimmer in the early days was considered a lunatic because coaches, with few exceptions, believed that exercise or weight work would destroy the loose, flabby muscles necessary for a competitive swimmer's success. However, Kiphuth was a physical educator who held fast to the concept that a strong, physically fit body was the key to athletic success. He brought physical training into swimming at a time when others scorned any type of physical activity for their swimmers. It was a novel approach for swimming. Other advocates had come and gone, winning little, if any, support for their cause. They had been theorists, not innovators or achievers. Kiphuth's dry land program was the result of personal observation, research, and experience.

The program was conceived on the principle that developing the proper mechanics of muscle and movement would create a strong and healthy body, beneficial to any athlete, including swimmers. This program, like any other, underwent changes and modifications as Kiphuth's knowledge expanded. In its most basic form the routine consisted of 60 minutes of exercise. Included in the 60-minute period were 45 minutes of calisthenics and 15 minutes of work with a 16-pound medicine ball. After that, the swimmers were encouraged to continue on their own with 20 to 30 minutes of pulley-weight exercises.

To partake in Kiphuth's program was, on the one hand, a physical experience and, on the other, an educational enlightenment. The coach, usually clad in either his white Yale sweat suit or his fireman red long johns, kept a rhythmic cadence by use of a bamboo pole. Mind and body responded automatically to the beat and tempo which was the dictum of either change of cadence or change of exercise. Occasionally, his deep baritone voice permeated the assemblage in order to chastise or encourage a fledgling student. The master's stick oftentimes missed a required beat in order to be put to better use upon the backside or personage of an incompetent performer. Whether standing in front of or strolling among the gathered guests, he seemed to possess an infallible ability to perceive even the most minute happening within the gymnasium. From the moment of commencement until the moment of termination, one was cognizant of the fact that Kiphuth seemed to be measuring both mental and physical capabilities.

When Mayer approached Kiphuth in the fall of 1917 requesting assistance, to Mayer's astonishment, Kiphuth recommended the radical concept of dry land exercise. Although this represented a revolutionary development, many swimmers accepted Kiphuth's invitation to "commit suicide." To the amazement of all, the exercises did not tighten muscles nor cause deficiency in performance. Instead, performance improved. His theory of a program of exercises successfully overthrew the long-entrenched concept that soft muscles made good swimmers.

Unfortunately, one can only speculate as to Mann's disbelief in January 1918, upon arriving at Yale, that Kiphuth had violated one of the cardinal rules of swimming. His astonishment, as verbally expressed, must have been a classic *reductio ad absurdum*. Destined to become the Michigan coach, Mann had traveled to New Haven on the weekends during the month of January in 1915, 1916, and 1917, to offer instruction to the Yale squad. During this period, he was dividing his time among at least four programs: the New York Athletic Club, Brooklyn Poly Prep, Lawrenceville Prep, and the Naval Academy.

While Kiphuth insisted on gym work and year-round training, Mann advocated loose muscles, mechanical rabbits, and swimming. According to Karl Michael, Kiphuth's endorsement of dry land formed a major portion of the professional debate between the two coaches. Fortunately for competitive swimming, this caused two schools of thought to develop. Finally in the early 1950s, when both concepts had undergone growth and modification, these seemingly distinct but conciliatory approaches raised the sport of swimming to new heights.

To Kiphuth's credit, he never shrouded any phase of his program in a cloak of secrecy. He publicly advocated his procedures and opened his workshop to the world of swimming. The coach was a true advocate for the advancement of knowledge at all levels of swimming. He never subscribed to the concept that he was the only knowledgeable aquatic luminary, but remained firm in his belief of a well-conditioned body.

Forbes Carlile, the world famous Australian coach, credited Australia's advance in the late 1940s and up to the 1956 Olympic Games as partially the result of reading, adapting, and modifying the Yale exercises to the needs of their program. In his book *Forbes Carlile on Swimming*, he mentioned a letter he received from John Marshall, Yale's Australian import. Marshall attributed his swimming success to Kiphuth's dry land program, and Carlile cited the letter as further proof of the importance of dry land exercise.

Kiphuth's dry land program found further disciples at Dartmouth, Princeton, Wesleyan, and various New England prep schools. John Miller of Mercersburg Academy (Pennsylvania) supplemented Kiphuth's program with cross-country running. Charles McCaffree, who coached at Michigan State from 1941 to 1969, stated that in 1952 his swimmer Bert McLaughlin decided to follow Kiphuth's program as outlined in his book *Swimming*. Misunderstanding the text, McLaughlin proceeded to double everything suggested and set a new NCAA record in the quarter mile.

Through the 1930s and into the early war years, many Yale athletic teams, with the consent or insistence of their coaches, took part in Kiphuth's program of dry land exercises. Yale's highly respected ice hockey coach Holc York collaborated with Kiphuth in May of 1937 to construct a series of exercises for his team to practice over the summer months to strengthen ankle and thigh muscles.

Bob Geigengack, the Yale track coach, credited Kiphuth as the pioneer who understood the principles of dry land exercise and increased workload. He felt it was due to Kiphuth's efforts and comprehension of anatomy and physiology that the gap between swimming and track began to narrow.

In general, there is consensus among leading authorities that Kiphuth was the first to institute a bona fide dry land program for swimmers. The concept was not only revolutionary, but also years in advance of its time and is responsible for the innovative practices in existence today. The executive director of the Swimming Hall of Fame, Buck Dawson, credited Kiphuth with bringing "physical training" into swimming at a time when others "scorned" the practice. The French swimming historian Francois Oppenheim credited Kiphuth with being "the first and undisputed leader of dry land exercises." He pointed out that, "until Kiphuth's organized approach, the practical application remained for the most part, an unpopular and untested theory in the evolution of competitive swimming."

At the conclusion of the bodybuilding program, two or three weeks were devoted to the review of stroke fundamentals. One thousand yards to one mile was the order of the day, mixed with starts, turns, body position, breathing, and stroke techniques. Kiphuth then utilized the middle third of the season to develop endurance and a sense of pace. He always stressed the importance of holding an even pace and employed mechanical means such as flashing underwater lights to ensure that his swimmers gained some knowledge and understanding of the concept.

James "Doc" Councilman, former Indiana University coach, credited both Kiphuth and Mann for utilizing "wind sprints" in the 1920s. Both coaches, toward the end of the practice session, would run their athletes through 10 to 15 50-yard repeats. Cecil Colwin indicated that the Australians adopted this concept from Kiphuth and it was instrumental in the development of their interval training program. In the late 1940s, Kiphuth employed 15 x 100-meter swims at 10, 20, or 30-second rest intervals for his middle distance swimmers. Unfortunately, he did not pursue this to the degree employed today.

In the Olympic summer of 1952, due to the large number of athletes training at Yale, Kiphuth utilized circle swimming, where athletes swim up on the right side of the lane and back down the left side. This allowed multiple swimmers to share a lane. Although innovative for its time, he did not continue this practice as he preferred to run heats. It was not until about 1960, when other coaches had perfected this technique of circle swimming and interval training, that Kiphuth added these practices to his program on a regular basis.

His conditioning concept was certainly unique. His water work, in itself, was not unique, except that he was one of the few to stress the importance of year-round training and mileage, especially for the distance swimmer. Kiphuth wrote:

> It should also be emphasized that the more mileage covered by a swimmer through the years, year in and year out, the greater the chances for success, especially in middle distance swimming. There is neither an easy road nor short cut to organic strength and vigor.... This constitutional power can only be built as in the case of the development of muscular power by intelligent application of work, work, training and work, ad infinitum. This is the sort of conditioning that cannot be bought in pill-form over the counter, and athletic achievement and success, like all good things in life, achievement and success can only be accomplished through hard work, sacrifice, and discipline.

COACHES KIPHUTH and BURKE WATCH MEDICINE BALL DRILL
MARSHALL, MOORE, McFAUL, THOMAN

# Building Yale's Legacy

In the first 12 years of Yale swimming from the fall of 1897 until the spring of 1909, deemed the pre-Kiphuth era, Yale competed in only 48 dual meets winning 28 and losing 20. The completion of Yale's Carnegie Pool in the fall of 1910 marked the beginning of Yale's dominant position in eastern collegiate swimming with a record of 55 wins and only 11 losses through the 1916-17 season.

The destiny of the team for these 12 years resided in the hands of a student-governed organization called the Yale Swim Association. The number of dual meets held each year was closely tied to the leadership exhibited by the captain, the team's student secretary, the ability to acquire necessary funding, and in many cases the train schedule. Often the season was only comprised of one to three dual meets.

Under Kiphuth's leadership from 1917-1959, Yale's overall record was 550 dual meet victories and a mere 14 losses (10 collegiate losses and four non-collegiate losses). During that span, Kiphuth won 10 of 18 Intercollegiate Swim League dual meet titles, won 17 Intercollegiate Swimming Association (ISA) titles, and won all 18 Eastern Intercollegiate Swim League Championship meets. The university captured four NCAA Championships (1942, 1944, 1951, 1953), eight runner up titles (1940, 1941, 1950, 1952, 1955, 1956, 1957, 1958) and a combination of 14 indoor and outdoor AAU titles for the Yale New Haven Swim Club.

## *The World, Yale, and Kiphuth: 1918-1929*

World War I ended with the signing of the treaty of Versailles on July 28, 1919. Objecting to the strident terms included in that treaty, the United States refused to sign and formulated its own treaty on August 25, 1921.

At the conclusion of the war, four major empires, Austro-Hungarian, German, Ottoman, and Russian, no longer existed. New and former independent nations emerged such as Poland, Finland, Lithuania, and Czechoslovakia. Rumblings of nationalism within the British Empire came to the forefront and Canada, Australia, New Zealand, and South Africa were moving towards independence.

On the home front, the ending of hostilities in 1918 caused an immediate 10-month recession, and finally a depression from 1920-21. The years from 1920 until 1929 impacted the national scene with the establishment of the League of Nations, unsigned by the United States; the Prohibition Amendment; the emergence of United States political figures Eugene V. Debs (Socialist Labor Party) and Robert La Follett (Progressive Party); the appointment of William Howard Taft to the United States Supreme Court; the passing of the Nineteenth Amendment which gave women the right to vote; the formation of the American Football League; the election of President Warren G. Harding; the passing of the Immigration Quota Act; the creation of the Appalachian Trail; the Teapot Dome Scandal (secret leasing of federal oil reserves by the Secretary of the Interior); the Capper-Volstead Act (agricultural exemptions from anti-trust laws); the Osage Reign of Terror (Native American lands and oil); the implementation of the eight-hour work day by U.S. Steel; the death of President Harding and subsequent swearing in of Calvin Coolidge and Coolidge's re-election by a wide margin in 1924; the Alaskan diphtheria epidemic; the Scopes Trial (concerning the teaching of evolution in public schools); the Billy Mitchell military trial; Richard Byrd's expedition to the North Pole; the Marines landing in Nicaragua; Charles Lindberg and the Spirit of St. Louis; President Coolidge stating, "I do not choose to run;" the Jazz Singer (Al Jolson) marking the end of silent movies; Henry Ford developing the Model A; Herbert Hoover's election using the slogan "a chicken in every pot, a car in every garage;" the St. Valentine's Day Massacre; and, finally, "Black Thursday" on October 24, 1929, followed by "Black Tuesday" on October 29, marking the beginning of the Great Depression.

Historian Brooks Mather Kelley, in *Yale: A History* noted that at the turn of the 19th century Yale faced a challenge from the new and powerful "private universities like the Johns Hopkins, Leland Stanford, and the University of Chicago" as well as the rise of "large public [tax funded] institutions." The Yale Presidency of Arthur T. Hadley, who was appointed in 1899, inherited the same problems that had plagued the university from its founding: "financial, organizational and attitudinal." Moreover, the students "were more interested in their games, newspapers, sports, and societies" than academics. Hadley's 21-year tenure was marked by failure and success. His biggest and most important contribution was "the shift of administrative and monetary power from the constituent elements of Yale undergraduate college to the professional schools of Yale University." In 1918, Yale was bequeathed a gift of $15 million from corporate lawyer John Sterling, class of 1864. This gift, thanks to competent trustees, mushroomed to over $25 million before it was given to Yale. It was used in part to build the Sterling Memorial Library, the

Law School, the Hall of Graduate Studies, Divinity Quadrangle, and the School of Medicine. Also included was an endowed chair for academic teaching, rather than a research professorship.

By 1921, after seven years of apprenticeship, Kiphuth, never one to be naïve, had paid close attention to the financial and political struggle for power and influence among students, faculty, and alumni. The importance of key faculty and administrative contacts, the development of strong alumni support and donations, and the consolidation of power within his domain, the Carnegie Pool, became the cornerstones of his existence.

When Yale selected James Rowland Angell as Yale's president in 1921, Kiphuth's future appeared to be guaranteed. Angell played a key role in the educational, financial, and physical growth of Yale during his 16 years. One of Angell's primary concerns was the development of first class graduate schools, a move assisted by a significant shift in power from the "college to the central administration." With the power of the purse now in the hands of the Provost, Yale became a place where "the existence of art, music, graduate, and other schools added immeasurably to the undergraduate experience."

By 1921, Kiphuth understood the importance of maintaining close dialogue with the powers within the university, especially the president. He and Angell were of the same mold, believing that greatness can only be achieved by the combination of unity of purpose with creative vision. These goals served as the basis for a strong bond between the two men.

President Angell in his annual letter of congratulations to Kiphuth on March 14, 1930, wrote: "You are too well aware of my general appreciation of your work for me to go into details in the matter. Nevertheless, accept my sincere congratulations and my best wishes for the continued success of your undertakings."

### *Kiphuth's 1919-1929 Seasons*

The *Intercollegiate Swimming Guide*, published by various entities through the years, only recognized the dual meet championship teams from both the Eastern and Western Conferences and the team and individual champions from the conference meets.

The program of swimming events in the Wilson Athletic Library's *Official Swimming Guide 1919-20* listed the order of events as the four man relay, the fancy diving, the individual events, which were the 40 or 50 freestyle, the 40, 200 or 220 breaststroke, the plunge for distance, the 220 freestyle, the 40 or 150 backstroke, and the 100 freestyle. In the relay the winning team scored five points. In the individual events, first place scored five points, second place scored three points, and third place scored one point. In addition, most meets were followed by either water polo or water basketball, which were more interesting to the student body because of the undisciplined rules in effect for those contests.

When Yale's 1919-20 season ended with victories in 10 dual meets as well as in four of five events at the ISA championships, Kiphuth declared that the team "must be the greatest college team in the history of the sport." The debate began for a dual meet swim off between the champions of the eastern and western conferences to determine the mythical national champion.

Success creates publicity and in turn publicity creates interest. In the fall of 1922, more than 100 swimmers responded when the announcement in the *Yale Daily News* called for all swimming candidates to report. More in line with his philosophy of year round conditioning, Kiphuth moved the start of the practice season from the second week of December to the third week of November. He offered three practice sessions a day: noon, three, and five to accommodate the large numbers and to avoid academic conflicts. In turn, he challenged the team with the words, "the fine record of last year's team will set the goal."

From 1918 until 1923, Yale won all six Intercollegiate Swim Association titles, and eclipsed 21 world records and 32 collegiate records. Yale now held every AAU world relay record except the 300 freestyle relay.

Kiphuth immortalized the road to national and international publicity for Yale and swimming by successfully making record performances the order of the day. The critics, imbued by jealousy and disbelief, tended to down play any of Yale's AAU world relay records. Many coaches called for a moratorium, arguing that collegiate swimmers should compete only in approved collegiate distances. To Kiphuth, criticism represented an ocean wave of little consequence and he deplored their lack of vision. Perhaps the words of T.S. Eliot fit the situation best: "Half the harm that is done in this world is due to people who want to feel important. They don't mean to do harm.... Or they do not see it...they are absorbed in the endless struggle to think well of themselves."

However, by the conclusion of the 1928 season, the NCAA, with pressure from a number of collegiate coaches, voted to eliminate any noteworthy performances by collegiate swimmers in swimming races that were not normally held in NCAA-sanctioned meets. There appears to be no question that narrowness of thought, human jealousy, the desire to maintain limited squads, and the attempt to maintain purity of events played a major role in this decision. Kiphuth and the ISA leadership

*Building Yale's Legacy*

**1921 Yale World Record 250-Yard Relay Team**

Holde, (Mgr.); Jelliffe; Gauss; Pratt; Banks; Solley: Kiphuth (Coach).

**1922 Yale World Record 250-Yard Relay Team**

Bundy (Mgr.); Jelliffe; Binney; Thurston (Capt.); Solley; Pratt; Kiphuth (Coach).

voiced strong dissatisfaction with the decision to no avail. However, coach Mann of Michigan in his quest to challenge Yale's superiority also ignored the edict.

Undaunted by this setback, Kiphuth embraced the opportunity under AAU rules to get an AAU sanction to surpass American records, American noteworthy records, and world records for both individual and relay events over any AAU recognized distance. Yale had the facility, Kiphuth had the manpower, and a major "Y" (the Yale varsity letter) under the Yale Athletic Association rules could only be earned with a world record performance. The motive of opportunity for his charges, the national and international publicity it would generate for swimming and for Yale were too much for Kiphuth to ignore.

At the conclusion of the 1922 season, the United States Naval Academy challenged Yale, through official channels as well as in the *New York*

*Times*, to prove its "superiority." On April 1, 1922, with approval from the Yale Athletic Association, Kiphuth inflicted a humiliating defeat on Navy, 31 to 13. Yale won four of the five races in front of a capacity crowd at Yale's Carnegie Pool.

In 1924, Yale was dethroned as champion of the ISA for the first time since 1913. Princeton reigned supreme by defeating Yale twice during the competitive season. The team suffered further humiliation when Navy, the Boys Club of New York, and the alumni made it the worst season in Yale's history, ending with a record of 10 wins and five losses. Navy had become a powerful force in collegiate swimming and would go on to win two unofficial NCAA championships in 1925 and 1926. The NCAA refused to sanction a scored team championship meet for swimming until 1937, and the Yale Athletic Association, on the grounds of the loss of academic class time, and limited funds, refused to allow Yale to compete in the unofficial championships. There was one exception in 1933 when Yale hosted the unsanctioned championship and showcased the new Payne Whitney Pool.

A new and significant era in collegiate swimming began when Mann, who had been the aquatic director at the Detroit Athletic Club, became the Michigan coach in 1925. He immediately prepared his "mermen" to challenge Yale's domination of collegiate and world relay records. The relay "dual in the pool" found Michigan surpassing five of Yale's recognized world relay records in 1927. Yale met the challenge with its amazing contingent of six sterling sprinters: James Bronson, E. W. Peterson, Stewart Scott, Ernest Clarke, Allison Choate, and Phil Bunnell. These swimmers set seven collegiate and world relay marks in 1928. In 1929, Michigan's 18-man contingent eclipsed Yale's revered 1926 mark for the mile relay (1760 yards) by over one second. As a result, Kiphuth and Mann enlivened the aquatic world by consistently striving, and usually succeeding, in lowering each other's collegiate and world standards in a variety of relay distances and strokes. The collegiate dual in the pool between Yale and Michigan spread to other collegiate and public teams. Northwestern, the United States Naval Academy, Minnesota, the New York Athletic Club, the Chicago Athletic Club, and even the Brooklyn Central YMCA began breaking AAU sanctioned relay records as well.

Kiphuth fully understood what this rivalry with Michigan meant to American collegiate swimming as a whole. He lived for the challenge and the opportunity it presented for national and international publicity for the sport. Coverage by major newspapers generated worldwide recognition for America's swimmers, as well as for collegiate programs.

In 1925, Kiphuth secured the ISA dual meet title in the final relay against Princeton by using Yale's quarterback, Philip Bunnell, on the final leg of the 200 freestyle relay. This marked a new era of Kiphuth's domination of the ISA, a domination that would include 12 consecutive championships and 165 collegiate victories before Harvard would terminate the streak in 1937. By 1926 student interest in Yale swimming hit a milestone. At the first preseason meeting, Kiphuth greeted over 250 candidates.

The college coaches' call for a dual meet between the eastern and western conference champions was finally heard by the NCAA in 1928. On April 2, the Carnegie pool had the distinction of being the site of the first ever national swim off. Although Yale led Michigan 31 to 23 and claimed five of the six individual races, the outcome depended on the victor of the 200 freestyle relay. With eight points at stake (the rule had been changed to eight points for the relay), and the potential for a tie score, the winner of the relay would emerge victorious, under NCAA rules. Kiphuth and Mann paced the pool deck both confident that their strategic maneuvering of manpower gave them the four finest relay men to secure victory. In the end, Captain House of Yale defeated his counterpart Captain Darnall of Michigan by a fingertip for a 39 to 23 Eli victory before an electrified capacity crowd. As was their custom, Kiphuth and Mann respectfully shook hands while already contemplating the next opportunity to cross swords. These two predestined titans of the collegiate world would meet again in 1930, 1938, 1939, 1940, and 1942. For, as Rudyard Kipling stated: "Oh, East is East and West is West...But there is neither East nor West...When two strong men stand face to face, tho' they come from the ends of the earth."

Perhaps the most distinctive aspect of the 1928 collegiate season occurred on March 6, when Kiphuth and his capable assistant Howard Stepp reported to Princeton to take charge of coaching the Princeton squad due to the sudden resignation of their coach, Frank Sullivan. The Yale authorities, learning of the resignation of Sullivan, offered Princeton the services of Kiphuth. Dr. Charles W. Kennedy, Chairman of the Princeton Board of Athletic Control, accepted the generous offer as headlined in the *New York Times*, "Yale Lends Coach to Princeton to Train Swimmers for Meet of the Two Schools." Kiphuth remained for two days, leaving Stepp behind to complete the remaining three weeks of the season. Needless to say, as the *New York Times* reported on March 6, 1928, Stepp remained on as the new Princeton coach until the conclusion of the 1953 season.

From 1925 through 1932, Yale continued to surpass over 36 world records and over 29 collegiate marks. The Yale-Rutgers dual meet in 1929 ended in a 31-to-31 deadlock; however, under the rules in place at that time, the tie was broken by assigning the win to the team that won the final relay. Yale, by winning the final relay, was declared the champion of the ISA.

Administratively, Kiphuth began a campaign in the 1920s aimed at improving the quality of eastern collegiate swimming and as a result American swimming. The formation of the College Swimming Coaches Association on November 22, 1922, predetermined the inevitable shift of the reins of power from athlete to coach and a new destiny for the sport of swimming. At this point Kiphuth took center stage and was elected secretary-treasurer. He knew that many collegiate coaches lacked any interest in international competition, believing that venue belonged in the realm of private athletic clubs. Using the tactics of "greater participation" and "conformity of a national dual meet schedule of events," he recommended to the ISA the elimination of the plunge for distance, the addition of backstroke and breaststroke events already contested in the western conference, and the replacement of the 220-yard freestyle with the 440-yard freestyle and the 200-yard freestyle relay with the 400-yard freestyle relay. The National Collegiate Coaches Association also considered his recommendations, and accepted some of his proposals, adding the 440 as well as the backstroke and breaststroke events. In addition, they wisely kept the 220, while adding a medley relay and finally allowing a 1500-meter freestyle event at the NCAA Championships to be contested on Friday morning at 10 a.m. as a time final event.

# The Yale Swimming Carnival

In the early nineteenth century, many collegiate swim teams featured water carnivals as a source of student entertainment and as a way to provide much needed revenue. Yale was no exception.

As late as 1922, the Yale Swimming Carnival was no more than an intramural aquatic show. By 1923, according to Phil Moriarty, Kiphuth's assistant coach, Kiphuth began to understand "the fine line between entertaining the student body" and the importance of engaging the faculty and the general public. By utilizing his "flair for showmanship" and realizing the importance of publicity, the head coach found avenues to include faculty children, clown diving, gown and candle races, water polo exhibitions, relay races, and the Yale Whiffenpoofs, a famous Yale a cappella singing group, founded in 1909. As a result, attendance increased dramatically. The Carnival attracted the attention of not only the Connecticut media but more importantly the New York media by featuring Olympic champion and world record holder Johnny Weismueller. The world record carnival was then featured in both national and international headlines. From then on the importance of newspaper headlines in the promotion of Yale and the sport of swimming became evident.

With the completion of Yale's Payne Whitney pool in 1932, the Carnival became a pageant of famous aquatic personalities and successful world record attempts. The event attracted a full audience and the publicity of the New Haven, Boston, and New York newspapers. Kiphuth continued to gain the attention of the Yale faculty by featuring their children, both girls and boys, in relay races and swim lesson exhibitions. He attracted interest from the student body by featuring a 200 freestyle relay race among Yale's six colleges. The 1930s carnivals featured Yale's continual and successful assault on American and World relay records and individual world record attempts by American Olympic swimmers Peter Fick, Princeton's Al VanDeWeghe, and Rhode Island high school sensation John Higgins.

On the 13th of February 1943, a capacity crowd reaching 2,187 spectators witnessed the breaking of 17 swimming standards highlighted by Alan Ford's world record lead off leg of 50.6 in a world record 400 freestyle relay. The additional members of the relay were Richard Baribault, Brewster MacFadden, and Richard Lyon. Ford continued his assault on the record book by surpassing the American and American noteworthy records in the 50 and 75-yard backstroke and the 300-yard medley relay, aided by Edwin Davidge and MacFadden. In 1947, LaSalle College's Joe Verdue set a world record in the 200-meter breaststroke in Yale's fifth floor 50-meter pool, while Yale established new American records in backstroke and freestyle relays in Yale's 25-yard Exhibition Pool.

From 1948 onward, the Carnival included a water ballet exhibition by featuring a collegiate team, and national AAU solo champions like Beulah Gundling, or the popular movie star Esther Williams. Comedy and exhibition diving by Olympic Champion divers such as Michigan's Bruce Harlan, collegiate champion Skippy Browning of Texas, or Ohio State's Bob Clotworthy were attractive features.

Kiphuth also entertained the public by having attractions such as the amazing Frog Man and aquatic stunt man George Hyde (Yale class of 1910) with incredible feats such as walking on the bottom of the pool and eating under water. In order to attract local interest, the coach featured a women's 100-yard freestyle championship race, the Connecticut boys' state high school championship 300-yard medley relay, and in 1960 added a 220-yard freestyle race in honor of longtime Naugatuck (Connecticut) high school coach Alex "Gimbo" Sullivan.

Moriarty, in reflecting on the many years that Kiphuth directed the Yale Carnival, stated that "everything fit in so well with Kiphuth's plan; the sport was young; new ideas were few and far between; and he was an imaginative man; so if there was a chance to give the public a world record and he had the team, Kiphuth took full advantage of it. It put the Yale name in all the record books in the world." Moreover, Moriarty pointed out that Kiphuth took "extreme pride in the fact that more records were set in the Yale pool, that more outstanding swimmers had swum in the Yale pool, that more championships had been held in the Yale pool, and that more foreign observers had come over to observe Yale swimming than anywhere else in the world. And although for over 25 years Yale was the center of the swimming world, Kiphuth always insisted that if his guest wanted a true picture of the American swimming scene, he should visit Ohio State and Michigan."

## The Beloved Gymnasium

The firm of Pope, Eggers, and Higgins was the recipient of the award for architectural excellence at the 1936 Olympic Games for the beautifully designed Payne Whitney Gymnasium. The award read in part, "For one of the world's most significant indoor athletic structures completed at the time of the 1932-1936 Olympiad." Pope, Eggers, and Higgins may have won the award, but the Gothic gymnasium bears the indelible mark of Robert John Herman Kiphuth. It was by virtue of his Socratic and Baconian inquiries that the completed structure blends beauty and utility under the same roof. Conducting his own personal research, Mr. Yale pre-examined, probed, and calculated every enigma of the gymnasium. For more than two years, he interviewed, researched, and conducted experiments in order to dictate what went into or did not go into the gymnasium. Not only the pool, but also the building in its entirety received his direct attention. In my interview with the firm's architect R. Jackson Smith, a 1936 Dartmouth graduate and a Yale architecture graduate, also renowned in the world of swimming and diving, he stated:

> Bob Kiphuth unquestionably played a significant role in the construction and planning of the Payne Whitney. The firm appointed two project managers, Rice and Frank, whose responsibility it was to work closely with Kiphuth. This factor, when coupled with Kiphuth's initiative, resulted in his being involved in even the minutest details of the structure.

Once construction began, Kiphuth and John Russell Pope lunched together at Mory's, Yale's legendary dining establishment, each Wednesday in order to discuss in detail the weekly progress and the proposed plans for the immediate future. Kiphuth, on many occasions, invited as his guest any member of the gymnasium staff who desired to confer with Pope and his project managers.

According to Harry Burke, Karl Michael, and Phil Moriarty, it was a wonder that the architect, the builder (Marc Eidlitz of New York), and Kiphuth, the little general, remained friends because "not a stone was laid unless Kiphuth approved." These men in no way wanted to discredit the architect, but rather wanted to stress the endless hours of travel and research by the coach.

Kiphuth's "Cathedral of Sweat" consists of the Main Tower which houses the facilities for general usage, and two competitive wings. The building is 510-feet long, 200-feet deep, and in the Tower, 200-feet in height. The main entrance lies below the Tower and leads to a spacious lobby. There are two adjoining lobbies which lead to the Amphitheatre and Exhibition Pool. Tennis and basketball are a part of the Amphitheatre, which also serves the needs of boxing, wrestling, and fencing exhibitions. This unit, as are all units and all floors, is self-contained and provides two home teams and three visiting teams with dressing, shower, and drying rooms.

The left wing contains the Exhibition Pool measuring 75 by 42 feet. This ultra-modern pool, built in the initial years of 1930, bears witness to Kiphuth's pedagogical attention to detail. The Exhibition Pool stands as his masterpiece. Perhaps Kiphuth's one great disappointment, according to R. Jackson Smith, was the necessity for utilizing demountable frames for the diving boards instead of hydroelectric controlled boards rising from the pool deck. Kiphuth had proposed this innovation for its instructional capability. A Yale trustee who insisted its only function was to encourage laziness on the part of the divers vetoed the proposal.

Kiphuth's aesthetic masterpiece deserves part of the credit for the early emergence of swimming from the "Dark Ages." He personally conducted innumerable experiments to determine the most innovative and practical solutions for solving "mechanical" problems encountered by the competitive swimmer.

Amid the bustling activity of the original Carnegie pool, the coach tested hypothesis after hypothesis. By dangling lights hung from poles, he reasoned the proper depth, angle, and number of lights necessary for illuminating the pool surface. Consequently, he realized the necessity for utilizing prism lights in order to avoid blinding reflection off the water. Kiphuth eliminated lighting at the ends of the pool because it proved to be unnecessary for illumination and both blinding and physically dangerous for the competitive swimmer. In order to determine the proper markings for the swimmer, he drained the Carnegie pool and instructed his staff to paint lines on the bottom of the pool and guide targets on the end walls.

Mr. Yale even subjected the crotch spray to a thorough inspection prior to its installation. Time after time, his assistants were required to test the operation of this innovative sanitary device.

Observing that the walls of the Carnegie pool at both the buttock and shoulder level were stained by blotches of human body oil, as swimmers swam nude in those days, Kiphuth chose Vitrolite, an opaque structural glass product, to line the six-and-one-half foot parapet surrounding the new pool. He noted that Vitrolite cleaned easily and that the 18 sections could be arranged to avoid buttock or shoulder contact with the joints.

Kiphuth also selected one-inch tile, instead of six by 12, to line the shell of the pool. This helped eliminate slippery walls. From water level to three feet below the surface he instructed the contractor to place the smooth edge toward the wall. Therefore, the swimmer gained additional support from the rough edged surface while turning.

In order to control the disturbance caused by waves, Kiphuth insisted on a bull-nose gutter with a curved wall on the inside which would cause the wave to hit the curve, drop down, and level out. He required six, seven-foot lanes, and pool markings which met NCAA and AAU standards for decades to follow. At the starting end of the pool he installed stainless steel starting blocks.

Realizing the perplexity of the problems instigated by the installation of windows, Kiphuth wisely concentrated the lighting in the 46-foot ceiling. This is ably supplemented by the 38 underwater lights. The six-story-high ceiling with its enormous skylight acts as a deterrent to the humidity problems of the past. The coach recommended having the spectator area at a 45-degree angle to encourage spectator crowds; however, this created an issue with keeping that area cool for the crowd, while having the pool deck temperature at 80 degrees for the comfort of the swimmer. This was solved when someone suggested and devised a system whereby steam could be released into the heating system, allowing the swimmers to stay warm, and the spectators to stay cool.

Kiphuth instructed the architect to conceive a five-story-high amphitheater seating arrangement. The 157-foot-wide ceiling is held aloft without the aid of supporting columns, which would have led to obstructed views. The pitch of the seats allows every spectator to have an individual hard back chair with an unobstructed view of the finish wall. Excluding the feasibility of temporary seating being installed at the top of the arena, the natatorium can seat 2,187 spectators.

These innovations, patiently researched and objectively tested by Kiphuth, allowed the Exhibition Pool to represent one of the first great modern pool facilities in the world. This new facility played a significant part in the removal of pools from the dark, damp, cold, dirty, and unsanitary cellars of the past. Ergo, the sport would now have a more appealing aura for both spectator and competitor alike or, as R. Jackson Smith termed it in 1973, "the Payne Whitney Exhibition Pool is unquestionably one of the most dramatic aquatic facilities then and now."

In addition to Kiphuth's innovations, the building boasts sporting facilities for various other teams and purposes. The three rowing tanks for crew practice are located in the rear section of the main tower. Below the tanks, in the sub-basement, are the rifle ranges. Nearby is the gymnasium laundry.

The second floor consists of the cashier's office, coat-check room, manager's office, and the trophy room. Located at each end are the locker rooms, shower rooms, and toilets. This is the first of four identical tiers of dressing facilities, each with the capacity of about 674 lockers.

The third floor houses the 167-by-35 foot practice pool. It is the world's largest suspended natatorium, with 330,000 gallons of water, weighing 2.75 million pounds. Kiphuth had the engineers devise a stainless steel movable bulkhead two feet wide and five feet deep and insisted that there be two gutter levels so that the water level could be dropped for instructional purposes. He had the side walls of both pools faced with a cream colored glass so that custodial staff could service the walls as if they were washing windows.

The fourth floor contains the faculty locker room, a room for rub-downs, the sauna, the steam room, and the staff room. The main corridor to the right or left contains 26 single squash courts, two double squash courts, eight full-sized handball courts, two golf galleries, and two equestrian polo cages. The squash courts are adaptable to accommodate handball.

The fifth floor houses the facilities for the required program of physical education. The 10 exercise rooms are divided equally so that five of them may be adjusted to accommodate basketball, volleyball, or badminton. Five of the rooms are provided with chest weights and Swedish bars, and one room with heavy apparatus. One also finds the general physical education office, examination room, photography room, and the director's office on this level. Also on the fifth floor, the wing off the exhibition pool roof contains a tumbling and diving pit filled with sawdust and loam. A 12-laps-to-the-mile jogging track with banked corners around the amphitheater is supplemented by a nine-and-three-quarters laps-to-the-mile jogging track around the pool.

The sixth, seventh, eighth, and ninth floors serve as the quarters for wrestling, boxing, fencing, and general training.

The building was dedicated in honor of Payne Whitney, a former Yale athlete and graduate, class of 1898. This $5 million masterpiece, a unique blend of Gothic beauty and American ingenuity, was the result of the Whitneys' generosity, the genius of Pope's firm, and Kiphuth's relentless research and experimentation.

## The Beloved Gymnasium

The Payne Whitney Gymnasium
Yale University

# The World, Yale, Kiphuth, and the Great Depression

The Great Depression would be the longest and most severe depression ever experienced by the Western industrial world. The United States had emerged from World War I as the major creditor and financier of postwar Europe; while the German economy was hit the hardest, and was weakened by the need to pay reparations imposed by the Treaty of Versailles. Many nations imposed tariffs and set quotas as a means of protecting domestic production. As a result, by 1932, the volume of international trade declined by more than half.

By the same token, more efficient farming methods and technological changes meant that the supply of agricultural products was rising faster than the demand and prices were falling as a consequence. As prices fell, interest rates rose making it too expensive for both businesses and consumers to borrow money.

The Depression had profound political implications. Germany became a fascist totalitarian state. Hitler's Third Reich, racist to its core, represented itself as the heir of an Aryan culture of classical antiquity embracing the concept of a Nordic-Germanic-Aryan Empire. Meanwhile, Japan's need for raw materials, and eventually its desire for a Pacific Empire, strengthened the militarist element within its government. By 1941, Hideki Tojo, an army general, a fascist, and a nationalist, became Japan's Prime Minister, but more importantly maintained his military rank.

A brief historical review of 1930s America found the completion of the Empire State Building; the founding of Birdseye's frozen vegetables; the opening of the Whitney Museum of Art; the Bonus Army march on Washington; the Model B; the 20th Amendment; election of President Franklin Roosevelt; the New Deal – known historically as the "3 Rs" (relief, recovery, and reform); the 21st Amendment, which ended Prohibition; the Glass-Steagall Banking Act; the Dust Bowl; Senator Huey "Kingfish" Long's "Share the Wealth" Society; the Social Security Act; the establishment of the FBI; the Neutrality Acts; the Hindenburg disaster; the completion of the Golden Gate Bridge; the Hatch Act; Orson Wells' *The War of the Worlds* broadcast; and the New York World's Fair, to highlight some major events.

## *Kiphuth in the 1930s*

In the 1930s, Kiphuth continued his assault on as many individual and relay records as possible. More importantly, however, in the minds of collegiate coaches, the four upcoming dual meets scheduled between Yale and Michigan for 1930, 1938, 1939, and 1940, took center stage.

In the first such match-up, a post season meet on March 31, 1930, east and west, Kiphuth and Mann, battled once again at Yale's Carnegie pool for the mythical national dual meet title. Both men realized it was more than a contest of dual meet superiority. This was the venue that would test each man's training methods: Kiphuth's gym work and year-round training versus Mann's loose-muscles philosophy.

Yale was victorious, winning five of the seven events. Michigan's victories were by Clarence Boldt in the 150-yard backstroke and distance ace Garnet Ault in the 440-yard freestyle. Yale's signature wins were by Robert Messimer in the 50 freestyle, Mahlon Glascock in the fancy dive, Nelson Millard in the 200 breaststroke, John Howland in the 100-yard freestyle, and the 200 freestyle relay of Donald Fobes, Bradford Butler, Messimer, and Howland. Yale defeated its western foe 42 to 20. It was a phenomenal start to what would be a new era for Yale swimming.

> John Howland's claim to fame was that he was the only collegiate swimmer to ever beat Rutgers phenom and Olympian George Kojac.

Kiphuth's initial duty when he was first appointed in 1914 was to conduct brief body building sessions for the students enrolled in Dr. Anderson's nationally recognized new "games" program. He also went on to conduct classes in gymnastics and dance. Appointment to the Carnegie Pool required the additional duties of administering the general swimming program as well as maintaining his commitment to the general physical education program. His subsequent involvement with the competitive swimming team and development of his body building classes were the result of his own initiative.

With the completion of the Payne Whitney Gymnasium, President Angell's commitment to and Kiphuth's belief in the principle of "athletics for all" created Yale's comprehensive required general physical education program, under Kiphuth's direction. This included a 16-week course in the "mechanics" of posture, the leisure skills program, and an extensive intramural program. Kiphuth was promoted to the rank of assistant professor, and appointed head of the general physical education program.

In addition to numerous team and pool records, in the four years following the opening of the Payne Whitney, Yale accounted for 24 new American, collegiate, and world records. Kiphuth realized that the Payne Whitney gave him the ability to realize two of his major objectives, publicity for collegiate swimming and the opportunity to train swimmers for international competition in an indoor 50-meter pool. The invitation went out to the finest collegiate, AAU, and foreign competitors to attempt world record swims at the pool. As was always the custom, free housing was available at the Ray Tompkins house, an arm of the Payne Whitney Gymnasium.

Between 1924 and 1936, thirteen unofficial NCAA collegiate championship meets were held. Northwestern won in 1924, 1929, 1930, and 1933; Navy won in 1925 and 1926, and Michigan won in 1927, 1928, 1931, 1932, 1934, 1935, and 1936. Kiphuth first entered the national championship fray when the NCAA awarded Yale hosting duties for the 1933 Championships, and the Yale Athletic Association lifted the ban on Yale's participation in the meet.

He was now excited that Yale would not only enter and host the meet, but also that he had the opportunity to showcase the Payne Whitney to the world of collegiate swimming. With The Great Depression as the most significant obstacle to a successful meet, Kiphuth persuaded his Yale family to host every athlete, coach, and official for free at the Ray Tompkins House.

At the 1933 NCAAs, Yale's strongest finishes were silver medals for A.T. Hapke in the 220 freestyle and Charles Pierson, Walter Savell, and David Livingston in the 300 medley relay. The remaining gold medal recipients represented Stanford, Rutgers, Navy, and Northwestern.

At the 1934 NCAAs hosted by Ohio State, Yale struck gold when Walter Savell won the 200 breaststroke and Norris Hoyt, Savell, and Livingston won the 300 medley relay. When Harvard hosted the championships in 1935, Yale did not win any gold but exhibited its team depth by placing competitors in all eleven finals. When the meet returned to the Payne Whitney in 1936, Yale picked up three silver medals: John Macionis in the 220 freestyle, Norris Hoyt in the 1500 meters, and the 400 freestyle relay of Donald Wilcox, Richard Cooke, Charles Rogers, and Macionis.

> In 1933, Kiphuth inaugurated his biennial dip in the Dartmouth pool as part of their swim carnival, disproving the Ripley's "Believe It Or Not" statement that Yale's famous coach could not swim a stroke.

In 1937, with pressure from the coaches, the NCAA sanctioned the first officially scored championship. Yale's NCAA record performances from

1937 through 1940 were a third place finish at Minnesota, a fifth place finish at Rutgers, a fourth place finish at Michigan, and a second place finish to Michigan (45-42) in 1940 at home. Michigan won the NCAA Championships for the first five years of the meet's existence. Princeton coach Howard Stepp in his Intercollegiate Review declared Michigan was "probably the finest intercollegiate team of all time." Prior to the 1940 meet Michigan had lost middle distance ace Jim Welsh to illness and Yale had lost backstroker Joe Burns to a broken ankle. Andrew Clark of Wayne State University, who was third in the 1500, second in the 220, and first in the 440, prevented Yale from outscoring Michigan.

Despite its run on NCAA championships, Michigan did not win the AAU title in 1937. There was a controversy over the disqualification of the Princeton medley relay team at the meet. Kiphuth avoided poolside mayhem by locking the officials, judges, and coaches in a conference room until they reached a settlement on the issue. Upholding the disqualification resulted in the Lake Shore Club of Chicago outscoring Michigan for first place honors.

On the regional front, although Yale went undefeated in all 15 of its dual meets in 1936, the ISA league disqualified Yale from being declared the ISA champion. Yale's Board of Athletic Control had disbanded the water polo team, a requirement for league participation. Apparently, the wife of Yale's Director of Athletics felt the sport was too brutal. Due to the rules of engagement at that time, her point was perhaps well taken. It should be noted that under Kiphuth's coaching, Yale water polo won six ISA championships. They won in 1918, tied in 1924, and won outright from 1925 to 1928. Kiphuth continued to coach that sport until its termination in 1936. According to Larry Hart, a former Yale water polo player and President of the USA Water Polo Foundation, Kiphuth taught his players the innovative tactic of placing the left hand under the goalie's armpit in order to twist oneself behind the defending goalie for the score.

As a result of the disqualification, Yale applied for and was admitted to the new Eastern Intercollegiate Swimming League. Due to problems in the formation of the EISL, no individual championships were conducted in 1937.

During the seasons of 1936-37 through 1939-40, Yale won 76 dual meets, losing only six. Yale's domination of the Ivy League took a brief hiatus with losses to Harvard in 1937 (39 to 37) and to both Princeton (38 to 37) and to Harvard (46 to 29) in 1938. Harvard added insult to injury by awarding their victorious merman a major "H" and declaring swimming a major sport. In turn Kiphuth and his team received a further loss when the Yale undergraduate athletic association refused a similar request by the Yale team. The association felt that swimming was not a popular national sport, and if the request were granted other minor Yale sports teams would want the same consideration. In another blow to Yale, Michigan inflicted the other three losses on Yale in 1938, 1939, and 1940.

By 1939, however, Kiphuth returned as king of Eastern swimming, and would lead Yale to 18 consecutive EISL titles. However, until the post WWII era, conference and NCAA championship meets, spectacular in their own right, did not garner the same popularity and interest as the head-to-head dual meet competition between two universities.

Mann's Michigan Wolverines dominated the collegiate scene from 1938 to 1940 and inflicted three devastating defeats on Kiphuth's Bull Dogs. On February 17, 1938, the *New York Times* reported that "After 8 years of agitation for a dual swimming meet between Yale and Michigan…to determine, once and for all, intersectional supremacy between these outstanding college aquatic squads…the Wolverines eked out a 41-34 decision." The Elis, who had been enjoying an undefeated season, faced a heavily favored Wolverine squad that had been undefeated since 1936.

> Yale almost suffered a defeat to Princeton in 1933, when Yale sophomore swimmer David Livingston, who had just set a pool record in the 220 freestyle, decided to take a walk about Princeton's spacious campus. Just prior to the 100 freestyle, Kiphuth realized that should the Tigers score first and second in the 100 and then win the final relay, Yale would suffer defeat. Livingston was needed in order for Yale to secure victory in the final relay. So while Kiphuth held his breath, the Yale swim team manager scoured the campus in pursuit of the wandering Eli. Returning just in time, Livingston was disrobed by his teammates on the pool deck and Yale proceeded to win the relay and the meet.

At the Payne Whitney pool, in front of a capacity crowd, the two teams "battled tooth and nail" in a meet that would not be decided until the final 400-yard relay. New Haven's radio station WELI presented a live broadcast, event-by-event score-by-score, including diving, to a national audience.

The truth of the story however was buried beneath the headlines and within the minute details known only within the minds of two of America's greatest swim coaches and a privileged few who understood the complexity of dual meet strategy.

Yale's path to glory rested with 1936 Olympian and NCAA 1500-meter titleholder John Macionis, the Brueckel brothers Pete and Johnny, Eric Perryman, backstroker Joe Burns, and diver Bill Danforth. On the other hand, as the *New York Times* pointed out, Michigan's road to conquest resided in the hands of national sprint title holder Captain Edward Kirar, 220-yard ace Tom Haynie, and Waldemar Tomski. After Michigan's expected victory in the first event, the 300-yard medley relay, Kiphuth and Mann became two chess players carefully filling out each entry card at the conclusion of the previous race before handing it to the meet referee. Both men had carefully calculated the points necessary for final victory, and what strategy could turn the tide of victory in their favor.

The Bulldogs were not ready to concede, and fought back when Macionis upset Haynie in the 220-yard freestyle, while Pete Brueckel took third. Eric Perryman's upset of Michigan's Tomski in the 50 freestyle, and Yale diver Bill Danforth's narrow victory over Michigan's Jack Wolin by 14 hundredths of a point tied the score at 16. An unexpected one-two finish by Kirar and Tomski of Michigan in the century (100 freestyle) broke the deadlock and set the stage for a Michigan victory prior to the final relay. Mann realized all he needed was second place in the 150 backstroke, a guaranteed sweep of the 200 breaststroke, and a second place finish in the 440 for 39 points and victory. But Kiphuth's fortunes changed when Burns and John Brueckel, both of Yale, responded with a one-two sweep in the 150-yard back to once again even the score at 25. At this point, both Kiphuth and Mann realized the 400 freestyle relay would decide the victor. Mann remained confident that an almost certain one-two finish in the 200 breaststroke would force Kiphuth to swim Macionis in the 440 while he could rest Haynie for the 400 freestyle relay. So a confident Mann, sensing victory was his, handed his entries for the 200 breaststroke to the meet referee.

Kiphuth realized the dark clouds of defeat were imminent unless he could block the Michigan domination in the 200 breaststroke, and have a rested Macionis for the final relay. In a masterful stroke of genius, and to the astonishment of Mann and the capacity crowd, he entered his distance ace, Macionis, in the 200 breaststroke, and Macionis did not disappoint. The score was Yale 30, Michigan 29. The Yale faithful sensed victory could be theirs.

Mann countered with a victory by Haynie over Howard Spendelow and Pete Brueckel in the quarter mile. The score, with only the 400-yard freestyle relay remaining, was tied at 34. Mann, although confident that his two sprint stars, Tomski and Kirar, could not be matched by any Yale swimmer, had strong trepidation about matching a tired Haynie, who had only eight minutes rest, against a rested Macionis on the anchor leg.

Mann's fear proved sound as Yale's distance ace, in a "desperate closing bid," just missed by a whisker the chance to bring a roaring Yale crowd the thrill of victory. Kiphuth, disappointed but always the gracious sportsman, applauded the Michigan swimmers and extended a congratulatory handshake to Coach Mann.

An opportunity for rematch didn't take long, as the teams met again on February 10, 1939, in Ann Arbor. An enthusiastic mostly Michigan home crowd watched Mann's Wolverines inflict a crushing defeat on Kiphuth's Bulldogs, 53 to 22. Yale's only victories were Dan Endweiss in the diving and Edwin Gesner in the 200-yard breaststroke. Michigan set four Big Ten records and took victory in the 100-yard freestyle (Tomski 52.1), 220-yard freestyle (Haynie 2:12.4), the 300 medley relay (Beebe, Haigh, and Hutchens 2:58.2), and the 50-yard freestyle, where Tomski swam 22.9 and equaled the national collegiate mark. Mann now had his second victory in four meetings; however, from the moment the customary hand shake and kudos to the victors were completed, Kiphuth's analytical mind began to envision the necessary steps to reclaim dual meet superiority over his worthy opponent.

The Payne Whitney would set the stage for a return encounter on January 19, 1940. The advantage favored Michigan, but Kiphuth had recruited a high-powered freshman foursome of Howie Johnson, Edward Pope, Richard Kelly, and Renee Chouteau. All were now sophomores and eligible for varsity competition. Mr. Yale was determined to erase the Ann Arbor debacle of 1939. His strategic plan was to garner enough points to allow the final 400 relay to determine the victor. Just a few weeks prior to this meet, the foursome of Kelly, Pope, Russell Duncan, and Johnson had established a new collegiate record of 3:21.6 erasing Michigan's record of 3:22.2.

In contrast to the 1939 debacle, although Michigan won seven of nine events, the meet was a closely contested affair. Most races were decided by inches, not seconds. Michigan won the first event, the 300 medley relay. Yale countered with Johnson's upset of Michigan's James Welsch in the 220 freestyle, but Michigan's Charles Barker set a pool record in winning the 50 freestyle. The Bulldogs' Jim Cook beat Michigan diver and captain Hal Benham in the one-meter dive to make the score Yale 14, Michigan 18. Then Michigan's Sharemet brothers took control with Gus defeating Johnson in the century, and John Sharemet defeating Gesner in the 200 breaststroke. Beebe of Michigan had won the 150-yard backstroke so the score now stood Michigan 34, Yale 25. If the outcome of the meet was to go to the final relay, Yale needed six points in the 440-yard freestyle. The experienced and tested Wolverine swimmer, Welsch, would not allow that to happen. Gus Sharemet, refusing to let

Yale taste even a moment of success, overtook Johnson on the final leg of the 400 freestyle relay for a one-foot victory, silencing the patrician crowd's chant of "Eli, Eli."

For the third consecutive year, Mann, in a hard fought but clean-cut battle, proved Michigan was the finest collegiate team in America.

However, Kiphuth regained a bit of pride when, on February 22, 1940, Yale's annual Alumni Day, meant to showcase Eli athletic power over that year's visiting Ivy League foe, was overshadowed by an epic swimming competition. Over 1,000 Yale alumni and President Seymour watched Yale defeat Princeton in basketball and hockey, but departed early from the wrestling arena to witness Kiphuth's mermen dominate Ohio State in the first clash between the two universities. Yale lost only the one-meter diving and the 200-yard breaststroke, and won the meet 55 to 20. The margin of victory most likely would have been larger but Kiphuth limited the services of Howie Johnson, Rene Chouteau, Edward Pope, and Russell Duncan to one event each.

By 1940, Kiphuth had completed his 23rd season. Despite the losses to Michigan, Yale had an incredibly successful run winning 18 ISA titles, and surpassing over 150 NCAA, American, and world records.

## Kiphuth's Philosophy of Athletics

Robert F. Geigengack, former Yale Track Coach and a product of a classical Jesuit education from The College of the Holy Cross, considered Kiphuth's philosophy of athletics to be "always sound and the application of the resulting principles (to be) steadfast." He compared Kiphuth's discerning thought process to a "rebirth of the great mind of antiquity, Aristotle, who defined the logic of the self-evident and unchangeable first principles." To Geigengack, Kiphuth was "not a politician but a statesman. A politician will seek approval and compromise, but a statesman remains tenaciously steadfast to his principles."

Kiphuth considered athletics to be an integral part of a young man's education as well as a preparation for life. Using this as his major premise, he logically concluded that athletics must be open and available to every member of the student body. Therefore, as an advocate of the ancient Greek concept of mind, body, and spirit, Kiphuth directed Yale's comprehensive program of collegiate and intramural sports.

In 1924, Kiphuth summarized the success of Yale's swim program into six main factors: physical training, large squads, good swimmers, an enthusiastic year-round program, the effective support of the faculty and the athletic officials, and Yale's excellent athletic facilities. Kiphuth could never accept the principle of scholarships for athletic achievement. He believed Yale represented the finest academic institution in the world, and therefore, his workshop would attract the scholar athlete without further inducement. It was not until 1944 that Yale offered a tightly controlled program of academic aid, tuition rebates, bursary employment, and student loans. However, a student athlete with proven need was not permitted to be employed by the Athletic Department, the Gymnasium, or the Intramural Office.

Amateur athletics was sacred to Kiphuth. He often spoke critically about "cheap money" and "sticky fingers," citing as an example the Connecticut AAU boxing scandal of the 1930s. He held firmly to the belief that money and the power of distribution of those funds represented the ultimate challenge to collegiate and amateur sport. Where money and sport were involved, he demanded a strict accounting. Like all great coaches, he inspired those who listened to be wary of finite goods and temporal horizons. He warned that the altar of greed and the lust for power were enemies of the purity of sport.

Kiphuth led by example. Kenneth Treadway an administrator with Phillips 66 and a former coach and founder of the Phillips 66 Splash Club in Bartlesville, Oklahoma, remembered how in 1961 Kiphuth invited him to attend the National Men's Indoor Championships at Yale: "At his feet, I learned how Yale promoted and conducted such smooth National Swimming Championships." At the AAU convention in 1961, both Yale and Phillips 66 bid for the 1962 Men's AAU Indoor Championships. Phillips 66 was the "new dog in town." Yale had hosted the championships countless times. Phillips was awarded the meet by a narrow vote margin. Treadway later wrote in a letter to Jeff Farrell: "I learned after leaving the convention that Mr. Kiphuth had given us his vote personally, and encouraged a few others to vote for our bid as he thought it would be a good thing for Swimming." This exemplified Kiphuth's philosophy that what was best for swimming should eclipse all personal gain. Treadway continued, "[Kiphuth] had a part in Phillips continuing its support and sponsorship of swimming even until this date at the local, state and national level."

Kiphuth believed sport should be an avocation, not a means to an end. He loved the quest for perfection. The conflict, the battle of man against man, not financial gain, must be the goal. Kiphuth envisioned and warned against the rise of a powerful plutocratic NCAA funded by television football money. He pointed out that the NCAA used the power of the purse – loss of television revenue – to keep universities in line.

The conflicts between the NCAA and the AAU were viewed as a battle between good and evil in the coach's mind. He realized that the battle would eventually define the future of athletics as amateur or professional. A powerful and entrenched NCAA usurping a university's institutional control of its academic integrity and athletic program represented in Kiphuth's mind nothing but a conquering empire of external regulations. He believed in Edmund Burke's "moral imagination," for a man either has virtue of heart or he does not. The NCAA had the facilities, the athletes, and, by the 1950s, the television revenue. The NCAA power base resided with the universities of the south, west, and far west. The AAU power base rested with the Ivy and the smaller colleges and universities along the Eastern Seaboard as well as the established and elite athletic clubs.

In contrast, the AAU had no facilities but rather had absolute authority over the non-collegiate sporting contests nationwide and internationally. In order to compete internationally, and in many cases nationally, an athlete had to be sanctioned by the AAU. In a counter-move in the 1950s, the NCAA began requiring that collegiate athletes obtain sanctions to compete in national competitions held by the AAU, and for the most part required the athletes to swim unattached, not claiming any university affiliation. As a case in point, each year the University of Michigan, before participation in the AAU Championships, had to apply for and receive an NCAA sanction. The last minute approval required Michigan coach Gus Stager to forward his entry by telegram to meet the deadline. In turn, Kiphuth, as the host of the indoor AAU Championships, waited patiently each year for the telegram, hoping that swimmers would not be punished by the blind greed of others. I witnessed this myself just days prior to the April 1961 AAU Championships, when I entered Kiphuth's office. In that moment, Bobbie Dawson was processing Coach Stager's telegram.

To Kiphuth, one of the greatest sins that an institution could commit was to allow itself to be caught up in the "football objective." To him, it was a vicious circle: the only objective of a football power was "to draw a bigger crowd in order to build a bigger stadium, in order to have more money to buy more athletes, to produce a better team, to draw more people, to build a bigger stadium, to buy more athletes." On many occasions, he cited the lethal dilemma of this objective.

Kiphuth believed both the institution and the coach must strive to keep a proper essence and to eliminate as many accidental evils as possible. When financial gain is the motive, the integrity of sport is the victim. The "false prophet," intent on destroying the "major premise" of sport for sport's sake, is the true enemy. Therefore, Kiphuth declared, "Retreat is not an option." Rather, it is a call to "muster your forces, exert your influence and prepare for battle."

There remains no question that Yale's President A. Whitney Griswald (1950-1963), prior to the adoption of the Ivy League Code of Athletics in the early 1950s, consulted with and was greatly influenced by Kiphuth. They had been friends from the time Griswald served as a professor of political science. The Code represents many of Kiphuth's philosophical beliefs.

Harry Hainsworth, retired AAU swimming chairman, felt that Kiphuth "had the highest of ideals of fair play." Believing in a strict amateur code, Kiphuth had absolutely no respect for a "man who posed as an amateur and was a professional."

In his concern for age group swimming, Kiphuth wrote to this author, "Isn't it too bad that you can't have a wonderful idealistic amateur movement, like Age Group Swimming, without besmirching with it commercialism. I suppose that humans being what they are, small and petty, can't do anything for its own sake, but always for the almighty dollar."

Kiphuth had a true love in his heart for all forms of athletic performance, as he followed all Yale sports teams and personally knew all of the coaches and athletes. He respected discipline, sacrifice, and dedication. Watching the superior athlete, friend or foe, from any country was a favorite pastime.

On two specific occasions, perhaps more, the coach defended the right of the superior athlete to compete unhindered by the powers that be. In 1960, Jeff Farrell needed an emergency appendectomy just prior to the Olympic Trials. Kiphuth immediately began the conversation and the administrative process to allow Farrell to either be granted an automatic waiver as a member of the Olympic team, or to be allowed the right of a post Olympic Trials swim off. Although Farrell, the ultimate competitor, refused both, Kiphuth was there by his side the entire time.

In 1964, Kiphuth went to bat for Murray Rose, a world and Olympic gold medalist, when Rose was unable to compete in the Australian Olympic trials and was therefore denied the right to represent Australia at the Olympics. Rose had a commitment to the movie *Ride the Wild Surf* that kept him from attending the trials, which were held eight months before the October Tokyo Olympic Games. However, Rose, still training under Coach Peter Daland set two world records in July of 1964: a 17:01.8 for 1500 meters at the USA nationals in Los Altos, and a week later for 800 meters in Canada. Australia, based on its selection process, still denied him the opportunity for Olympic representation.

> This author was deck side in 1964 in Los Altos as an assistant to Peter Daland, during Murray Rose's first world record swim. At the finish of the race, a timer exclaimed to Rose, "Wow do you know what time you just did?" Rose, the ultimate competitor, had a tremendous sense of pace, and responded, "17:02." Perhaps the stop watches were incorrect or the timers were lapse in their duties but Murray missed the official time by only two tenths of a second.

The prolific defender of athletes then contacted Australia's Olympic powers on behalf of Murray, requesting that he be allowed to represent Australia despite missing the trials. Kiphuth's argument was based on the precedent established in 1952 by Australian authorities in allowing John Marshall's world record performances as an automatic ticket to their national team. Berge Phillips, the icon of Australian swimming, rejected this appeal outright. When this failed, Kiphuth, not one to accept defeat, without hesitation and in defiance of and certainly to the ire of Phillips requested that FINA, the international governing body for aquatic sports, allow Rose to compete under the flag of the International Olympic Committee. Of course, this too failed. Kiphuth's proposal of an athlete competing under the IOC flag was 16 years ahead of his time. In the 1980 Moscow Olympics, independent athletes were permitted to compete due to the United States' boycott.

Kiphuth's unwavering support of Farrell and Murray represented his philosophy that the welfare of the athlete should reign supreme. He believed that advances in swimming knowledge, like academic knowledge, belonged to the universal world of swimming. Refusal to share knowledge or access to one's facility was pure selfishness.

He believed that competition defined the character of the man in victory or defeat. Kiphuth told this author personally, on many occasions, that the true character of the athlete was not in the public honor of victory, but whether he wore that mantel with dignity and humility. He preached a firm and unrelenting message of truth to his charges, with the age-old quote borrowed in part from Arthur Murray's Dance studio: "applause dies, awards tarnish, achievements are forgotten, and accolades and certificates are buried with the owner."

## Man of Taste, Man of Letters

*"I have never let my schooling interfere with my education"*
*- Mark Twain*

Kiphuth and his wife Louise married in June of 1917. While Louise dedicated herself to the home and the professional ambitions of her husband, she played a significant role in their choice of cultural pursuits. In order to feed their varied and intense interests, they not only attended the academic and athletic offerings at Yale, but also often traveled to New York for its great cultural offerings.

Kiphuth's initial preoccupation with, participation in, and digestion of materials and books concerned with the history of dance, were stimulated by Louise's personal friendship with Ruth St. Denis, a pioneer of modern dance. Mostly because of their own interest and partially because of Miss St. Denis, they became devotees of, and on occasion friends with, such renowned performers as Mary Wigman, Ted Shawn, Isadora Duncan, and Martha Graham. Consequently, Kiphuth's teenage introduction to dance developed into an intense and life-long interest. While they went to the Gotham City to see and renew their friendship with the renowned dancers of that era, they did not ignore significant athletic events such as the Dempsey-Firpo fight, nor the distance running of the Flying Finn Paavo Nurmi.

There is evidence to suggest that a second source of income, belonging to Louise, may have provided the funds necessary for the couple to enjoy the performing arts, sporting events, and travel. A document discovered in the Yale files and signed by Louise Delaney Kiphuth, witnessed by Oscar Kiphuth, Bob Kiphuth's brother, and dated June 26, 1926, appointed Chapin S. Newhard as power of attorney over a St. Louis, Missouri, bank account. Newhard, who was from a wealthy and politically influential St. Louis family, was founder, president, and chairman of a stock brokerage firm, the Newhard Company, and a former Brown University swimmer, class of 1922.

By 1924, the Yale School of Art hired George Pierce Baker, America's foremost playwright, to be the first chairman of Yale's new drama department. Kiphuth and Louise did not allow the resulting on-campus opportunities to escape them. In addition, New Haven's Schubert Theatre provided the convenience of attendance at pre-Broadway productions.

During the summer of 1925, the Kiphuths traveled to Germany to study Dr. Bess Mensendieck's system of therapeutic movement. It was a technique of exercises, both corrective and preventive, to reshape, rebuild, and revitalize the body. On a future trip Kiphuth and his son Delaney, returning from Europe aboard the U.S.S. York, developed a lasting friendship with Dr. Mensendieck, who was also a passenger. The Kiphuths learned that she was en route to the United States in order to introduce her system of exercises.

As a consequence of this meeting, Kiphuth and Louise traveled three days a week to New York to fully learn the Mensendieck Method. Shortly thereafter, all gymnasium employees were required to take the course from Al Motely, a student of Mensendieck, whom Kiphuth hired to conduct the university program in corrective exercises. Motely, himself quite frail from rheumatic fever as a child, had been rehabilitated by a firm commitment to this method. By the middle 1930s, the popularity of the Mensendieck System had captured the interest of not only America's social elite, but also of such Hollywood celebrities as Ingrid Bergman, Fredric March, and Gloria Swanson.

Joe Brown, a former Temple University football player, who later boxed-professionally, became Princeton University's boxing coach in 1937. Brown continued as Princeton's boxing coach, but with the completion of a seven-year apprenticeship in sculpture under R. Tait McKenzie at the University of Pennsylvania, he also became Princeton's artist in residence and gained full professorship in 1962. Famous for sculpting many sports figures, such as Duke Kahanamoku (swimming), Jack Kelly (rowing), Jesse Owens (track), Bill Bradley (basketball), and busts of poet Robert Frost, Supreme Court Justice Louis Brandeis, and author John Steinbeck, Brown upon his appointment to the National Art Museum Of Sport (NAMOS) became a colleague of Kiphuth.

Brown's wife, Gwyneth King Brown, mentioned Kiphuth's love for dance and his excursions to the New York theatrical scene when she wrote:

> Bob loved to watch dancers and having seen many performances at home and abroad he had saved a number of programs and photos; those of the 1920s and 1930s I found most interesting because I drew and painted dancers, and had studied ballet. Bob, my husband and I, found we liked [Mary] Wigman, Hanya Holm, Gene Kelly, Ray Bolger, and (if we had seen them) Nijinsky, Isadora Duncan, and Pavlova. Bob saw the film *Damn Yankees* three times because he enjoyed the baseball ballet number, in which the choreographer for the

first time used authentic baseball movement. He agreed with us that dancers could learn a lot from watching the athletics, perhaps introducing more virility into the roles of the male dancer.

The three of us saw several dance performances in New York including the first appearance of the Jose Greco and [Igor] Moiseyev troupes. We arrived somewhat late for the Moiseyev and once inside Bob ran ahead of us up the stairs to the balcony saying 'Hurry or we'll miss the first number.' At the time he had had a heart attack and was not supposed to exert himself. We saw a remarkable film at the Thalia cinema called *Flamenco* featuring Antonio, the great classical dancer of Spain.

*Flamenco* was a documentary spotlighting the best Flamenco dancers in Spain such as Pilar Lopez, Maria Luz, Pacita Tomas, and Roberto Ximenez. Mrs. Brown continued, "Bob was so thrilled by this film that in 1959 he wrote 'still trying to get our little theater (in New Haven) to show the film but without success. We will have to go down to the Thalia again to see it. I still think it is the greatest dance film I have ever seen.'"

The Director of the Frick Collection in New York City and former Yale swimmer Edgar Munhall reminisced on the many occasions when Kiphuth would attend the cultural offerings at Yale. The concert and ballet performances at Woolsey Hall found Kiphuth and his collective entourage of athletes in constant attendance. Kiphuth loved to perform and he loved the performer. To share this love with Kiphuth was a journey down the long road from education to learning. On one occasion, this author attended a Robert Frost lecture at Yale and was not surprised to see Kiphuth in attendance. He could recite or quote from memory phrases from many major works of Victorian and Contemporary poetry.

His many swimming trips to Japan resulted in an intensive study of Japanese culture. He became an authority not only on Japanese music, the history of the Geishas, and Japanese prints, but also the Kabuki dance theater, the Bunraku puppet theater, and the Kano School of Art.

Kiphuth projected his early enjoyment of the theater and dance into an earnest and sincere academic interest. Because of this, he also cultivated an interest in the contemporary playwrights, especially Eugene O'Neill, who was just stepping into the limelight. As a result, Kiphuth acquired a collection of O'Neill's plays right off the book stands. O'Neill won three Pulitzer Prizes in the 1920s for *Beyond the Horizon*, *Anna Christie*, and *Strange Interlude*. The fourth Pulitzer came in 1957, after his death. In 1936, O'Neill became the first and only American playwright to win the Nobel Prize for Literature. Kiphuth's favorite was O'Neill's *Long Day's*

*Journey into Night*, a largely autobiographical tragedy of a family's journey in time, both past and present. When Random House, honoring the wishes of the deceased O'Neill, refused to publish the play, his widow gave the rights to the Yale University Press in 1956.

Kiphuth's attention to contemporary American Literature was stimulated by his reading of *The American Mercury* and the *Smart Set Magazine*. This generated exposure to the writings of H.L. Mencken, George J. Nathan, Ernest Hemingway, F. Scott Fitzgerald, and Theodore Dreiser, among others. Kiphuth had personal friendships with Alistair Cooke, Archibald MacLeish, and Thornton Wilder. On many occasions one could find Kiphuth at a table down at Mory's, listening intently to or contributing to chatter regarding modern day literature including the latest student fad, *Winnie-the-Pooh* by English author A. A. Milne. Owing to Kiphuth's interest in the works of H. L. Mencken, Deane Keller, a Yale professor of painting and drawing and Kiphuth's long-time friend, gifted Kiphuth with a collection of correspondence between Keller's father and Mencken.

Kiphuth was equally interested in studying the roots of America. Ken Treadway, a Native American and longtime coach, AAU, USS, and USOC representative, and executive at Phillips 66, recalled: "I could not send him enough history about the American Indians, the history of Oklahoma, of Mr. Frank Phillips and the Company, and the oil industry in general."

The wisdom of his intellect was rooted in the curiosity of self-education. During his early years at Yale, Kiphuth's unquenchable thirst for manuscripts usually found him low on funds as the end of the month approached. He became a collector of rare books and accumulated a personal library of over 15,000 volumes on a wide variety of subjects. His son, DeLaney, recalled that the collection became so large they were forced to build an addition onto their Cleveland Road home in 1936.

His book collection concentrated on historical aspects of swimming, various areas of international sport, general physical education, contemporary American literature, as well as books from the Limited Editions Club and the Nonesuch Press. In reviewing the volumes in Kiphuth's personal library, this author found a great diversity of literary taste. There were books on ancient and modern history, art history, classical and operatic music, anatomy and physiology, posture, ballet, modern dance, philosophy, and many works on Japanese culture, history, and music.

Munhall, who had been a graduate guest in residence at Kiphuth's Timothy Dwight apartment from 1955 to 1957, recalled that Kiphuth had an "excellent art library containing all of the standard reference works." The library also contained many rare and remarkable art publications put out in the teens and early twenties. The library was arranged so that one could easily find what one was looking for. In the evening when Kiphuth returned to his apartment he immediately went to his library and began to immerse himself in his latest acquisitions. He loved to discuss art. His major interest seemed to be paintings and sculpture of the Renaissance period and the early 20th century painters, primarily Picasso and Matisse.

Keller considered Kiphuth's art library a fantastic collection, especially with respect to well-illustrated color prints of the Renaissance period. According to the professor, the modern paintings of both Rouault and Miro commanded much of Kiphuth's interest.

Due to Kiphuth's assimilated knowledge and concern for the worlds of art and sport, Yale commissioned him the Curator of Sporting Art in 1937. By the agency of self-education and constant association with Yale's art professors, Kiphuth had long since completed his apprenticeship. However, the entrusting of the Francis P. Garvin collection of sporting art to his personal care awakened his curious and inquisitive mind even further. As if overnight, he became an authority on the paintings, drawings, and lithographs of George Bellows, the lithographs of Currier & Ives, and the sport sculptures of Tait McKenzie. Among Kiphuth's favorite repertoire was a prolific dissertation on scenes depicted by Currier & Ives prints, especially those on hunting, fishing, whaling, yachting, trotting, and winter activity, as well as Bellows' *Dempsey and Firpo* and *Stag at Sharkey's*, on Thomas Eakins' *John Biglen in a Single Skull*, on William Morris Hunt's *The Ball Players*, and on Rembrandt's *The Golf Player*. Kiphuth was as familiar with the ancient sports art of Greece as he was with the American sporting scenes depicted by Norman Rockwell.

On December 16, 1959, the *New York Times* announced the formation of the National Art Museum of Sport (NAMOS) under its founder and president Germain G. Glidden, a prominent portrait painter and former Harvard tennis captain. The purpose was to foster the already close relationship which existed between sport and the fine arts. Kiphuth was chosen to serve as vice president and chairman of the Board of Trustees. The first exhibition in November 1962 entitled "Fine Arts in Sports" was followed by the opening of its New York gallery in Madison Square Garden Center in March of 1968.

Kiphuth audited numerous Yale undergraduate classes from 1914 to 1917. And often times in later years, he would attend art or literature classes with some of his pupils. He seldom missed a Yale literary lecture series. Al Hapke, Yale swimming captain in 1933, wrote that Kiphuth strove to improve his own mind, had a deep appreciation and understanding of the liberal arts, and had a fine collection of modern press books. Upon completion of the newest book, Kiphuth never hesitated to consult with a noted authority, usually in residence at Yale. Kiphuth's charges, aware of his love for literature, presented him with two handsome volumes of the plays of Euripides at the 1936 swimming banquet. To Kiphuth's great satisfaction and with his approval, Yale's great man of the theatre, Monty Woolley, produced an Aristophanes play, *The Frogs*, within the Payne Whitney pool.

It meant a great deal to him to have people visit and appreciate his various collections. On one occasion, Forbes Carlile (Australian Olympic coach) recalled how Kiphuth, noticing his interest in Ralph Thomas' classic *Swimming* (1904), gifted the book to him. This particular edition commanded a most important place in the Carlile library.

Kiphuth received many honorary degrees, including a Master of Arts from Yale University in 1950 and a Doctor of Laws from George Williams College in 1960. His own literary endeavors on swimming and physical education are found in American and English magazines as well as in his four books: *Swimming*, *How to be Fit*, *The Diagnosis and Treatment of Postural Defects*, and *Basic Swimming*.

During his world tour in the summer of 1957, Kiphuth arranged to meet Munhall, who at the time was a graduate art student in Florence, Italy. Munhall had the following to say concerning the incredible physical energy and enthusiasm of Kiphuth over the four days. "Together we saw every major collection and monument in the city and many very obscure churches. Although I kept trying to lure him to a café for refreshments, he would only do so under duress. At the end of the four days, I must say I was a physical wreck."

The local, and sometimes New York, cinema offerings presented an insurmountable attraction that Kiphuth seldom, if ever, resisted. It was not uncommon for him to take in two movies in one evening. Although he loved best the movie reproductions of popular Broadway plays which he had seen, he did indulge in the latest social craze. As Gwyneth Brown wrote, "Kiphuth was greatly amused by Bridgette Bardot when she was the sexpot rage and he would ask apropos of nothing, 'Have you seen B. B.'s latest?' Kiphuth had."

So meaningful were his contributions to Yale, that in 1958 investment banker John M. Shiff (class of 1925 and a former business manager of the campus humor magazine, the *Yale Record*) presented to the Yale University Library in honor of Robert John Herman Kiphuth, the oldest English language book on swimming, *A Short Introduction For to Learne to Swim* (1595).

# THE WORLD, YALE, AND KIPHUTH: 1941-1950

World War II dominated the years 1941-1945. Some of the major events of that era were: the Alien Registration Act; the Lend-Lease Act; a peace-time draft; the Bugs Bunny and Tom and Jerry cartoon debut; Pearl Harbor; World War II; the Atlantic Charter; Roosevelt's Executive Order 9066 (creating Japanese internment camps); Office of Price Administration; the movie *Casablanca*; the Cairo Conference; the Tehran Conference; Operation Overlord (D-Day); Battle of the Bulge; Battle of Okinawa; Roosevelt's 4th term victory; the G.I. Bill of Rights; the Yalta Conference; the Truman Doctrine; the German surrender; the Atom Bomb and the Japanese surrender; the Philippine Independence; the Taft-Hartley Act; the Marshall Plan; the Berlin Blockade; baseball's first black athlete Jackie Robinson; Truman's re-election (in spite of the *Chicago Daily Tribune's* false headline: *Dewey Defeats Truman*); and the Korean War.

Notable on the literary front were F. Scott Fitzgerald's *The Last Tycoon*, Thornton Wilder's play *The Skin of Our Teeth*, Tennessee Williams' *The Glass Menagerie*, Richard Wright's *Black Boy*, Eugene O'Neill's *The Iceman Cometh*, and Norman Mailer's *The Naked and the Dead*.

Before the war, in 1937, the Yale Corporation had elected Yale graduate Charles Seymour as president of the university. As noted by Kelley, while Seymour was a skilled diplomat and educator, his "quiet efforts to develop 'the normal functions of the university, especially the course of study and the strengthening of faculty,'" were interrupted by World War II.

"Seymour believed that 'the justification of a university is to be found in the service which it gives to the nation.'" In 1939, he called for the entire university to unite behind "the necessities of national defense." On December 15, 1941, Seymour announced that, as part of Yale's wartime plans, a three-year degree program for undergraduates was now in effect.

All of Seymour's positions on faculty, academics, and student participation fit well with Kiphuth's belief in Yale as a great educational bastion. Believing firmly in the concept of teamwork, Kiphuth understood what his contribution to the war effort would be. In 1918, Kiphuth had organized a swimming tournament for more than 900 servicemen. His plan for the 1940s required all ROTC and NROTC cadets to undergo a comprehensive program of swim instruction and/or to participate on service swim teams. All Yale undergraduates were required to pass the mandatory swim test prior to graduation.

## *Personal Tragedy Strikes*

Kiphuth's life, blessed with precious memories of the past, as well as hope for the future, was shattered on June 7, 1941, while visiting the family home in Orlando, Florida. Kiphuth and his beloved wife Louise had arrived in Florida on June 2. Louise entered the Florida Sanitarium Hospital on June 5 and passed away at the age of 65 from anemia and acute nephritis. According to Phil Moriarty, the death of Louise was a terribly painful event for Kiphuth, and the void it created in his life at first seemed insurmountable.

During the summer of 1941, Kiphuth, as Director of Camp Timanous, a summer camp in Maine, hired one of his swimmers, Dick Peters, as a counselor. Peters recalled that Kiphuth was very lonely following the death of Louise. While Peters helped Kiphuth review the proofs of his new book *Swimming – The Barnes Dollar Sports Library*, Kiphuth would talk about his close family ties and his devotion to his son, Delaney.

In the fall of 1941, Kiphuth, previously honored in 1936 as a Fellow of Timothy Dwight College (TDC), received further recognition when Yale bestowed upon him the title of Professor in Residence at TDC. This move onto campus provided some initial respite from his grief. Kiphuth, evidently the only sports figure so honored in the history of Yale, now became a splendid representative of TDC and the influence of his presence added greatly to the prestige of this College.

On December 8, 1941, one day after the Japanese attack on Pearl Harbor, President Franklin Roosevelt delivered a brief but powerful speech before Congress *A Date Which Will Live in Infamy*. It was concurrently broadcast over the airwaves to the American people.

By early 1942, the university announced as part of its wartime plans the firing of the tennis coach of 29 years, the baseball coach of 20, and the golf coach of 10 years with the statement "the university must stress sports on a group basis."

The dynamics of "group think" did not escape Kiphuth. The result often led to irrational and dysfunctional decisions. Early on in his career, Kiphuth realized that tenure belonged to the faculty, not to coaches. If he was to remain a central part of Yale's future he must maintain an image and a presence within the university structure that identified him as more than a "swim coach." He made it his mission to be a prominent figure on campus investing his time and energy into efforts that extended well beyond his duties within the Payne Whitney. Kiphuth often would audit courses, or if he heard the swimmers discussing a great class he would suddenly appear to listen in on lectures. There was no enigma to his rise in stature within those beloved Gothic walls for even the medical students seeking assistance with their anatomy lessons found Kiphuth as the perfect professor in residence.

In 1940, President Seymour eliminated the inefficient administrative committee of three, composed of the directors of University Health and Athletics and the comptroller of the university and appointed Kiphuth as the sole director of Yale's "cathedral of sweat." Kiphuth's rise to the seat of power received final affirmation in 1941, when President Seymour bestowed on him the title of assistant professor of athletics. This was most significant because Kiphuth's academic appointment gave him the essential credential necessary to breech the portals of academia.

He kept Yale in the forefront of the international scene by being a productive member of national and international sports committees and organizations, including as a member of the swimming committee of the AAU of the United States, a member of the United States Olympic Swimming Committee, and being appointed the United States delegate to international swimming meetings in London. He kept Yale relevant in the Connecticut community through his participation in city and state organizations and committees, including serving on the board of the YMCA of New Haven and the New Haven Chapter of the American Red Cross, being a member of the National YMCA Physical Education Committee, being a member of the National Council of the Boy Scouts of America, and the Cheshire Reformatory parole board.

In 1949, Kiphuth's man President Seymour announced his retirement. In February 1950, after extended negotiations and to the surprise of everyone, the Yale Corporation chose A. Whitney Griswold, a 43-year old Yale professor of history, as its next president.

The coach and Griswold had become close friends years prior to Griswold's appointment as president. Yale historian Brooks Kelley ascribed the following traits to Griswold's dossier: the man had "wit, gaiety, and a gift for mimicry." He "was independent, opinionated, and had a passion for education." His "soft shoe routine with cane and straw hat" as part of his lecture on Derby Day (a student celebration) became legendary. Kiphuth and Griswold were definitely two peas in a pod. Thus, Kiphuth's future remained in good hands.

## An Epoch of Victory

The commencement of the 1940-41 season marked the initial year of Kiphuth's final 19 years as Yale's coach. During this period Kiphuth would win four NCAA, seventeen EISL, and fourteen AAU titles. He would also coach two of the finest collegiate teams ever assembled: the class of 1942 and the class of 1953. From March 10, 1945, through the 1958-59 season, Yale never lost in head-to-head competition, winning a total of 183 straight dual meets. Some of the most outstanding individual performers from 1941 to 1959 were Howie Johnson, Rene Chouteau, Alan Ford, Alan Stack, Don Sheff, Dennis O'Connor, John Marshall, Wayne Moore, Jimmy McLane, Kerry Donovan, Rex Aubrey, Dick Thoman, Sandy Gideonse, Roger Anderson, and Tim Jecko.

The 1941 team broke multiple pool and Yale records, and on two occasions surpassed the world record in the 400-yard freestyle relay. On February 15, 1941, Kiphuth's Eli would journey to Columbus, Ohio, to face Peppe's forces on his home turf. Peppe, still in the process of building his empire, once again found that his Buckeyes were not yet up to the task, falling 51½ to 23½ to the Elis. The defeat occurred even though Kiphuth had restricted his stars to only one event each. As the *New York Times* reported, "Yale placed first in six of nine events, but Dick Cook... Eli diver, was nosed out by Earl Clark, Buckeye captain, in the diving competition.... John Leitt won the 100-yard free-style test for Ohio State...(and) Al Hirsch, Buck sophomore, beat Yale's Fairhurst in the 200-yard breast stroke.... The rest of the meet was all Yale." Peppe even lost the final 400-yard freestyle relay to a reserve Yale foursome of John Vreeland, James Cook, H. Y. Wilson, and Everett MacLeman.

Despite their impressive dual meet winning streak, Yale struggled at major competitions in the first couple of years of the decade. Only three points decided the 1940 NCAA meet – Michigan 45 to Yale 42. As for the 1941 NCAA Championships, the March 30, 1941, *New York Times* headline screamed, "Michigan Outscores Yale, 61 – 58, For Eighth Straight Swim Crown." The article went on to report: "Michigan, turning on the heat when points were needed most, tonight won its eighth consecutive National Collegiate Athletic Association swimming championship in a fight to the finish with Yale." Michigan won four individual titles: James Welsch, 440-yard freestyle; James Skinner, 200-yard breaststroke; Francis Heydt, 150-yard backstroke; Charley Barker, 50-yard freestyle. They also won the 300 medley relay in the two-day event. "The outcome of the meet actually was decided before the final event. It was just as well... because Yale, which had thrown a scare into the Wolverine camp by piling up unexpected points, won the last race, the 400-yard free style relay, by a touch from Michigan." Yale's victories were the result of Renee

Chouteau in the 1500-meter freestyle, Howard Johnson in the 220-yard freestyle, and the 400-yard freestyle relay team of Johnson, Kelly, Pope, and Thomas Britton.

The year 1942 marked Yale's return to the pinnacle of collegiate swimming, and they were given the honor of being labeled by Mann as "the greatest swimming team that has ever been gathered together. It's a truly great combination and much stronger than any of our previous Olympic teams."

This was definitely the finest swim team up to this point in Yale history. Marked by an undefeated season, Yale had defeated Michigan in a dual meet, for the first time since 1930, 59 to 16, and won the NCAA title with a resounding 71 to 39 victory over 2nd place Michigan, winning five of 11 events. Then, in April of 1942, Yale added the national AAU crown to its list of laurels.

Now, however, the dark clouds of war were about to inflict a painful toll on the world, Yale, and collegiate swimming.

> At the 1942 NCAA Championships, a motion of interest was proposed by Coach Joseph Nill of the United States Military Academy (West Point) "that the Army, seeking to conserve silk for defense purposes, had asked that silk racing suits be discarded in favor of tights." The motion passed. Also the coaches voted to defeat a motion by Robert Miller, Coach of Bowdoin College, that the diving event be eliminated or drastically altered.

By 1942, both Yale and Yale swimming would be greatly impacted by the Selective Service Act of 1940. Anyone eligible for military service or any member of the ROTC program faced an accelerated academic schedule and would graduate in two and a half years.

### *The Panamanian – Alan Ford*

In the fall of 1942, Alan Ford, known as the Panamanian, enrolled at Yale with high praise from legendary Mercersburg Academy (Pennsylvania) coach John Miller. More importantly, the NCAA, due to World War II depleting collegiate athletic ranks, had lifted its long-standing ban on freshman eligibility. Surprisingly, Yale agreed with the NCAA, and allowed its freshmen to compete on the varsity level. This was done in spite of the more rigorous two-and-a-half-year academic schedule for graduation that Yale had imposed due to the war.

At the same time, Kiphuth's hopes for defending Yale's NCAA title at Ohio State and its EISL title at Harvard in the spring of 1943, ended when the Yale Athletic Association imposed war time travel restrictions. These restrictions also limited Kiphuth to eight home meets and four away meets and banned Yale from both championship meets.

Undaunted, Kiphuth refused to allow anything to deter the opportunity for Ford to showcase his talent. On January 8, 1943, Ford equaled the Yale and pool records for the 50-yard freestyle in 22.8. Then on January 30, Ford broke Johnny Weissmuller's world and American record in the 100-yard freestyle with a 50.7. On February 13, 1943, skeptics who adhered to a "fast watch theory" (in the era before electronic timing systems) were even more astounded when Ford led off the relay team at the Yale Carnival, and broke the record again with a time of 50.6. He went on to establish collegiate, AAU, and world marks at an alarming rate. He would eclipse American, world, and NCAA standards from 50 yards to 200 meters in backstroke and freestyle events.

Ford, denied the opportunity to compete in the 1943 NCAA Championships due to Yale's travel restrictions, did not disappoint the home crowd at the 1944 meet by winning the 50-yard freestyle in 22.1 and immediately returning in the next event to win the 150-yard backstroke. This was an outstanding, unprecedented feat. It was unheard of at that time in collegiate swimming for anyone to swim back-to-back events, as there was little break in between each event. On the final evening of competition, March 18, 1944, Ford, before an overflowing crowd, became the first swimmer in the world to surpass the 50-second barrier in the 100-yard freestyle with a 49.7 performance. By winning three individual events, Ford gave Kiphuth his second NCAA crown in a 39 to 38 win over Michigan, temporarily silencing most of the critics.

One week prior to the start of the 1944 AAU Nationals, the Navy, in charge of Yale's pools, closed the facilities because of a polio epidemic. In spite of "no water" and a travel restriction that required the team to return 85 miles each evening to New Haven from the New York AC, Yale defeated Ohio State for the AAU team title.

Ford's final and only NCAA appearance would be in 1944, due to his graduation in February of 1945. Since the championships were in March, he was declared ineligible by the dictatorial powers within the NCAA. The year 1945 also marked Yale's first dual meet defeat in five years, when they lost to a great West Point team in the final relay. In spite of pleas from fans and team members to protest the results of the meet, because of what they felt was questionable human judging, Kiphuth, true to his innate nature of an ordered society and fair play, remained faithful to his dictum that coaches coach, swimmers compete, and the integrity of officials is not to be questioned "[f]or never the twain shall meet."

John Knowles, of the *Saturday Evening Post*, vividly recalled the scene and Kiphuth's reaction as Ford valiantly tried to overcome an Army lead of 10 yards.

> Kiphuth who had been lurking quietly in the background, charged past me. He had held himself under tight control until the last crucial instant, but now he wanted to see the finish.... No one who knew Kiphuth's will to win could doubt his disappointment. But he turned quietly away, showing no emotion at all. In fact, there was only one thing to indicate how he felt. In the bus going back to New Haven he lit a cigarette. The rest of us stared in awe. Kiphuth neither smokes nor drinks. But he lit this cigarette and puffed amateurishly on it for a while, without inhaling. Up in its smoke went this loss to West Point.

Rumor states he obtained the cigarette from the bus driver.

**Left: Kiphuth and Alan Ford**

**Below: 1942-1943 Yale Swim Team**

## Kiphuth's Post War Years

Peace returned to the world in late 1945, but for the most part, collegiate swimming would be unable to return to its prewar level of operation until 1947. In 1945, for the third straight year, the EISL failed to hold the individual championships. Due to the lasting effects of the world conflict, the league did not operate with its full list of eight teams during the 1946 campaign, so no team title was awarded.

Yale competed in only seven dual meets during the 1945-46 season. It was a year that lacked the glamour associated with record performances. Further disappointment occurred when Yale hosted the NCAA Championships but failed to score any swimming points. Their only points came from a fifth place finish by Harry Lockery in the three-meter diving.

In 1946-47, Yale returned to a portion of its prewar form by establishing three world marks, seven American records, an EISL title and domination of the individual championships, finishing first, second, third, and fourth in both the century (100-yard freestyle) and furlong (220-yard freestyle) events, and first and second in the 50-yard freestyle and 150-yard backstroke. The future looked bright heading into the 1947 NCAA meet. But, upon arrival in Seattle, the entire eight-man squad of Edward Hueber, Alan Stack, Paul Girdes, Al Ratkiewich, Richard Baribault, Richard Morgan, J. Selden, and F. P. Heffelfinger was stricken by illness. As a result, the team only managed a fifth place finish.

During the 1947-48 season, Yale went undefeated in dual meets, enjoyed world record performances by Alan Stack in the 400-meter and 440-yard backstroke events and again dominated the EISL championships. Although Stack earned the gold medal in the 100 backstroke, setting an NCAA record, the season ended on a sour note when Yale finished sixth at the NCAA title meet behind Michigan, Ohio State, Michigan State, Iowa, and Stanford.

To highlight the 50th anniversary of competitive swimming at Yale, the 1948-49 team won all 13 of its dual meets, winning the EISL dual meet title, and dominated the individual EISL championships held at Princeton. However, Stack's eligibility ran out and, with Paul Girdes limited by illness, Yale finished fourth at the NCAA meet held at North Carolina. Nonetheless, the season concluded with a national AAU crown at Yale.

During this same time, the tide of influence had shifted when Kiphuth was appointed as Yale's athletic director in March of 1946. Payne Whitney was no longer his only realm of influence. The fate of Yale's athletics, and perhaps the Ivy League's future, and a simmering battle with the NCAA, had just fallen into the hands of a man absolutely dedicated to the philosophy of amateurism. Unfortunately, it would be short lived.

## Yale's Finest Team – The Class of 1953

In the fall of 1949, Kiphuth's expectations for the future were bright. The varsity squad was most formidable with backstroke ace Captain Al Ratkiewich at the helm. The coach and athletic director was pleased that Yale, with strict guidelines, had expanded its policy to allow for student aid and work-study for incoming students. Perhaps even more importantly, the Yale Board of Admissions had admitted a group of freshman swimmers with excellent potential.

Leading off this impressive class were the "three M's." The first was former child swimming star and 1948 Olympic 1500-meter freestyle champion Jimmy McLane. McLane and Kiphuth met for the first time at the 1944 National AAU outdoor long distance championships in Williams Lake in Rosendale, New York, in the Catskills Mountains. McLane was a mere 13-years old. According to the swimmer, after he beat Keo Nakama to win the four-mile swim, he was resting on the dock. Kiphuth came up behind him and put his finger on McLane's neck. When McLane turned and asked him what he was doing, Kiphuth responded, "I'm Robert Kiphuth, coach of the Yale swimming team, and I'm taking your recovery rate." Kiphuth then invited McLane to New Haven to see Yale and meet the great Alan Ford. This meeting was nothing short of prophetic, and serves as an indication of Kiphuth's effective approach to introducing the incredible program at Yale to talented young swimmers. In a telephone interview in May of 2016, McLane stated that "Kiphuth was one of the greatest recruiters ever in sports."

One year after that first meeting, the 14-year-old McLane swam at the Outdoor Championships at the Cuyahoga Falls municipal pool near Akron, Ohio. He once again successfully defeated Nakama, then considered to be Ohio State's prolific distance ace, in the 800-meter freestyle. McLane, in a phone interview, described this time in his career: "I was going through a bad period.... I was having difficulty with my coach at Akron Firestone Swim Club (Hal Minto).... I was looking for another coach. I called Matt Mann and Bob Kiphuth, and Kiphuth said 'for Heaven's sake come on down to New Haven....' He basically became my father for the next 10 years." Initially, McLane moved to New Haven with his mother. Then, concerned about his education, Kiphuth helped him gain acceptance to the prestigious Phillips Andover Academy in Massachusetts. "He got me into Andover which was a really lucky thing. His interest went beyond you being a trained seal. He was interested in your future. That was the thing that made him such a marvelous man." Until he finished prep school, the young swimmer spent the school years at Andover, and vacations and the summers training at Yale and living with Kiphuth.

The second of the "three M's" came in the form of a man named Marshall. Kiphuth's initial meeting with the Australian Olympian John Marshall occurred at the 1948 London Olympics. It was here that Marshall won the silver medal behind McLane in the 1500-meter freestyle and placed third in the 400-meter freestyle. Marshall possessed an outstanding combination of physiological traits: an unorthodox but powerful arm stroke, great flexibility, and a propulsive rhythmic kick. According to Forbes Carlile, Marshall was an exception to the rule when it came to training. Prior to training for the Olympics, Marshall was trained by Tom Donnett in Melbourne. The training consisted of only 2000 meters a day: 1000 meters swimming and 1000 meters kicking. Despite the limited training regimen, he won all the freestyle events from 200 meters to 1500 meters at the 1947 Australian Championships. Kiphuth initially felt Marshall would be a potent force behind McLane.

Rounding out the "three M's" was underrated Bridgeport, Connecticut, Boys Club champion and Warren Harding High School distance freestyler Wayne Moore. Moore had originally joined the diving team in high school, but after he broke his collar bone, his coach decided he should swim instead. He placed second in the two-mile Bridgeport Captain Max A. Baum cross-harbor swim when he was only 15 years old. Although initially scheduled to enroll at Dartmouth, his high school coach talked to his father, and convinced him that Moore should swim for Kiphuth at Yale.

Along with the "three M's," the team also consisted of freestyle sprinter Don Sheff from New York, destined to become one of America's premier sprinters, and six-foot-five backstroker Dick Thoman out of Cincinnati. Donald Byck, Stanton Smith, J.H.K. Norton, J.A. Joslyn, William Duncan, W.H. Milroy, and Michael W. Stuhldreher (son of the famous University of Notre Dame four horsemen quarterback Harry Stuhldreher) also added to the Yale ranks.

Sheff confirmed what a significant role the factors of esprit and competitiveness played in the success of the class of '53:

> Kiphuth never babied us, and we all wanted to win. We wanted to win as individuals...and as a team. We competed against each other when appropriate. But when it came to

**Yale Swimming Class of 1953** (L-R): Byck; Moore; McLane; Smith; Norton; Thoman; Joslyn; Duncan; Sheff; Marshall; Stuhldreher; Milroy

> NCAA or AAU championships, if we were not competing in the same event, we cheered for one another like crazy. We were a team!...I enjoy looking back on those halcyon days and tweaking my memory of long-forgotten – but, in a way, glorious – events.

Sheff said that since "there was no other world-class sprinter at Yale at the time" Kiphuth had him swim with Marshall, Moore, and McLane.

> Kiphuth usually had us freestylers swim together. You know Kiphuth would bark: 'Marshall, Moore, McLane, Sheff – do 20.' And we'd dive in and do 20. But, usually, it wasn't just a 20-lap workout. It became a race! Every time we hit the water together, each of us wanted to finish first. Even during practice. Yes...there was esprit, but swimming, as you know, is a lonely art. *'Swim your own race!'* Each of us wanted to win.

There is always the unknown factor. The one dynamic discovered only when a voice from the past speaks. Don Sheff in the following monologue describes the significance each member of a team, many times unknowingly, contributes to the success of the team. The other two swimmers in their workout heat were Frank Chamberlin, an "unheralded swimmer from a Southern military prep school," and Marty Smith. As Sheff pointed out:

> Marty had awful form. He swam like a crab. But he had determination. Mad, unyielding determination...! This became a problem on those occasions when the M's and I did not feel up to an all-out race...there were times when we wanted to dog it. But Marty prevented that. Our unspoken motto was, *"Don't ever let Marty come out ahead!"* Each of us carried that creed as Gospel. So, no matter how much we wanted to cruise at neutral, Marty made it impossible. We had to beat him. And that meant we had to race whether we wanted to or not. For the record, Marty *never* came out ahead of any of us. But he was always damned close.

This followed Kiphuth's philosophy that there always had to be a leader of the pack.

At the conclusion of World War II, the NCAA once again prohibited freshmen from being eligible for varsity competition, so the class of '53 could not compete on the varsity level until their sophomore year. There were great expectations for the freshman swimmers' subsequent three years of varsity eligibility.

Kiphuth began the start of the 1949-50 season with a renewed enthusiasm. The varsity outlook was very optimistic; however, a year from now, with the addition of the class of 1953, Yale's varsity swimming team would be virtually unstoppable.

Despite the lack of athletic scholarships, Kiphuth realized that Yale swimming presented a clear and imminent challenge to Peppe's formidable Ohio State team. But fate is the hunter, and tragedy struck on November 10, 1949, when Kiphuth suffered a coronary occlusion while playing handball. The 59-year-old coach suffered further damage when a second attack occurred at the hospital. Therefore, when the swimmers entered the pool for their first practice of the season on November 16, Phil Moriarty, Kiphuth's assistant and diving coach, was in charge.

In December 1949, Kiphuth, on the advice of his doctors and faced with reality, had a decision to make. He chose to resign as director of athletics, keeping his beloved positions as swim coach and director of Payne Whitney. In order to keep in constant contact with his swimming staff at Yale while he recovered, he brought his secretary, Eileen Wall, to his mother's home in Orlando.

Physically incapacitated, but optimistic for his return to the helm, Kiphuth put the immediate future of Yale swimming in the hands of his two trusted aides. He found he had little to worry about as Moriarty and Harry Burke carried on the beloved traditions of the past. Moriarty guided the varsity team through 13 dual meets, the EISL team title, a second-place finish at the NCAA Championships at Ohio State and a third-place finish in the AAU Championships held at Yale. Moriarty's team carried on the Eli tradition by breaking five EISL standards, two world and American records, one intercollegiate, and one NCAA meet standard. The standard bearers were William Farnsworth, Larom Munson, Raymond Reid, and John Blum in the 800 and 400 relay (world marks), and Al Ratkiewich, Robert Essert, and Reid's 300 medley relay NCAA record.

On the other hand, Burke found that he had a full time job on his hands handling the talented but unique freshman aquatic stars. Perhaps the class of 1953 stated it best in their memoir: "[T]he Dean's Office, the lure of Poughkeepsie [Vassar College], and bursary jobs, all took their separate tolls, but Harry managed to keep us in line with parables from the days of [his barnstorming travels with and managing the clairvoyant] lightning calculator, Pat O'Neil. He alone needled, cajoled, and psychoanalyzed us to our National [AAU] Championship."

Kiphuth, always mindful of the role that superior lieutenants play in a successful campaign, informed the Yale alumni of the invaluable service both Burke and Moriarty contributed in his 1951 *Yale Swimming News*

# Yale's Finest Team – The Class of 1953

*Letter:*

> Harry Burke, with his added responsibilities as Freshman Coach continues to build better and better Yale swimmers, and more than that, is always the jolly companion and great educator "without portfolio." His value to the Yale Community is without reckoning. Phil Moriarty, the strong right arm of the Yale Varsity swimming program, has through the years grown into one of the country's fine swimming and diving coaches, and Yale is most fortunate to have these two men who have done so much to further the educational, as well as athletic, success of Yale swimming.

Burke helped heal Kiphuth's heart when Yale's freshman team eliminated 18 opponents and broke or re-broke 19 national collegiate freshman records, 14 world records, and 13 American records. The onslaught of record breaking began on December 7, 1949, in an AAU sanctioned time trial over the 25-meter course in Yale's fifth floor practice pool. A team of McLane, Moore, Marshall, and Thoman lowered the world record for the 800-meter freestyle relay, previously held by a Japanese national team. With the addition of Sheff, they broke the 1000-meter freestyle record as well.

Then, on December 14, Sheff, Joslyn, Thoman, and McLane lowered the collegiate record for the 400-yard freestyle relay. Team Burke kept things relatively calm until February 11, 1950, when Marshall, the Australian fish, broke world and American marks for the 300-yard, 300-meter, and 400-yard freestyle distances.

In a dual meet against Hopkins Grammar School (New Haven, Connecticut) on February 21, Marshall, 220-yard freestyle, Moore, 440-yard freestyle, and Thoman, 150-yard backstroke all set collegiate records, and the relay team of Marshall, Sheff, Thoman, and McLane eclipsed the collegiate record for the 400-yard freestyle relay. The record onslaught continued on February 24, against West Haven High, when the 300-yard medley team of Thoman, Duncan, and Sheff set a collegiate and American mark. Thoman set the records again in the 300-yard individual medley. The following month, on March 1, Thoman, Stuhldreher, and Sheff eclipsed the freshman record for the 300-yard medley relay while Marshall annihilated the world, American, and collegiate marks for the 220-yard freestyle. Between March 4 and 13, the class of 1953 lowered a total of 11 collegiate freshman records over the 25-yard and 50-yard courses. On two occasions Marshall lowered the world, American, and collegiate freshman records for the 400-meter and 440-yard freestyle.

Despite this historic streak, Burke's finest and happiest hour occurred on April 1, 1950, when his freshmen, led by the "three M's," wrote a unique chapter in the annals of competitive swimming by winning the national indoor AAU Championship meet held at Yale. They competed under the banner of "Yale Freshmen" and defeated the current reigning NCAA champion Ohio State Buckeyes and the combined Yale varsity and New Haven Swim Club team. The "three M's" led the individual victories with Marshall winning the 1500-meter, 440-yard, and 220-yard freestyle. McLane finished second in all three. Moore finished third in the furlong, fourth in the quarter, and sixth in the metric mile. Marshall, Sheff, Thoman, and McLane secured the meet title with a second place finish in the 400-yard freestyle relay.

Just prior to that meet, Kiphuth had arrived back in New Haven. There is no question that the final decision for the decorated class to swim under the banner "Yale Freshmen" and not "Yale's New Haven Swim Club," rested with Kiphuth. As always, he viewed it as an opportunity for Yale, Yale Swimming, and for his loyal assistant Burke to have his moment in the sun.

Mr. Yale looked with great anticipation toward the 1950 Outdoor AAU Championships in Seattle and the resulting competitions in Japan in August of 1950, the first since the end of war hostilities in 1945.

Yale's Australian import and his teammates continued their record onslaught during the summer of 1950. Prior to Seattle Marshall broke seven world records and with the assistance of Sheff, Moore, and McLane established a new American standard for the 800-meter freestyle relay and an American noteworthy record for the 880-yard freestyle relay.

Unwilling to waste any opportunity for record setting opportunities, Kiphuth arranged for two AAU sanctioned time trials prior to the team's departure for Seattle. The quartet of Marshall, Sheff, Moore, and McLane set two new American standards in the 800-meter freestyle relay, over a 25-meter course, and for the 880-yard freestyle relay, over a 55-yard course.

As anticipated, Seattle was not a disappointment to Kiphuth, as Marshall continued his record pace by erasing two world (mile and half mile freestyle), five American (mile, 1000-yard, 1000-meter, 880-yard, and 440-yard freestyle) and two American noteworthy (550 and 1320-yard freestyle) records. McLane accounted for one American standard in the 220-yard freestyle and the relay team of Marshall, Moore, McLane, and Sheff surpassed the American record in the 880-yard freestyle. The team victory in Seattle found six members from Yale earning berths on the Japan-bound squad. (This trip is covered in the chapter *Kiphuth Inter-*

*national.*) This onslaught of attack on world, American, and collegiate records by one university team from December of 1949 to July of 1950 was unprecedented in the history of swimming.

After returning from Japan, the head coach undertook the 1950-51 collegiate season with renewed vigor. His heart attack was behind him and the great freshman team had reached varsity status. Kiphuth, understanding the psychology of competition, realized that these were self-motivated and highly competitive individuals. Therefore, his strategy was to use psychological warfare, combining the fastest swimmers in the same heat during workouts, so that they would compete against one another daily. This competitive training combined with Kiphuth's famed calisthenics culminated in collegiate, national, and world record swims. He directed this sophomore loaded team through 13 dual meet wins to the EISL team title, to eight of 14 individual firsts at the EISL championships, to an NCAA victory and to the Indoor and Outdoor AAU Championships. During the season Kiphuth guided his mermen to 11 world records, 25 American records, 15 noteworthy performances, and 16 collegiate marks. To quote Phil Moriarty, "[Kiphuth] was not one who would give you great help with your strokes…he offered a special ingredient, perhaps of greater importance. It was his knowledge of the Mind and Body and his ability to glue them together, which enabled him to make a person perform beyond their potential, as he himself did throughout his own life. A special gift not given to many."

While Wayne Moore had shown promise in December of 1949 by swimming the fastest 200-meter split in the 800-meter world record relay, it wasn't until January of 1951 that he notified both Marshall and McLane that he was a force to be reckoned with. In Yale's first dual meet of the year against Fordham Moore smashed the national, intercollegiate, and American marks for the 440-yard freestyle. Moore's sophomore season would be a banner season as he lowered collegiate, American, and American noteworthy standards for the 220, 300, 400, and 500-yard freestyle, and the 400 and 500-meter freestyle.

However, Marshall, not content to play second fiddle to Moore, also established world, American, collegiate, and American noteworthy performances for the 400, 500, and 1500-meters, and 220, 300, 400 and 440-yard freestyle. This is not surprising because, as noted by Morgan Murphy of the Ballarat Swimming Club (Australia), "[i]n one training session, he swam a set of 5x400m Freestyle and reputedly broke the World Record…in each consecutive swim." The Australian import's self-discipline and "a natural understanding of his body's capability," allowed him to recognize "the signs that would over stress and over train his systems." Yale's third distance ace, McLane, had just returned to

Yale from participation in the Canterbury Centennial Games in Christ Church, New Zealand over the Christmas holidays to witness Moore's rise into the limelight.

Kiphuth's competitive workout strategy was contagious, and other members of the class of 1953 were not to be denied individual accolades during the 1950-51 season. Thoman contributed collegiate marks over a 20-yard and 25-yard course for the 100 backstroke and Stanton Smith established new standards for the 100-yard and 100-meter breaststroke. Kiphuth's team continued its attack on world, American, and collegiate records for the following distances: 160, 400, 500 and 600-yard freestyle relays for 20-yard pools and 1000-meter freestyle relay and 300-yard medley relay over the 25-yard course. At the Yale Carnival on February 17, 1951, the 400-yard freestyle relay of Thoman, Sheff, Farnsworth, and Reid lowered the world, American, and collegiate standard in a time of 3:21.6, averaging 50.4 per man. On March 21, the 800-yard freestyle world and American records fell to a team of Sheff, Moore, McLane, and Farnsworth.

At the EISL Championships held at Harvard University during the third week of March, Kiphuth's squad swept the first four places in the metric mile, quarter mile and furlong. Sheff won the 50 and 100-yard freestyle, adding to the point total and leading Yale to a team victory.

One week later, Kiphuth and company departed for Austin, Texas, for the NCAA Championships. A late plane arrival, coupled with the hotel awarding their rooms to another team, caused the team a chaotic last-minute search for new quarters. With the problem solved, they settled down to the task at hand and easily defeated runner up Michigan State for the team trophy 81 to 60. The "three M's" led the way with a sweep in the 440-yard and 220-yard freestyle events. Marshall won the 440-yard and 220-yard freestyle, and also the 1500-meter freestyle, with McLane in third place in all three. Moore won the silver in the 220 and 440. En route to his three victories, Marshall set three world, American, and collegiate records. His performance received high praise from Michigan's coach Matt Mann, "he has a style like nothing you ever saw. He has streamlining, but mostly he just gets in the water and goes like hell." Mann attributed his style to great stamina and superb conditioning (Kiphuth trademarks). Mann predicted that other coaches would rise to the challenge and demand more of the same from their swimmers. Thoman won the 100-yard backstroke and placed second in the 200-yard backstroke. He placed fifth in the 150-yard individual medley. Sheff placed third and Raymond Reed fourth in the 100-yard freestyle. Sheff was fifth in the 50-yard freestyle. Frank Chamberlin, Larom Munson, Sheff, and Reed also placed second in the 400-yard freestyle relay.

Immediately after the NCAAs, the team embarked for Columbus, Ohio, to compete in the National Indoor AAUs. Ohio State's Mike Peppe played host and the Olentangy Club served as the place of residence. Yale was seeking its third crown in three weeks and Kiphuth was determined not to allow anything to interfere. The team did not disappoint.

In the first event of the meet, the 1500-meter freestyle, Marshall set a world record of 19:19.8 and over the next two days he won the 220 and 440-yard titles with teammate Wayne Moore finishing right behind him in second place. McLane, who had by-passed the metric mile, placed fourth in the 220 and third in the 440. Victory was secured by Yale winning the 400-yard freestyle relay with a team of Thoman, Sheff, Reid, and Farnsworth, and the 300-yard medley with a team of Thoman, O'Connor, and Sheff. Kiphuth and his contingent of superpower swimmers returned triumphantly to New Haven, undefeated in both collegiate and AAU competition, to complete the school year and prepare for summer training.

The Yale New Haven Swim Club, led by Moore, also won the 1951 Outdoor AAU Championships in Detroit. Moore secured victories in the 200-meter and 400-meter freestyle. The relay team of Sheff, Marshall, McLane, and Moore won the 800-meter freestyle relay.

The 1951-52 Yale varsity season began with great expectations. Yale once again had an undefeated dual meet season. They also dominated the EISL individual championships by securing 25 out of a possible 75 finalist positions.

Unfortunately for Kiphuth and company, the NCAA had once again reinstated freshmen eligibility for varsity competition, but the Ivy League rejected the proposal. This meant that non-Ivy League teams could swim their freshmen in varsity competition. However, Yale's recent incoming freshman luminaries (Kerry Donovan, Malcolm Aldrich, Jerald Felder, DeMaurice Moses, and Edgar Munhall) were forced to compete only on the freshman level. In contrast, Peppe's tenacious Ohio State team would be able to add the potent punch of its new freshmen, who were two of Hawaii's best, Ford Konno and Yoshi Oyakawa. The above duo, backed by sprinter Dick Cleveland and their backstroke ace Jack Taylor, plus the perennial points from its divers, upset the Yale squad 94 to 81 at the 1952 NCAA Championship meet at Princeton University.

With an excited and overflowing crowd looking on, Konno led the "three M's" home in the 1500-meter and the 440-yard freestyle, but Moore and Marshall reaped revenge by defeating Konno in the 220-yard freestyle. Ohio State added valuable points when Dick Cleveland won the 50-yard freestyle and placed second behind Clark Scholes, known as the "hom stretch ace" of Michigan State, in the 100-yard freestyle. Peppe's Taylor and Oyakawa limited Yale's Thoman to second place in the 100 and 200-yard back. Although on the final event on Saturday evening, Yale's 300-yard medley relay team of Thoman, O'Connor and Sheff set an NCAA record of 2:48.9, it was not enough to claim victory, as Ohio State had captured three out of six places in the one-meter, and three out of six places in the three-meter diving, for a total of 18 points. Yale's Roger Hadlich finished second in the three-meter, scoring five points.

The memoirs of the team of 1953 summed up the experience:

> Looking back on it now, it seems that Thoman must have a compulsion for self-mutilation. He had the habit of finishing wind-sprints with either his forearm or his skull, and showed for the finals of the collegiates with his arm in a sling. As a part of his calculated psychological warfare he casually undid the bandage and jumped into the water, but to no avail since Yoshi was unaffected by these theatrics and beat him twice (sic). It was in this meet that John (Marshall) got bored with Konno and McLane's company in the mile and decided halfway through it to take a crack at the world record for the three-hundred yards. If he had not already swum 800 yards he undoubtedly would have gotten it, but as it turned out all he got was tired and a third place. The following night, however, Wayne (Moore) and John upset Konno in the 220, but we could not make up the big lead Ohio piled up in the dive, and lost the meet, the only Yale team loss of our careers.

The national indoor AAU meet was scheduled be held in New Haven the following week. Konno was superb in winning three titles: the metric mile, the quarter-mile and the furlong. McLane, Marshall, and Moore finished second, third and fifth in the metric mile and third, fourth and second in the quarter. Moore, McLane, Don Sheff, and Frank Chamberlain were second, fourth, fifth and sixth in the 220. Dick Thoman outclassed the field in the 100 and 150-yard backstroke. Kiphuth's Yale New Haven Swim Club completed the campaign by finishing first and third in the 300-yard medley relay and first, fourth, and sixth in the 400-yard freestyle relay. Yale successfully defended its AAU crown to conclude its 1951-52 season.

Returning from the Olympic Games, Kiphuth made arrangements for the short trip to Newark, New Jersey, and the outdoor AAU nationals in August of 1952. The meet was marked by the entry of future and past champions, most notable of which were Bill Woolsey, Richard Tanabe, Bill Sonner, Yoshi Oyakawa, Bowen Stassforth, Sandy Gideonse, and the "three M's." In a gallant try to secure the team title, Kiphuth attempted to bolster the "three M's" with Richmond Curtiss, Anthony DuPont, Steve Burness, and Martin Smith. In need of a backstroke swimmer, he phoned this author at the YMCA summer camp in Watertown, Connecticut, and invited me to become a member of the elite Yale NHSC. Unfortunately, the Olympians were tired and the newcomers suffered from inexperience, and the Yale New Haven Swim Club lost the meet to Ohio State. So it was back to Yale and the commencement of the final season for the class of 1953.

In their final year, the class of 1953 did not let Kiphuth down. They started off the year slowly, but picked up momentum along the way, winning the EISL, the NCAA, and the AAU titles. As the team swept through 14 dual meet opponents they surpassed seven recognized world marks, while also establishing many pool and championship records. Moore accounted for four new world records in the 300-yard, 440-yard, 300-meter, and 400-meter freestyle. Thoman entered the picture by surpassing the world and collegiate record for the 100-yard backstroke on two occasions. The season highlight occurred on February 14 at the Yale Carnival before a capacity crowd, when a team of Moore, McLane, Sheff, and Smith set a world record in the 800-yard freestyle relay.

> Marshall's fall from prominence occurred in the summer of 1952. According to McLane, and verified years later by my high school coach, hall of famer Jim Farrar, a group of swimmers training at Yale managed to manipulate their way through the tunnel connecting the Ray Tompkins house to the Payne Whitney's third floor practice pool after hours. The swimmers, competitive by nature, went too far with their daring antics. Marshall's foolish leap from the third floor balcony to the pool below caused an injury to his back from which he never fully recovered. Kiphuth, true to his nature, considered this incident as a family matter, never to be divulged for public consumption.

Yale went on to dominate the EISL and won a decisive victory at the NCAA Championships, 96½ points to runner up Ohio State's 73½. Ohio State's chances of a team title suffered a severe blow when Peppe limited his distance ace Konno to one event: the 400-yard freestyle relay. Konno had fallen victim to mumps three weeks prior at the Big 10 Championships. Yale, on the other hand, lost valuable points when Marshall, reportedly suffering from a severe sinus infection since December, also suffered a back injury (known but to a few) and contributed only two points to the team effort. Led by "the sensational little Buckeye"

Yoshi Oyakawa's two individual titles in the 100 and 200-yard backstroke, Ohio State joined Michigan and Yale in winning three swimming events each. But, as stated in the *New York Times* on March 29, 1953, "Bob Kiphuth's Bulldogs, scoring in all but two of the...fourteen events... and completely dominating the three distance free-style tests" reigned supreme. Ohio State once again swept the diving.

This would be Kiphuth's fourth and final NCAA team championship. The 1953 team exemplified all that he ever preached about the importance of team unity, and the major role it played throughout the years in Yale's success. This would be the season that McLane would return to the pinnacle of collegiate swimming. Swimming a superb tactical race, McLane won the metric mile and the furlong, finishing second to teammate Moore in the quarter mile. To quote the *New York Times* from March 27, 1953, "This was McLane's first national title since entering Yale four years ago. As a schoolboy prodigy...Jimmy won twelve national AAU distance crowns and the 1948 Olympic 1500-meter championship. But although he himself was swimming better than ever, he was overshadowed in varsity competition until this year by Marshall, Moore, and Konno." As noted by his International Swimming Hall of Fame biography, "seldom a world record beater...McLane relished the tactics and strategy of gamesmanship." Kiphuth labeled McLane as a competitor who thoroughly enjoyed the cunning and calculated pre-race mental preparation.

During the first three days of April 1953, McLane joined a select group of triple winners taking the blue ribbon in the 220, 440, and 1500 freestyle at the National AAU Indoor Championships. Unfortunately, the Big Ten boycott, a result of the renewed NCAA and AAU differences, turned the meet into a Yale rout.

This author recalls how Kiphuth loved to reminisce about each of his great distance stars and their moments of glory. Kiphuth enjoyed highlighting the "mental toughness" that led to the fantastic comeback of McLane in his farewell to collegiate swimming.

Kiphuth emphasized Marshall's initial inability to do more than one push-up prior to his exposure to the dry land program. Marshall then used his unorthodox stroke and superb kick to set the swimming world on fire. He was reported to have a resting heart rate of 35 beats to the minute. Don Sheff recalls that Dr. Tom Cureton, a former Yale swimmer in 1925, known as the father of physical fitness, and a professor at the University of Illinois, claimed Marshall had the quickest recovery rate of any athlete in any sport he had ever tested. Marshall burst upon the world scene with an unprecedented assault on world records from 1949 to 1951. According to his biography at the International Swimming Hall of Fame, this was "a record breaking performance unsurpassed in the annals of speed swimming."

Next was the rise into national prestige of the unassuming Moore. Kiphuth pointed to his qualities of grit and perseverance, and celebrated his rise to stardom beginning in January of 1951. Although Moore was pleasant and humble in nature, he had an innate competitive drive. His determination led him to a world record onslaught that January. Due to his high moral values and leadership ability, he was elected captain of the 1952-53 team. This was impressive because Yale tradition dictates the election of only one individual to lead the team.

The class of 1953 had written an indelible record in the pages of competitive swimming history. Although the three M's, along with Thoman and Sheff, received the majority of the publicity, and perhaps rightfully so, they understood the significant role each member of the class of 1953 played in the team's success. In the face of all obstacles, perhaps the most obvious being pre-ordained greatness, the team tasted defeat on only one occasion. But, true greatness can only be appreciated after one has been humbled by defeat. In conclusion, the class of 1953 wrote the following in their memoir, *Our Four Years With Bob*:

> We were undoubtedly the most talented aggregation in the history of the sport, and it is difficult to judge whether or not we fulfilled our potential, for there is no means of comparison. We have reason to feel satisfied about our accomplishments, but not smug, for in terms of Kiphuth's philosophy of sport, it matters not how superlative our past performances may have been, they are nevertheless finite, and beyond them lay possibilities that are infinite.

For many coaches, the success enjoyed by Kiphuth in that season would have created a great temptation to rest on one's laurels and to be content to reminisce about the past. But 36 years of successful coaching had enlightened him to the instability of living in the past. In commenting on previous athletic and academic achievements, Kiphuth, in his *Yale Swimming News Letter* in the summer of 1953, challenged the returning team members "to accept the responsibilities of the present in light of Yale's tradition of the past."

# Kiphuth International

During Kiphuth's 45-year coaching career, he conducted clinics for the United States Department of State in Iceland, Israel, and South Africa, and supervised the U.S. Army European Swimming Clinic on four different occasions in the 1950s. He led international and Yale teams to competitions in Hawaii, Japan, Germany, Cuba, Bermuda, and Mexico.

The U.S. Olympic Committee appointed him Olympic coach in 1928, 1932, 1936, 1940, and 1948. The 1940 and 1944 Games, scheduled for Helsinki, fell victim to World War II, thus Kiphuth's final tenure as Olympic coach occurred at the 1948 London Games.

## *International Recognition*

The journey to international recognition for Kiphuth and Yale swimming began at the conclusion of the 1921 season. The year proved to be one of victory, records, and Hawaiian leis. Yale went undefeated for 14 dual meets, establishing two world records, 12 collegiate, and eight pool records. As a result, Yale swimmers were for the first time awarded a major sport "Y" for setting world records in the 200 and 250 freestyle relays. The awarding of a major "Y" had been a bone of contention among Yale athletes. Only athletes in "major" sports could earn a major "Y." Athletes in "minor" sports, such as swimming, could only earn a minor "Y," unless the athlete set a world record. According to Kiphuth, to attach the label of "minor" performance on a Yale sportsman or sports team did not fit the vocabulary of true gentlemen. All athletes, regardless of their sport, deserved the "major" designation.

Cognizant of the importance of publicity to promote the sport of swimming, Kiphuth always allowed a sports writer to have access to the pool deck during the Yale Carnival, the national AAU meet, or the NCAA Championships. Any swimming performance worthy of national or international attention immediately was telegraphed to all major newspapers, especially the *New York Times*. Kiphuth and Yale swimming reached the pinnacle of success and publicity when Louis de Breda Handley, renowned sportsman, sports writer, and coach of the internationally recognized Women's Swim Association of New York, declared the Yale team of 1920-21 to be the "finest aquatic varsity aggregation ever gathered together."

After the completion of the season, Captain Lorrin Thurston approached the coach with the idea of a transcontinental-Hawaiian swimming tour. A receptive ear was found in Professor Clarence Mendell, who served as an advocate of foreign educational opportunities and chairman of the English Department and Board of Athletic Control. After securing financial guarantees from the Hawaiian AAU and various athletic clubs, the team held an exhibition at Yale's Carnegie pool in early May during commencement week to secure additional funds.

Team members began practice in early May and held two intramural meets one for Yale students and faculty and one on Alumni Weekend with the dual purpose of selecting the team members and to raise funds. After the team was selected R. F. Solley was forced to withdraw due to illness, and F. de P. Townsend, Jr. took his place. E. T. Hetzler, 1923, was the rooter and general aide. In order to accommodate the annual cleaning of the Carnegie pool, Kiphuth, beginning on June 25, 1921, trained 13 members of the squad in the cold waters of the Long Island Sound for nine days. Kiphuth and the team were hosted by swimmer Ed Bin-

ney's parents at their home in Sound Beach, today known as Old Greenwich, Connecticut. The training site was most likely Tod's Point Beach, a long thin peninsula at the southwest end of the neighborhood where the Binney's had a private swimming course.

The opportunity for additional revenue revealed itself on June 25 at the 15-acre Brighton Beach (Brooklyn) Bath and Racquet Club's open-air pool. The Club was a middle class Mecca, subway accessible to New Yorkers, serving mostly the nearby first and second generation Jewish-American population. It also served as the entertainment center for well-known vaudeville entertainers of that era. At an aquatic show that day, before a large crowd, Yale's 200-freestyle relay team of William Leeming Jelliffe, C. Dudley Pratt, David Gauss, and Lorrin Thurston competed against an intercollegiate all-star aggregation of Vic Hulst and Phil Genthner of Pennsylvania and Paul Lockwood and Walter Eberhart of Columbia, who were all lifeguards at nearby New York beaches. On June 26, 1921, the *New York Times* deemed the race "the principal attraction on a card of four events." Jelliffe for Yale and Hulst for the "All Stars" were the lead-off swimmers. Hulst touched out Jelliffe, while Pratt out swam Lockwood on the second leg. Gauss increased the lead over Eberhart on the third leg, and Thurston defeated Genthner by seven yards for a Yale victory in a time of 1:41 2/5. Yale diver John Pollard, however, lost to Columbia's 1920 Olympic bronze medal diver Louis Balbach.

A second fund-raising exhibition took place at the luxurious Stamford Connecticut Country Club on July 2, under the auspices of the Stamford Civic Association. Finally, on July 4, the team departed by rail for Chicago. The transcontinental portion of the trip involved meets against such formidable foes as the Chicago Athletic Club, the Milwaukee Athletic Club, the Minneapolis Athletic Club, the White Bay Yacht Club of St. Paul, the Los Angeles Athletic Club, the Venice Beach Club, the Santa Barbara Club, and the Olympic Club of San Francisco. At each checkpoint the benevolent and obliging alumni extended a warm welcome.

While competitive meets composed a major portion of the trip, the 15-man delegation enjoyed social receptions in the form of luncheons, dinners, and supper parties. In response, the team presented exhibitions before Yale alumni and friends at such places as the Chicago Athletic Club (Chicago AC), Mr. J.B. Bell's estate at Lake Minnetonka, Minnesota, and at the home of S.F.B. Morse in Del Monte, California. Morse was captain of the undefeated 1906 Yale football team and voted most popular in the graduating class of 1907. As the first environmentalist on the Monterey coast, he became a most significant and influential figure in the development of the Monterey Peninsula and the Pebble Beach Golf Club.

It was a most stimulating transcontinental journey. However, there was little opportunity for swim practice during the 17-day train trip. While the team competed in 10 meets against the best competition American athletic clubs could offer, there is little substitute for time spent in practice; however, the team successfully raced in 20, 25, and 33 1/3-yard pools, and in a straight course under heavy seas in Santa Barbara. Yale won nine of 10 competitions, losing only to the older and more mature swimmers of the Chicago Athletic Association.

The Chicagoans humiliated the Yale squad 31 to 19. However, Kiphuth and Yale pride gained some atonement with Edward Binney's victory in the 50 freestyle that tied the world record of 23 2/5, and then forced the AA team to fracture Yale's recent world record in the 160-freestyle relay for the gold, with a time of 1:15 to Yale's 1:15.2. The Eli's successfully defeated a slew of opponents: the Milwaukee Athletic Club, 33 to 8, the Minneapolis Athletic Club, 32 to 18, the White Bear Yacht Club, 43 to 6, the Los Angeles Athletic Club, 30 to 14, and the Venice Beach Club, 29 to 15. Against the Santa Barbara Club, in a course parallel to the city pier on a day with very heavy seas, Yale dominated 40 to 4. In their final meet against the Olympic Club of San Francisco at Idora Park, Yale won 33 to 17.

Kiphuth learned many lessons from the sojourn. He witnessed the results of year-round training, the superiority of the mature athlete, and the necessity for some standardization in competitive pools. More importantly, he learned the social advantages to be gained by cultivating the support of Yale's influential and prosperous alumni.

On July 20, 1921, the 17-day transcontinental portion came to an end when Kiphuth's entourage embarked from the mainland on the S.S. Manoa. The blue waters of the Pacific would be the team's only companion for the next seven days. The swimmers' dreams of sun-filled, lazy days of rest were soon shattered when Kiphuth, undaunted by the lack of pool facilities, conducted two-a-day dry-land exercises.

It would be difficult to imagine a coach today even considering having his swimmers take a transcontinental train excursion lasting 17 days, engaging in 10 competitions against the best of American athletic clubs, and then undertaking a pool-less, seven-day ocean journey prior to a major competition.

The pier-side reception on July 27 was at the time unique to the island paradise. The reception committee included many local dignitaries such as Ezra Crane of the Pacific Advertiser, the AAU Commissioner George "Dad" Center, Yale alumni Carter Gault, P. Young, H. von Holt, William Thomas Rawlins, and Olympic swimmer Duke Kahanamoku. The reception was initiated by a momentous "Brek-ek-ek-ex, ko-ax, ko-ax! Brek-ek-ek-ex, ko-ax, ko-ax! O-op, O-op! Par-a-ba-lou! Yale! Yale! Yale!" – a salute from the local Yale alumni.

To the enjoyment of its island alumni, the team after two days of practice went on to defeat the best Hawaii had to offer in an "all-comers" meet at the University of Hawaii's new pool. The final score was Yale 24; Outrigger Canoe Club 19; Hui Makani 18; Hui Nalu 2. It was an amazing feat that Yale's swimmers competed so successfully following the 24-day journey.

Yale's initial success would give way to tired bodies and lack of experience in open-water competition. Over the next two days, in the open-water meet conducted in the Honolulu Harbor, Yale (15 points) finished third behind the Hui Makani swim club (28 points) and the Outrigger Canoe Club (20 points). At this meet, the Hawaiian teenager Pua Kealoha, who represented the Hui Makani club, equaled a world record of 53 seconds for the 100-yard freestyle.

> Brek-ek-ek-ex, ko-ax, ko-ax, Brek-ek—ek-ex, ko-ax ko-ax, O-op, O-op! Par-a-ba-lou! Yale! Yale! Yale! known as Yale's Long Cheer, was born in 1884. Yale students, influenced by the study of Greek (but perhaps embellished by a bit of libation), decided it would make a great cheer. The cheer was first heard in an 1880s Yale baseball game, and the revelry appeared to lead the team to victory. Henceforth, the cheer became a long-lasting part of the Yale repertoire that survived until the 1960s. (Mark Alden Branch, "Greek Revival" *Yale Alumni Magazine*, July/August 2008.)

The transcontinental tour had great significance for swimming, Yale, and Kiphuth. First, Yale swimming moved from the campus and the eastern seaboard across the continent to the Pacific paradise. Moreover, Yale alumni across the United States and in Hawaii had the opportunity to observe a successful Yale program within their own communities. The trip made headlines in the *New York Times* and other newspapers. In turn, Kiphuth received the good fortune of being able to exhibit the results of his labor and his gracious manners before a national audience of alumni and the swimming public. Perhaps even more importantly, this was the first time in intercollegiate athletic history that a series of coast-to-coast athletic contests had ever been scheduled. Unique was the fact that a college team traveled 13,000 miles, crossing the Pacific to compete against Hawaii's best.

The journey for Kiphuth's and Yale's international reputations continued on April 17, 1923, at the swim team banquet, when team manager and toastmaster D.H. Bigelow announced that, with unanimous approval of the team, the funds raised from the recent Yale aquatic carnival would be used to send Kiphuth to Europe to study European swimming in the summer of that year. The coach took full advantage of this opportunity to be schooled in the art and culture of the old world and in the process made very valuable life-long contacts with the established powers that controlled European and world swimming.

In 1926, the Yale Alumni Association of Hawaii invited Kiphuth and his squad to compete in two international meets, but the Yale Athletic Association rejected the bid for another transcontinental trip. Undaunted by the rejection, instead eight Yale swimmers applied for and received AAU sanction to compete in Europe during the summer of 1926. In the end, seven swimmers made the trip. The plan was for Kiphuth, team captain Phillip Bunnell, who was also captain of the Yale football team, John House, W.S. Meany, Allison W. Choate, William S.K. Stage, G. Grant Mason, and H.G. Phillips to depart individually for Europe as circumstances allowed. They would meet in late June in London, train there for a few weeks, and conclude with competitions in five European countries: England, France, Belgium, Germany, and Switzerland. This successful venture expanded Kiphuth's image as America's respected international swimming voice.

The coach's appetite for foreign travel and especially for a return visit to the Hawaiian paradise became a possible reality when the Yale Club of Honolulu proposed an east vs. west collegiate dual meet between two prominent international universities, Yale and Japan's Meiji University. AAU open competition would also be included in the trip. The contests were to take place in the summer of 1930. However, Yale had imposed travel restrictions on all athletic teams due to the world-wide depression. The centerpiece of the invitation, certainly influenced by Kiphuth's input, highlighted the cultural and educational components involved for Yale's student athletes.

In spite of the travel restrictions, Dr. George Nettleton, chairman of both Yale's Athletic Association and English Department announced on February 26, 1930, Yale's acceptance. Evidently, Nettleton sanctioned the trip because of strong alumni interest, the fact that financial expenditure was not required on the part of the athletic department, but more importantly because of his affiliation with Yale's cultural study abroad program.

Once again, the 1930 journey required train travel across the United States to San Francisco and travel by ship to Hawaii. However, Kiphuth found that in spite of alumni interest, at the last minute it was determined that a barnstorming tour of the magnitude conducted in 1921 would not be sanctioned by either Yale or the AAU.

Honoring the restrictions, Kiphuth limited the dual meets to Buffalo and Milwaukee and exhibitions to Detroit, Omaha, and Denver – cities that coincided with the transcontinental train route. Upon arrival in Los Angeles, Yale competed in only the first two days of the National AAU Championships before departing for San Francisco and Hawaii. The team traveled from San Francisco on the brand new luxury liner, S.S. Malolo, complete with an onboard swimming pool, which was commissioned in the Port of Philadelphia in 1926.

In Honolulu, the Meiji University team greeted Kiphuth and team with miniature Japanese flags and leis. Dudley Pratt who had been a member of Yale's 1921 swim team, and was now President of the Yale Club of Honolulu, led the Yale delegation, while Francois D'Eliscu of the *Hawaii Advertiser* represented the press. Kiphuth and the team graciously accepted their offerings but, within two hours, Kiphuth, wasting no time, had his charges in the Waikiki War Memorial Natatorium. Over the next two days, Kiphuth scheduled workouts at 9:30 a.m. and 4:30 p.m.

The 100-by-40-meter salt water Memorial pool was the brainchild of the Sons and Daughters of Hawaiian Warriors. The pool, first proposed in 1918, was built to honor the over 10,000 volunteers from the Territory of Hawaii who contributed to the efforts of the Great War (World War I). The 1921 Territorial Legislature passed a bill, first introduced by Senator L.M. Judd, to commission the building of the pool. Faced with the usual bureaucratic delays, it was finally completed in 1927. Unfortunately, although beautiful in appearance, the San Francisco architects, unfamiliar with pool construction, built a facility along the Hawaiian shoreline that was in reality unfit for sanctioned competition. It was a poorly constructed saltwater pool open to the ocean tides, seaweed, and many ocean creatures. As Julie Checkoway stated in her book *The Three Year Swim Club*, "Schools of fish, slithery eels...octopuses...blowfish, hard-shelled sea turtles...stinging jellyfish....[and even] sharp-toothed barracuda" invaded the waters of what became known as "the Nat." In spite of these conditions, swimmers came to swim, coaches came to coach, and spectators took delight.

This historic pool was the location where, for first time in the history of the sporting world, two university swimming powers, champions of their conferences from two ends of the globe, would meet in head-to-head competition. The open portion of the meet featured Hawaiian Buster Crabbe, who later would become a movie star, and diver Mickey Reilly (also known as Michael Galitzen), both of the University of Southern California. It also featured the local Hui Makani AAU team, coached by

**Official Program 3rd KEO NAKAMA Simming Meet, July 5-8, 1950**

the "infamous" Harvey Chilton, a former Waikiki beach boy who would dedicate 45 years to initiating greatness into the annals of Hawaii swimming. He played an important role in the golden age of Hawaiian swimming, coaching 45 Olympic competitors who won 50 Olympic medals. Eighteen of those athletes were inducted into the International Swimming Hall of Fame.

Prior to the start of competition between Yale and Meiji University, radio station KGU broadcast a half-hour interview of the two collegiate coaches, Shakhi Muramatsu and Kiphuth. The meet drew over 3,000 spectators to the opening ceremony and featured a "Parade of Nations" behind the Rising Sun of Japan, the ancient flag of the former Kingdom of Hawaii, and the Stars and Stripes. The military band played the national anthems of Japan, Hawaii, and the USA (the *Kimigayo*, *Hawaii Ponoi*, and *The Star Spangled Banner*). The collegiate meet between Yale and Meiji ended in a 70-70 tie.

In the open section of the competitions, the Hawaiians once again showed their ability to dominate world swimming. The Hui Makani Club, a pool-less team prior to the completion of the Nat, had trained along Pier 7 in the Honolulu Harbor and completed long distance swims in front of the Ala Moana Hotel. These practices were always under the watchful eye of the (legendary) Chilton, stopwatch in hand. The Club dominated the meet with 65 points to Meiji's 36 and Yale's 31. The open meet featured record after record performances by Buster Crabbe, Maiola Kalili, Yoshiyuki Tsuruta of Japan, and Yale's Nelson Millard who defeated the Olympic champion Tsuruta in the 400-meter breaststroke. Kiphuth was intrigued by the image, demeanor, and reputation of the

Hui Makani coach with his signature bow tie and diminutive stature. Kiphuth took note of both Coach Chilton and the talented swimmers and expressed how Hawaii's location near the warm waters of the Pacific was a rich source of available talent.

As in 1921, Kiphuth, due to the interest and generosity of the alumni, was again able to initiate a "first" for intercollegiate and world swimming. In spite of restrictions imposed by the Yale Athletic Association, the last minute necessity to alter the route of the continental portion of the trip, and the urgency for rules of conduct for this new era of international dual meets, Kiphuth played a significant part in writing a new chapter in the histories of Yale, collegiate and international swimming.

In March of 1931, the AAU announced that it would choose a 13-man delegation, selected on the basis of trials held in each section of the country, to compete at the dedication of Japan's new Meiji University pool in the first ever AAU international dual meet to be held that summer. Although years of legend dictated otherwise, it was regional competition, not Kiphuth, that would determine team personnel. Although the athletes had in the past been required to obtain permission from the AAU for prior international swimming events, including those in Hawaii, those meets were not official AAU dual meets. The *New York Times* reported in May that Kiphuth would serve in the dual capacity as coach and manager of this historic team.

From every possible standpoint, the meet proved to be a total success, drawing approximately 40,000 spectators. So enthusiastic were Japan's swimming fans that they were willing to purchase standing-room-only tickets. With the absence of two of America's finest competitors, Olympic gold medalist George Kojac from Rutgers and Walter Laufer from the Lake Shore (Illinois) Athletic Club, Japan emerged victorious with a final score of 40-23. Kojac, an excellent pre-med student, had bypassed the trip to secure the necessary income for his final year at college. Laufer, now married, had other responsibilities outside of swimming. Kojac and Laufer, Olympic gold and silver medalists in the 100 backstroke, and both world-class freestyle swimmers, certainly would have stolen victory for the Kiphuth-coached USA team.

This was not unusual in the early decades of competitive swimming: for athletes to be unable to compete on the world stage for lack of financial support. This was a theme all too common in that day and age for both swimmers and coaches.

Kiphuth's next journey to the land of the rising sun took place in 1934 when he accompanied a delegation of three American swimmers, Albert VanDeWeghe from Princeton, Jack Medica from the University of

Washington, and Arthur Highland from the Lake Shore Athletic Club, to the Japanese National Championships in Tokyo on August 11, 12, and 13. Although Ed Kennedy coach of Columbia University admitted to being considered for coach of the United States team to Tokyo that year, the always affable Kennedy relinquished the honor when the Japanese specifically requested Kiphuth. The visit by Kiphuth and his delegation of American champions proved once again to be tremendously popular with the Japanese public. This opened the door for Kiphuth to return with an all-star team in the summer of 1935.

The 1935 team was selected based on the results of the Outdoor AAU Championships held in Detroit. Finally, and of major importance, head-to-head competition, not regional competitions, and not a political selection process within the AAU, would determine the American delegation for foreign trips. En route to Tokyo, and with the blessing of the AAU, Kiphuth, once again, took advantage of the opportunity to promote the sport of swimming. Competing in meets in Denver, Los Angeles, San Francisco, and Honolulu, the AAU all-stars captured headlines and thrilled the public by establishing three American relay marks in the 800 freestyle, 400 freestyle and 300 medley, and one individual American mark in the 100 breaststroke.

After defeating a delegation of Japan's finest in a dual meet in Osaka in torrential rain, the team moved on to Tokyo. Interest in the August 17-19 dual meet reached tremendous proportions. Lines formed each morning at 6:00 a.m. in front of the pool to purchase the remaining standing room only tickets that went on sale at 3:00 p.m. More than 13,000 fans filled the Meiji pool each evening. The general populace received up-to-date reports from all the Japanese radio stations as to the progress of the meet.

The meet itself was an extremely exciting affair. The outcome was fully in doubt right to the final event. Taylor Drysdale from the University of Michigan, after apparently snatching victory for the American team in the 200-meter backstroke, was disqualified due to a difference in interpretation of the rules. In the view of Mercersburg Academy Coach, John Miller, who was at the meet, the ever-gracious Kiphuth "hid the mist in his eyes," and congratulated his "worthy rival." In victory or in defeat, Kiphuth always stood as "Kiphuth, the Man."

After a three-year hiatus, Kiphuth's next international assignment would be to lead a delegation of seven swimmers and one diver on a tour of Germany in August of 1938. An agreement between Dan Ferris secretary-treasurer of the AAU (noted for his tendency to procrastinate) and his German counterpart, Otto Brewitz was necessary before the team could travel or competition could take place. The slow and tedious manner in which Federation International de Natation (FINA) and the AAU functioned was always a bone of contention with Kiphuth. He clearly understood that the affluent with the freedom of prosperity and time reigned supreme within the halls of national and international amateur sport. Therefore, Kiphuth realized diplomacy, not irrational behavior, resulted in a more favorable outcome.

On June 5, 1938, Kiphuth wrote to Max Ritter, the prominent AAU official and one of the founders of FINA. Kiphuth expressed, as diplomatically as he could, the concerns of the coaches and swimmers who had contacted him. There was distress about the impact the delay presented on the availability of America's talented pool of swimmers. The letter further addressed the difficulty delays of this nature cause for securing adequate travel arrangements. Kiphuth, in his usual manner, had made his point that it was time for those in charge to take care of business.

**Max Ritter, founding father of FINA, and Coach Kiphuth**

On June 25, 1938, the *New York Times* announced that the Foreign Relations Committee of the AAU had arranged and sanctioned 18 days of competition to take place in Germany. The Americans would compete on 13 of 18 days in the German cities of Bremen, Hanover, Magdenburg, Breslau, Munich, and Stuttgart. They would also compete in the Hungarian capital of Budapest. The final competition would be against a European all star team composed of swimmers from England, Sweden, Hungary, France, the Netherlands, and Germany at Berlin's Olympic pool.

The selection of team personnel, greatly affected by the procrastination of Dan Ferris, did not go without some controversy as only a squad of seven swimmers and two divers would be chosen. The winners at the National AAU Championships to be held in Louisville, Kentucky, in July would receive first priority. Pool and weather conditions, always a factor, tested the capacity of the athletes to adjust. The contestants' initial concerns of humid air and warm water gave way to the burden of cool rain showers and water temperature of 78 degrees. The first six swimmers earning a ticket to Europe represented a cross section of America's finest: Adolph Kiefer, America's premier backstroker and a proficient all around swimmer, freestyle sprinter Peter Fick of the New York AC, distance ace Ralph Flanagan from Miami, middle distance swimmer Paul Wolf of Southern California, sprinter Otto Jaretz from Chicago AA, and breaststroker Jim Werson from Cal Berkley. The divers were Elbert Root of Detroit and Al Patnik of Ohio State.

With the exception of Wolf and Jaretz, each athlete had won his respective event at the AAU nationals. Jaretz and Wolf finished second and third behind Fick in the 100-meter freestyle, and had qualified in accordance with AAU rules governing the necessity for additional relay members. When Kiefer declined the nomination in favor of a job in Chicago, the task of replacing Kiefer and to choose the seventh nominee fell to the AAU selection committee. The final two swimming spots went to Ohio State's William Neunzig, a backstroke specialist (replacing Kiefer) and to 15 year old Hawaiian teenager Halo Hirose who had placed behind Kiefer in the 200-meter freestyle. Unfortunately, Hirose's teammate Kiyoshi Nakama, a victim of Flanagan's dominating the three distance events, was not selected. Kiphuth supported Hirose's nomination because he saw it as an opportunity for the young Hawaiian to gain the necessary experience to compete on the world scene, prior to the 1940 Olympics.

Ignoring the fact that his swimmer Ralph Flanagan was a member of the German delegation, Steve Forsyth, coach of the Miami Biltmore Club, seized the opportunity at the AAU Championships to disparage the name Kiphuth before the swimming world. Forsyth's conduct exposed his own wounded vanity. His long standing dislike for Kiphuth had reached crit-

Ralph Flanagan, left, 3-event winner, and Pete Fick, 100-meter champ, test the temperature of the Lakeside water and discover the rain has cooled the pool to 78 degrees. Contestants had complained of the warmth of the water previously, but they had no kick Sunday about the heat, in or out of the pool.

## Kiefer and Flanagan Each Captures Third National Title At Lakeside Pool

ical mass at the 1936 Olympic Games. In spite of Kiphuth's support for Forsyth's appointment as assistant coach, Forsyth blamed Kiphuth personally, not the AAU or the USOC (Olympic Committee), for the fact that funding was not part of the package. Perhaps he was ignorant of the fact that appointment as either head or assistant swimming coach in those ancient times bore only the honor of prestige and rarely, if ever, remuneration.

Forsyth's verbal barrage before his coaching peers, and anyone within ear shot, attacked Kiphuth's professional credentials and centered on his false belief that Kiphuth secretly controlled not only the reigns of AAU swimming but the allocation of funds. Not content with venting to his peers, Forsyth went public in the *New York Times*. In the article "Swim Coach Complains," published on July 31, 1938, Forsyth lamented the choice of Kiphuth as the coach for the trip to Germany. Kiphuth responded with a deaf ear, and his usual shake of the head indicating ignorance of facts allows little room for rational discussion. After all, the scene was "Full of sound and fury signifying nothing." Thus, Kiphuth maintained his gentleman's decorum.

The team boarded the Bremen from New York to Germany on August 5, 1938. In spite of both cold weather and chilly water, the Americans performed very well in all 13 competitions, setting a world record in the 400-meter freestyle relay. More than 10,000 spectators remained in their seats during a torrential downpour to witness the conclusion of the Berlin meet against a European all star aggregation, the final competition of the tour. Although the Americans had built up a 24 to 18-point advantage over the first six events on day one, they faltered on the second day but still edged out a narrow victory for the USA 38-36. The typically European policy of unheated pools combined with the chilly and wet weather (with the exception of Budapest) proved testament to Kiphuth's dictum that survival of the fittest depends on the mindset.

With war clouds looming over Asia and Europe, foreign travel came to a halt until 1946 when Kiphuth accepted an invitation from Cuban officials to compete against an all-Cuban team in Havana. Kiphuth selected Eileen Wall, his secretary, and Harry Burke, the Yale freshman coach, to be members of the 18-member party, which also included the United States' 15-year old Jimmy McLane, who had been a swimming sensation since the age of 13.

### Japan Re-enters the World Scene

Although Japan had been banned from the London Olympics of 1948, at Kiphuth's urging the AAU invited Japan to compete in the 1949 Outdoor AAU Championships in Los Angeles. This was to be the first time Japan competed internationally in any sport since World War II. General Douglas MacArthur, the American viceroy of Japan and the former President of the 1928 United States Olympic Committee, had ordered the recall of all Japanese diplomats throughout the world and the ending of diplomatic ties. MacArthur, however, stabilized the Japanese government by refusing to charge Emperor Hirohito with war crimes and by wisely refusing to micromanage the bureaucrats and technocrats in charge of Japan's economy.

The General had been a high school tennis, baseball, and football athlete and played left field for the West Point baseball team. Since Japan's sports programs received strong support from the business establishment, MacArthur's policy of non-interference played an important role in Japan's post war sports history.

The Japanese delegation of six swimmers, determined to silence the "rumors of short pools and slow stop watches," was eager to verify Japanese superiority and perhaps play a part in healing the wounds of war. Scholar and writer, Pete Parsons, e-mailed this author from his home in the Philippines about how his father, Commander Chick Parsons, a member of MacArthur's Tokyo headquarters, with the assistance of his close friend, General Courtney Whitney, also on staff, "was instrumental in getting to MacArthur to allow these [world-record holding Japanese swimmers] to travel." He did this by convincing the General that the "young men would only help in the reconstruction of Japan." As Parsons points out in his article, *Commander Chick Parsons and the Japanese*, his father learned of the plight of the swimmers through his friendship with Takizo "Frank" Matsumoto, a member of the Japanese Diet, the government's legislative branch. Matsumoto's wife, Mary, was often referred to as the "[swim] team's social manager."

On August 8, 1949, the *New York Times* reported "Diet member Frank Takizo Matsumoto, who has many friends in Honolulu and California, will head the swimming delegation." The designated "[h]ead coach will be former Olympic 100-meter-backstroke champion Masaji Kiyokawa" and "Hihon University swimming coach Katsuyoshi Murakami will [also] make the trip."

> In 1952, as a young child, Pete Parsons was invited to join the Japanese Olympic training camp in Usuki, south of Tokyo. The team took up residence in an old temple and slept on futons on a tatami floor. As a result, he developed a close and lasting friendship with many Japanese Olympic hopefuls including Shiro Hashizume, Yoshihiro Hamaguchi, Hiroshi Suzuki, and the "Flying Fish," Furuhashi, who would later visit him in the Philippines.

Prior to the departure, Japan's swimming sensation Hironoshin Furuhashi, with dignified humility, expressed that "It will be my first experience competing against Americans and I'm not so sure I will win." A reporter told him "you should have no trouble winning the 800 and 1500 meter free-style events." Furuhashi responded: "I don't know about that – Americans are strong competitors."

Questioned as to Furuhashi's ability to shatter world standards, Tetsuo Hamuro, a former Olympic Champion, replied that he "has a powerful stroke and a phenomenally strong six-beat kick which is deceptive because there is little or no splash above water. There is terrific driving power in his left kick as he completes his right stroke, something which few swimmers have."

On Thursday, August 11, McArthur's Allied headquarters sanctioned the overseas junket. On August 12, the delegation departed by Pan Am Clipper from Haneda Airport to compete in the AAU outdoor championships to begin on August 16.

The Japanese swimmers did not disappoint, winning five of six freestyle gold medals and establishing five world records: Hironoshin Furuhashi in the 400, 800, and 1500-meter freestyle; Shiro Hashizume in the 1000-meter freestyle; and the 800-meter freestyle relay of Yoshihiro Hamaguchi, Shuichi Murayama, Shigeyuki Maruyama, and Furuhashi. The American media labeled Furuhashi, "The Flying Fish of Fujiyama" as he anchored the relay to a 24-second victory, with his seemingly unorthodox straight arm, windmill-style stroke and his drag kick.

When Robert Gibbs won the 100-meter freestyle, Olympian Alan Stack, the 100-meter backstroke, and Olympian Joe Verdue, the 100-meter breaststroke, respectively, American pride was salvaged.

In 1950, the Japanese Swimming Federation, respectfully requesting that Kiphuth head the delegation, invited and sponsored a 12-man United States team to compete in eight days of competition, beginning on August 4th and concluding on August 24. The main dual meets were to take place in Tokyo August 4 through 6 and in Osaka on August 12 and 13, followed by a meet in Yawata on August 15, Kura on August 20, and Nagoya on August 24.

In order to have the four finest distance swimmers in the world competing, the Japanese sent a special invitation to Yale's Australian import John Marshall to compete against fellow Eli Jimmy McLane, the 1948 Olympic 1500-meter gold medal winner, Ford Konno, the rising Hawaiian distance swimmer, and their own "Flying Fish," Hironoshin Furuhashi. Yale contributed four additional athletes, Allen Stack, Dennis O'Connor, Dick Thoman, and Wayne Moore, ably supported by Ron Gora from the University of Michigan, Clarke Scholes from Michigan State University, Dick Cleveland from the Ohio State University, and Bowen Stassforth from the University of Iowa.

At the conclusion of World War II in 1945, two young U.S. State Department aides had drawn a line across the 38th parallel of Korea, previously a Japanese colony. Russia initially occupied territory north of the line and the United States, fearing the advance of communism, sent a small occupying force to the south. On June 25, 1950, the Korean conflict began. President Truman ordered General Douglas MacArthur to assume command and to send additional troops from Japan.

The start of the Korean Conflict impacted the September 10-15, 1950, best-of-seven baseball series between the Fort Wayne Capeharts and the Japanese. The American baseball players were required to be sworn into active duty for the duration of the tournament. A brief but mild earthquake delayed the opening day festivities. General MacArthur's wife threw out the ceremonial first pitch. The Fort Wayne club featured a pair of southpaw pitchers, Pat Scantlebury, and Jim LaMarque, both all-star veterans of the Negro League.

In contrast, the swimmers were not required to be sworn into the military, and the Korean Conflict did not appear to have any effect on the international swim meets held in Japan in 1950.

With Japan's sponsorship of the trip, America's governing body, the AAU, was free of all financial responsibility. Therefore, the AAU had only two main responsibilities for the meets: grant the required sanction for the swimmers to compete, and determine the selection process for choosing team members. Unlike in previous trips, Kiphuth was free from AAU administrative oversight and able to field a full and competitive team. As in 1934, Japan, always the perfect host, provided to all team members first-class transportation, a per diem of $5.00 per day stateside, $2.50 per day while on the ship, and $10 per day while in Japan.

Upon arriving in Tokyo, Kiphuth requested masseurs for the team. The Japanese, always ready to accommodate, but wise to the nature of Western man, provided two lovely masseuses instead. Much to the dismay of the team, Kiphuth insisted on supervising.

Jimmy McLane, by then a mature and experienced competitor, outperformed his Yale counterparts by taking second in the 200 and 400-meter freestyle and later teaming with Ron Gora, Clarke Scholes, and Dick Cleveland for victory in the 400-meter freestyle relay. The overall strength and versatility of the American team proved to be the deciding factor in the victorious outcome before crowds numbering up to 80,000.

But, the Flying Fish of Fujiyama brought the home crowd to its feet screaming "Furuhashi ganbare (fight)" as he easily defeated John Marshall by 10 meters in the 400 and Ford Konno by 3 meters in the 800. John B. Holway (known as the baseball guru and famous for his books on the Negro Leagues), was in attendance, and in his article *Japan Beat Us In Baseball*, remembered the crowd turning and bowing respectfully at the conclusion of each victory by Furuhashi:

> At the end of the race, everyone stood up, faced me, and bowed. I said, 'What the heck is this?' Then I turned around and saw Emperor Hirohito standing up and waving...To my mind, he (Furuhashi) was one of the great sports heroes of the 20th century, the way he raised a whole nation up out of its post-war depression.

The Osaka meet, in the middle of the trip, was held in a 50-yard pool. The highlights of the meet were an American mark in the 800-freestyle relay by Wayne Moore, Jimmy McLane, Ford Konno, and Ron Gora and concluding with a world mark by a 300-medley relay team of Dick Thoman, Bowen Stassforth, and Dick Cleveland. Kiphuth was in his glory coaching a team of the best swimmers representing the finest American universities.

These first post-war, Japanese-American swimming competitions were incredibly successful. Although gratifying to the Americans from the standpoint of victory, the 1950 meets, more importantly, contributed significantly to post-war healing and signaled a continuation of renewed Japanese and American sporting exchanges. The quadrennial dual meets with Japan were the only open international competitions except the Pan Am and Olympic Games.

At the beginning of the summer of 1951, at the request of the national AAU office, Kiphuth began preparing to accompany a select group of swimmers and divers to a meet in Hamilton, Bermuda, to be held at the conclusion of the Outdoor AAU Championships. Some members of the contingent were Cornell University swimmer Robbie Ord, Colgate University swim captain Garry Hoyt, divers John McCormack of Pasadena, California, and Ralph Trimborn of Chicago, along with swimmers John Marshall and Wayne Moore of Yale. Marshall and Moore broke world records in the 440-yard freestyle and the 300-yard freestyle respectively. According to the *New York Times*, in a unique turn of events, Marshall, who won the 100-yard breaststroke, disqualified himself by reporting to the officials that he had used an unorthodox kick.

At the same time, Mexican authorities contacted Yale with a request for a team of swimmers to compete against their all-star team. Immediately upon his return from Bermuda, Kiphuth departed for Mexico City. Among the contingent were Kenny Smith, Marshall, Moore, and Sheff.

From 1952 until 1955, Kiphuth remained extremely active in the international swimming picture. He conducted clinics in Germany and Iceland for the U.S. State Department and the Army, and also for the U.S. Committee for Sports in Israel.

In 1955, with strong support from the Japanese officials, Kiphuth was again selected as the American coach for the Japanese-American competitions to be held in Japan. On April 8, 1955, the vice-president of the AAU, Nick Barack, from Columbus, Ohio, had sent a letter to Louis G. Wilke president of the AAU. He copied Mike Peppe, Dan Ferris, who was the secretary-treasurer of the AAU, Charles Roeser, the Olympic swimming chairman, and Kiphuth. The letter served as a protest against Kiphuth being appointed as the coach for the 1955 Japan trip. On April 15 of the same year, the NCAA national office also sent a letter to Wilke requesting that Ralph Casey of the University of North Carolina receive consideration for the appointment. Secretary Ferris responded to Barack that Kiphuth's appointment was unanimous.

The team members were all selected from the Outdoor AAU Championships conducted in Los Angeles, and included 14 swimmers and one diver. The swimmers were Yoshi Oyakawa, Robert Mattson, Albert Wiggins, Reid Patterson, George Onekea, George Breen, Frank McKinney, Bill Yorzyk, Bill Woolsey, Ford Konno, David Armstrong, George Harrison, Dave McIntyre, and Sandy Gideonse. The lone diver, Don Harper of Ohio State, would later become the only athlete in NCAA history to win national championships in two different sports in the same year, diving and trampoline. He accomplished this feat twice, in both 1956 and 1958.

The 1955 team took part in five exhibitions and two dual meets, in Tokyo and Osaka, losing 44-to-35 and 43-to-27. The Japanese hospitality included its usual adventures of sightseeing, visiting shrines, and a geisha dinner. When Harper expressed his interest in Japanese prints and art, Kiphuth, excited to share his passion, invited Don on his excursions to Japan's finest art galleries.

This Japan trip marked Kiphuth's farewell to international coaching. While the protests did not change his 1955 appointment, they did not fall on deaf ears. Many of America's turn-of-the-century coaches were retired or close to retirement. Whereas it had previously been financially difficult for many coaches to volunteer to coach international teams, the newer coaches, more financially secure, as professional coaches, were able to accept the international appointments. The selection process for overseas coaching assignments was no longer what some coaches felt had been a closed and hidden book. The absolute authority of the AAU was being challenged. A full and complete renaissance in domestic and international swimming was on the horizon.

The emerging conflict between professionalism and amateurism in collegiate and international sport needed a voice of reason. A Cold War of politics had entered the arena of international sport. The NCAA and the AAU were locked in a heated battle. Avery Brundage, President of the International Olympic Committee, faced strong pressure from many sources, including the media, to step aside. However, Kiphuth, undeterred, continued to be a strong voice for America's presence in international competition. He saw his role as a bridge between the past and the present. He maintained a place on America's Olympic Committee, serving as America's representative to FINA, and continued to conduct international clinics for the U.S. State Department. When a number of American coaches called for the exclusion of foreign nationals in the United States AAU Championships, Kiphuth ended the discussion with a few simple words: "What! Are we afraid of competition?"

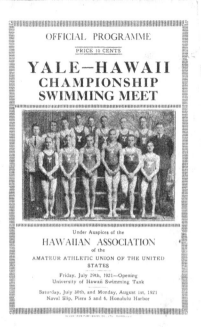

**Left: Coach Kiphuth and Son, Delaney in Hawaii**

**Above: Kiphuth and Frank McKinney - Indiana University**

Kiphuth International

*Kiphuth International*

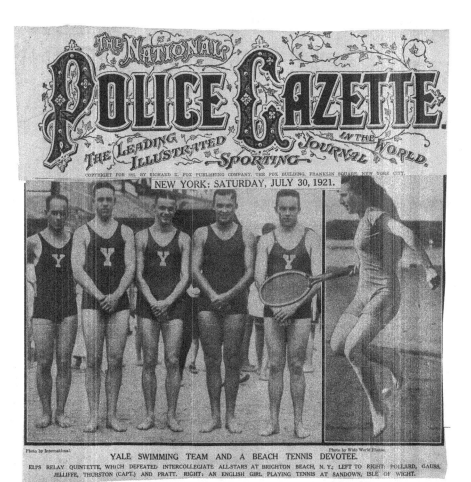

YALE SWIMMING TEAM AND A BEACH TENNIS DEVOTEE.
ELI'S RELAY QUINTETTE, WHICH DEFEATED INTERCOLLEGIATE ALL-STARS AT BRIGHTON BEACH, N. Y.; LEFT TO RIGHT: POLLARD, GAUSS, JELLIFFE, THURSTON (CAPT.) AND PRATT. RIGHT: AN ENGLISH GIRL PLAYING TENNIS AT SANDOWN, ISLE OF WIGHT.

*Kiphuth International*

**1930 Yale - Hawaiian Team**

*Kiphuth International*

**Left: Kiphuth holds a Japanese Baby**

# The Olympic Experience

Kiphuth attended every Olympic Games from 1924 through 1960, either as a FINA official or as head coach. His first tenure as an Olympic coach came in 1928 when he was appointed to the helm of the women's team. In 1932, Kiphuth served in a dual capacity as men's and women's coach. In 1936, 1940, and 1948, he served only as men's coach. The 1940 and 1944 Helsinki Games were canceled due to World War II. For the 1964 Olympics, the Japanese Olympic Committee honored him with an invitation that included a first-class airline ticket, housing, full admission to all events, a chauffeur, an interpreter, and carte blanche in the city of Tokyo.

In spite of the perceived notion that Kiphuth's Olympic experience was a mantel of fame, honor, and glory, the facts paint a more realistic picture. Kiphuth and Harry Hainsworth, of the Buffalo Athletic Club, arrived at the Paris Olympiad in 1924 as the United States' appointed diving officials for FINA. However, at the time, the privileged and the elite of society controlled the reins of international sport. Neither professional coaches nor common laborers would be allowed to discredit amateur sport. Consequently, despite their appointment, FINA disqualified them, on the basis that, as professionals, neither one was a bona fide amateur under the existing rules.

## *1928 Olympics: Amsterdam, The Netherlands*

Kiphuth's appointment as women's coach in 1928 apparently resulted from his prestige as coach at Yale, his winning record, his impressive demeanor, his willingness to sacrifice monetary gain for the sport, and the unwavering support of the powerful Louis de Breda Handley, coach of the Women's Swim Association of New York.

Kiphuth's initial introduction to Olympic coaching provided him with the opportunity to be front and center before the entire swimming world. He was blessed with the finest women's freestyle swimmers and divers of that era, and a disappointing performance could have tarnished his Olympic debut. Despite the pressure, the Americans dominated three of the five women's swimming events. The talented 17-year-old

Albina Osipowich established a world record with a gold medal swim in the 100-meter freestyle, and Eleanor Garatti glided in earning silver. Teammate Martha Norelius had a 400-meter freestyle gold medal finish, with Josephine McKim earning the bronze. The swimmers put the finishing touch on their performance with a world record 400-meter freestyle relay in both the prelims and finals. In the prelims the team of Adeline Lambert, Susan Laird, McKim, and Osipowich finished in 4:55.6, and in the finals Lambert, Garatti, Osipowich, and Norelius finished 4:47.6. The divers dominated by capturing all three medals in the three-meter spring board: Helen Meany (gold), Dorothy Poynton (silver), and Georgia Coleman (bronze). They also captured gold (Betty Becker Pinkston) and silver (Coleman) in the platform diving.

## 1932 Olympics: Los Angeles, California, United States of America

In 1932, the same prestige that led to his 1928 appointment, combined with his success in Amsterdam, once again emerged as reasons to appoint Kiphuth as both men's and women's Olympic Coach. The other factor, just as important, was the economic impact of the Great Depression, requiring greater fiscal consideration and further limiting the pool of available coaches.

The Los Angeles Games in 1932 showed the rising superiority of the Japanese male swimmers. Out of a possible 16 medals the Nippon swimmers accumulated 11. The United States' only places were gold by Buster Crabbe, a former University of Southern California swimmer, in the 400-meter freestyle; a silver by the 800-meter freestyle relay of Frank Booth of Stanford University, George Fissler of the New York AC, and the two Kalili brothers, Maiola and Manuela, from Hawaii; and two bronze medals by Albert Schwartz, a former Northwestern swimmer, and Jim Cristy, of Michigan, in the 100-meter and 1500-meter freestyles, respectively.

The absence of the defending 100-meter backstroke champion, Kojac, now a medical student at Columbia University, also contributed to America's poor showing. Nonetheless, American divers won all six diving medals. Michael (Riley) Galitzen won the three-meter spring board, followed by Harold Smith and Richard Degener. Harold Smith won the 10-meter platform, with Michael Galitzen and Frank Kurtz taking silver and bronze. Although disappointed in the overall performance on the men's side of the ledger, Kiphuth felt that with more emphasis on long-course training and Olympic events, the United States men could regain the dominant position in Olympic swimming.

On the other hand, the women's team maintained their premier position in world swimming. America's newest rising star, Helen Madison, coached by Seattle's future women's Olympic coach, Ray Daughters (1936 and 1948), did not disappoint and brought home the gold medal individually in the 100-meter and 400-meter freestyles. She also led off the 400-meter freestyle relay. The team of Madison, McKim, Helen Thomas, and Garatti swam a world record 4:38.00. Since, due to the Great Depression, only five other countries sent women's relay teams, the event was held as a final only. Those swims, along with Eleanor Holm's gold medal in the 100-meter backstroke accounted for the women's team winning four out of five swimming events. In turn, the women's divers captured all six diving medals. Coleman, 14-year old Katherine Rawls, and Jane Fauntz finished in that order in the three-meter springboard. Poynton, Coleman, and Marion Roper were the 10-meter platform medalists.

Although the coaches and swimmers were grateful for the large and enthusiastic crowds at each session at the 10,000-seat Olympic Stadium, more important was the fact that for the first time in Olympic history they welcomed the opportunity to compete in a facility with clear, high-quality (not cloudy) water.

## *1936 Olympics: Berlin, Germany*

In April of 1896, the first modern Olympics, the vision of Frenchman Pierre de Coubertin, took place in Athens, Greece. The Games were based on de Coubertin's dream of a world event dedicated to the principles of peace and sportsmanship among all nations. In his *Edict on Professionalism*, de Coubertin expressed his belief "in the noble and chivalrous character of athletics against professionalism." But by 1936, a mere 40 years later, the Games succumbed to the ideology of athletic nationalism. Hitler, through the implementation of nationalized scientific training centers for his athletes, and the use of Joseph Goebbels' office of Nazi propaganda, would change the Games forever. Hitler believed the showcasing of a "master race" dominant in athletic performance would

> The citizens of Berlin experienced the first sports on television when, to showcase the "master race," Goebbels had 25 large television screens placed throughout the city of Berlin so the citizens could watch the Olympics for free. The games were also broadcast via radio to 41 countries. German filmmaker Leni Riefenstahl, renowned for her propaganda film *Triumph of the Will* (1934), was commissioned to film the games. Her two-part documentary *Olympia* pioneered what are now common techniques for sports filming. (Nicholas Barber, *How Leni Riefenstahl Shaped The Way We See the Olympics*, www.bbc.com/culture/story/20160810-how-leni-riefenstahl-shaped-the-way-we-see-the-olympics and www.olympic.org/berlin-1936)

be a precursor to his dream of a German empire. What followed was the U.S.S.R., East Germany, and other Eastern Bloc countries attempting to use Olympic dominance to idealize the utopia communism seemed to offer.

Kiphuth, a proponent of de Coubertin's philosophy of amateurism, constantly fought against the eroding of the amateur status of sport to the demagogues who would use sport to promote the national interest and the almighty dollar. He was dogmatic and unwavering in his stance against professionalism.

For the 1936 Olympic Games in Berlin, Kiphuth was not only named Men's Olympic Swimming Coach but also named Director of Aquatic Sports, a position that gave him final authority over Olympic diving, water polo, and swimming. There is no doubt that Kiphuth's collegiate and AAU endeavors, combined with the successes of his Hawaii and Japan ventures, were instrumental in this appointment. His attendance at crucial AAU and Olympic Committee meetings, in the sometimes smoke-filled meeting rooms of the New York Athletic Club, and his association with the powerful elements involved in swimming, certainly were also major factors. However, one can never disallow the image of the man himself – always professional, always poised, and always confident.

Prior to the departure of the Berlin bound American Olympic team, newspapers, politicians, and sportsmen called for a boycott of what had become known as Hitler's Games. According to Iris (Cummings) Critchell, a member of the 1936 Olympic women's swim team, Charlotte Epstein of the Women's Swim Association of New York "made it very clear that…[the WSA] club would do nothing to help the Olympic team to raise money for [the Olympics] because of her personal political beliefs." Critchell went on to say that, "The Olympic Committee relied heavily on the Jewish community… as major supporters, and many withdrew support." When Avery Brundage, President of the United States Olympic Committee, declared that politics had no place in sport and that no country had the right to "restrict participation by reason of class, creed, or race," the Games and Kiphuth's position as head of aquatics was secured. Germany's greatest ally in securing the '36 Games (Hitler was not yet in

> By the 1984 Los Angeles Olympics, although nationalism was still front and center, commercialism and professionalism began to take hold. This was the first privately funded Olympics. Under the leadership of Peter Ueberroth, the current Olympic sponsorship program was introduced. This led to a surplus of $250 million at the conclusion of the L.A. Games.

power when the decision was made in 1931) was the belief by Brundage that Communism, not the rise of German nationalism, represented the greatest threat to the world order. An article by Harold Lloyd Varney (The American Mercury) gave strong support to the existing threat of the Bolsheviks in the Soviet Union. Brundage took full advantage by disseminating the article to every available media outlet, and every person of influence.

Although certainly an honor to be named Olympic coach or to earn the privilege of representing Team USA, in the early years there were many obstacles to overcome in preparing the team prior to and once arriving at the Olympic site. From its inception and at least through the XV Helsinki Olympiad in 1952, there were many necessary and unnecessary impediments, aside from funding, to a successful Olympic experience for both the coaches and the athletes. The athletes had to travel by boat, the competition swimming pools were unheated, the water was cloudy, and the accommodations, as well as the meals, were not up to today's standards.

The title of Olympic Coach was void of financial remuneration. Faced with obstacle after obstacle in order to properly prepare Team USA for competition, the coaches still wore the mantle with pride. But even more astonishing, athletes were expected, in most cases, to sponsor themselves for the privilege of representing Team USA.

Critchell states it best with the most revealing account, unheard of and unappreciated by today's Olympians, that an introduction to the Olympic swimming team in 1936 consisted of a verbal congratulations, and "a letter that said yes, you've qualified for the team and yet we do not have the funds to send the whole team…'If you want to go, get out and try to raise some money.'" As a result "they dropped the two alternates [for relays]…[and] the third placers in a lot of these events were put on questionable standby."

"[In those 10 days prior to boarding] we had been wandering around trying to raise money, not training…I didn't even get in a pool, I never saw a coach…We were 10 days on the SS Manhattan…there was just one swimming pool which was about 20 feet x 20 feet x 9 feet deep. And they pumped the [cold sea] saltwater into it….[The coaches] kept alternating [athletes] for the use of the pool. They used long pieces of rubber which they'd tie around our waists and then we'd swim and the coaches would hold us back. Sometimes they tied them to a post." She went on to say there was no "adapting to the [German] environment - the rain, the cold…We'd not traveled to a place with a climate like Berlin." And with modest exclamation, she also stated, "Well, of course, the essence of it was thrilling."

When the boat arrived in the Harbor of Hamburg "they ushered us into a train to Berlin." From there the women Olympians were taken to an athletic center called the "Friesenhaus" walking distance to a "cold and unheated" 50-meter practice pool.

According to Critchell, the athletes "were given enough food, but it was boiled cabbage and boiled potatoes and boiled beef-things we weren't really used to. And it wasn't training food...very few green vegetables, no salads, and no fruit...I got to saying to mother, 'I'd love an orange.'" Kiphuth's theory that psychological preparation is the final and ultimate weapon to victory was tested under these conditions. He believed that the ultimate victor ignores distractions, since the existing conditions are the same for all athletes. Three of the top American male swimmers, Jack Medica, Adolph Kiefer, and Al VanDeWeghe were experienced and mentally prepared. Thus they were able to overcome these difficult obstacles. Not all of the athletes were as successful. Kiphuth's theory held true: all things being equal, psychological preparation is the ultimate weapon for ascending to the top of the podium.

The 1934 and 1935 United States-Japanese dual meets, as Kiphuth had warned, predicted the logical outcome of the 1936 Berlin swimming events. With the exception of gold medals by USA's Medica in the 400-meter freestyle and Kiefer in the 100-meter back, silver by VanDeWeghe in the 100-meter backstroke, and gold by Hungary's Ferenc Czik in the 100 freestyle, the Japanese reigned supreme. However, the American divers were led by Richard Degener, Marshall Wayne, and Alan Greene finishing first, second, and third on the three-meter springboard, while Wayne and Elbert Root finished first and second on the 10-meter platform. Hermann Stork of Germany took bronze on the platform.

When Alan Gould of the Associated Press conducted a poll to find out what was regarded by Olympic officials as the outstanding feature of the Berlin Games, almost everyone, including Kiphuth, selected the centralization and permanence of facilities. In the category of an outstanding highlight, Kiphuth, in line with his love of distance runners, selected the record performance in the 1500 meter by Jack Lovelock of New Zealand.

At the conclusion of the 1936 Games, Kiphuth praised America's indoor competitive swimming program but expressed concern over the fact that both Europe and Japan conducted far superior long-course programs training in 50-meter pools, while Americans trained in non-regulation pools, lakes, and various other venues. He stressed the fact that if America was to regain a leading position in world swimming "all interested parties must exert a greater effort to further the cause." Due to the Depression and later the war effort, the United States was not then in a position to heed the warning, nor to implement an increase in long-course training facilities.

## *1940 and 1944 Olympics become 1948 Olympics: London, England*

Kiphuth, by 1936, was ahead of his time in realizing the importance of looking at the overall Olympic experience to maximize the athletes' psychological preparation. In 1920, swimmer Norman Ross, who was the Olympic champion in the 400, 1500, and 800 relay, had led a successful strike of Olympic athletes to avoid returning to the United States "on the cattle boat we went over on." The Olympic athletes had traveled by steerage. The "ruling" aristocrats had traveled in first class cabins. Significantly, in a letter to the Foreign Relations Committee of the AAU, Kiphuth took that one step further and requested consideration of the possibility of the 1940 Olympic swimming team traveling to Helsinki as a separate unit from other Olympians. He wrote in part "there is an esprit and morale possible on this type of trip that is never in evidence when the group is submerged as a part of the entire Olympic Team." Kiphuth, always the diplomat and fully aware of the Olympic Committee's sensitivity to public scrutiny, was very careful to state that, "this is not a criticism of the Olympic administration. It is merely expressing an arrangement which this writer feels would produce a finer team and get better results." Unfortunately, this dream would not come to fruition during Kiphuth's tenure as coach.

Japan, in celebration of the anniversary of the founding of the Empire, desperately wanted to host the 1940 Games. In June 1937, the IOC, meeting in Warsaw, awarded the XIIth Olympiad to Japan. Politically, the bid was under severe scrutiny since Japan had invaded Manchuria. Brundage, in an attempt to save the Games, made an emergency visit to Japan, wisely taking Kiphuth with him because of his relationship with Japanese authorities. However, the Japanese military war machine settled the issue by withdrawing Japan's bid in late 1938. Brundage now threw his support in favor of Helsinki. Hitler's invasion of Poland on September 1, 1939, would result in the cancellation of both the 1940 and 1944 Olympics scheduled for Helsinki. Helsinki then relinquished the 1948 Games in favor of London with the promise of hosting the 1952 Games.

Once hostilities in Europe became uncontrollable, in a surprise move the AAU and the United States Olympic Association (presently known as the United States Olympic Committee) made an unsuccessful bid to host the swimming portion of the 1940 Games at the New York AC's Travers Island outdoor 50-meter saltwater pool in Westchester County.

During the summers of 1946 and 1947, Kiphuth once again took on America's leadership role and attended the international swimming meetings in London, conducted by FINA, in preparation for the 1948 Games. He also attended the European Championships in Monte Carlo in 1947. In the fall of 1947, the United States Olympic Committee announced that Kiphuth would once again serve as swim coach, while Mike Peppe of Ohio State would serve in the capacity of diving coach.

As in previous Olympics, despite strong objection from Avery Brundage, certain countries were not permitted to partake because of political considerations. In order to heal the scars of war, Kiphuth hoped that political considerations would be put aside. However, when Helsinki bowed to the choice of London, a city still bearing the scars of Hermann Goering's Luftwaffe, as the preferred site, political and emotional factors dictated that the two major Axis Powers, Japan and Germany, would be excluded from participation.

Kiphuth's shining hour occurred in 1948 when the United States completed a grand slam in the men's competition by winning every gold medal in both swimming and diving, and accumulating 16 of a possible 22 medals. Although a great moment in Olympic and American sports history, Kiphuth once again recognized the role circumstance plays in the finite nature of victory.

The Japanese swimming federation, barred from the Games, conducted their own meet to coincide with the competitions in London. In most instances, the Japanese times were superior to the gold medal standards of 1948. When Doug Kennedy of the *New York Tribune* questioned the impact on American success, Kiphuth replied "perhaps those Japanese banned from international competition lifted the psychological barrier just by the incentive brought on by their exclusion." Once again, Kiphuth verbally expressed his belief that "all things being equal, superior mental preparation wins the day."

### *1952 Olympics: Helsinki, Finland*

As another Olympics came onto the horizon, the public outcry among many coaches came to the forefront. Coaches like Matt Mann and Mike Peppe deserved consideration, but the appointment as Olympic Coach bore no fruit, except the honor of the appointment. So, what coaches were willing to forgo summer employment for the honor? For the 1952 Helsinki Games, the electorate chose Mann.

Kiphuth's era as Olympic Coach had come to an end. Undeterred, as was his nature, he redefined his Olympic role by serving as an official of FINA. After arriving in Helsinki, Mr. Yale was questioned by a reporter as to why he was not on the pool deck. He simply stated that it was not his role to be on deck.

Based on his open door policy of free coaching, free housing, and full access to Yale's 50-meter indoor pool, Kiphuth saw the opportunity to concentrate his efforts on training any swimmer, friend or foe, with national or Olympic aspirations. During the summer of 1952, prior to the American Olympic Trials, Kiphuth offered "all Olympic hopefuls" the opportunity to train at Yale. According to the account given by the class of 1953, Kiphuth's full house included "a stable of Texans, a delegation of Canadians and South Americans and practically the entire University of Michigan varsity."

After all, in the final analysis, Kiphuth believed the contest resided in the mind of the competitor as to whom the victor would be.

Four members of Yale's class of '53, Wayne Moore, Jimmy McLane, Don Sheff, and Frank Chamberlin, along with Yale graduate Alan Stack, earned berths on the Helsinki bound team.

### *1956 Olympics: Melbourne, Australia*

Forbes Carlile revealed that Kiphuth, through his friendship with famous Australian swimmer Frank Beaurepaire, played an important part in obtaining the 1956 Olympic games for Melbourne. Sadly, Beaurepaire passed away in May of 1956, just six months before the opening ceremonies.

That year, the powers of influence chose the road of least resistance and appointed Robert Muir, a former swim student of Mann and a close associate of Kiphuth to be the Olympic swim coach. Muir was certainly worthy of the honor. As a FINA official, Kiphuth was deck-side as the United States won only two gold medals, one by former Ohio State diver Robert Clotworthy, who was then training under Phil Moriarty at Yale, and the other by Yale NHSC member Bill Yorzyk, a non-swimmer until coaches Charlie Smith and Dr. Red Silvia took him under their wing at Springfield College.

### *1960 Olympics: Rome, Italy*

At the Detroit Olympic Trials in 1960, Kiphuth's swimmer, Jeff Farrell, considered a "shoo-in" for the Olympic Team, underwent an emergency appendectomy just six days before the meet. Because of his intimate knowledge of human anatomy and his understanding of the physical recuperative powers of a superior-trained athlete, Kiphuth convinced a surgeon to avoid cutting through muscles to remove Farrell's inflamed appendix. Farrell was the fastest sprinter in the world at the time and this played a significant role in his unbelievable account of his return to competition in six days, as documented in his autobiography, *My Olympic Story*.

Kiphuth had petitioned the Olympic Committee to grant Farrell's automatic nomination to the team, if a marked improvement in his condition became evident. Approached by Ray Daughters, Chairman of the Men's Olympic Committee, Farrell showed the highest level of sportsmanship by refusing automatic or "swim off" appointments to the Olympic Team. Instead, he earned an indelible place in American swimming history by qualifying for the team with a sixth place finish in the 200-meter freestyle. This allowed him to compete as a member of the 800-meter freestyle relay and the 400-meter medley relay.

Just like the two Olympics before, Kiphuth was pool-side as an official while his swimmer, in his eyes *America's* swimmer, Jeff Farrell, anchored the United States to two relay gold medals.

# An Analytical Mind

Kiphuth was able to analyze all of the elements necessary to produce outstanding swimmers and record swims. He knew that coaches willing to initiate competitive training programs that would prepare the athlete physically and psychologically for the competitive challenges ahead were necessary for developing world-class swimmers.

In 1930, at the conclusion of the Yale vs. Meiji swim meet, in response to *Hawaii Advertiser's* Francois D' Eliscu's question regarding the major elements necessary for producing a champion swimmer, Kiphuth replied: "There are four: a climate, either real or artificial, to allow year-round training, a large competitive base, proper coaching, and community involvement." Citing Hawaii's teenage swimmer Maiola Kalili as an example, Kiphuth continued, "The ocean at your door, the mild climate all year round, the ability to swim 365 days a year [and the endless supply of youngsters] should make Hawaii, as it is, the center of the swimming world."

At the conclusion of the 1932 Olympic Games, American sports writers accused their country's swimmers of complacency. In response, Kiphuth identified the Great Depression as the major contributor to the lack of success. He pointed out that over the past 10 years, "Our great swimmers have largely been members of wealthy clubs, located near large metropolitan areas, which fostered year round programs." As a result of present economic conditions, "expenditures have been limited."

Kiphuth's conceptual analysis of the conditions necessary to a productive and successful age group competitive swim program was initially implemented in California, allowing those youngsters to dominate world swimming by 1964. Confirmation of Kiphuth's reasoned position came in the 1950s when coaches such as George Haines, Peter Daland, Don Gambril, and Sherm Chavoor, all from California, and Don Watson, from Illinois, implemented successful age group and senior programs based on the above premise. This propelled America into the forefront of world swimming. Just as Kiphuth predicted, the necessary elements to maintain the "continuity so necessary for the development of the highly trained athlete" was now in place.

As early as 1934, he concluded that, "The most important factor in breaking a record is psychological rather than physiological or anything else." The coach declared that the major stumbling block for any athlete is "mental attitude." All things being equal, he firmly believed that "mental conditioning" constitutes 75 percent of pre-race and race strategy.

Observing Arne Borg's astonishing world record 1500-meter swim in Bologna in 1937, Kiphuth attributed Arne's incredible speed over the first 100 meters, the resulting evenness of pace maintained for the next 700 meters, and the subsequent increase in pace over the remaining meters to be the result of exceptional psychological preparation.

While analyzing Japan's emergence as a world swimming power in 1934, Kiphuth pointed out that Japan had a powerful coordinator of swimming, assisted by dedicated and interested amateurs. Swim meets drew large crowds and those gate receipts added to the financial stability already in place. Also, geographically, all swimmers had access to the seat of power in Tokyo. He further noted the development and adaptation of "a new swimming stroke, structured to the length of their arms, legs and trunk and the importance of dietary considerations, as well as mental attitude and the willingness to sacrifice for cause and country."

In contrast, the coach noted the poor economic conditions in the U.S., the lack of a strong and financially secure Swimming Federation, the stress on individual performance rather than a national program, the lack of professional swim clubs and the fact that the Olympic coach served as nothing more than a morale booster. In addition, once an Olympic Team was chosen, athletes disbanded to train individually and would not meet again until departure for the games. He felt all the above were issues in dire need of being addressed by the AAU and the U.S. Olympic Committee. Although Kiphuth did not believe in profiting from athletics, he did feel that financial stability allocated responsibly to the competitor was an integral part of success in international swimming.

In 1931, Kiphuth responded to Silas B. Fishkind's (the *New York Times*) question as to the limits of man's aquatic ability by stating: "The sport is improving all the time...as we become more expert and teach the correct stroke the general excellence and standard of performance will be raised...Of course, improved pool design and construction must also be considered." He emphasized the importance of buoyancy and flexibility in swimming.

> I mean flexibility of ankles, knees, arms and shoulder girdle. Then there is the physiological side, the constitutional vigor of the man, and thirdly we have the psychological side the mental drive which enables a man to fight on in the stress

of competition and give all he has to the finish. Given a man with this dynamic quality, with the other factors added, and you have the perfect swimming type. Even if he has never swum before, with the proper coaching and teaching he can be developed into a great swimmer.

Unknowingly, Kiphuth had predicted the emergence of Doc Councilman's great distance swimmer George Breen.

The *New York Herald Tribune*, on February 4, 1949, featured Kiphuth's declaration that the onslaught on records would continue "indefinitely." "We haven't come close to the ceiling of swimming achievement." Kiphuth cited the Japanese movement of the bar from 19:20 to 18:30 in the metric mile as proof that "barriers are purely psychological." Inhibitions to present standards, improved technique, and the intelligent application and understanding of pace and personal endurance play important roles in the development of the superior athlete.

One of Kiphuth's most astute observations involved an analysis of Japan's Flying Fish Furuhashi's non-conventional leg kick:

> All the theories of the conventional crawl leg beat are shattered. In the opinion of many he would be even faster if he kicked in the conventional rhythm, but like many great competitors he establishes his own style, which is based finally on his superb condition and balance and power in the water. His stroke cannot be imitated by anyone but another Furuhashi.... It is a spectacular conquest of the water by a greatly talented young man.

He believed firmly that coaches should respect the creativity of their athletes.

Kiphuth believed a man had to test himself physically if he was to learn his mental limitations. The purpose of athletics was to prepare man for the adventure of life. While the pool was his medium, Kiphuth's personality was the motivator. Kiphuth believed firmly that an older mature athlete, who could continue to compete as an amateur while working for a graduate degree, could achieve great success. He always cited the success of American swimmers Norman Ross, Tedford Cann, Duke Kahanamoku, Bowen Stassforth, and the phenomenal, but not recognized, swim of 48.5 by Weissmuller at age 36, while working for Billy Rose's World's Fair Aquacade in 1940. The swim was not recognized because Weissmuller was a professional and once again the skeptics screamed foul. Kiphuth wrote the following to this author in 1964:

Last week I went to see the trials and finals in the single sculls and eights in rowing. I saw exemplified what I have always believed, that an athlete in good, mature physical condition, at 25 or 26, is better than an athlete at 20 or 21 years of age. This was also true and evident to me in the AAU and Olympic Trials for Track and Field. If our swimmers would continue, I am sure we could have the same results we [meaning his ROTC team] had with Farrell, McGill, McIntyre; the same results the Australians had with Dawn Fraser, and now with Murray Rose.

We have a great example of that here at Yale, with a fellow like Jay Luck who is, at the moment, the best man in the world at 400-meter intermediate hurdles. He just worked very consistently as an undergraduate and in the past two years, while working here for his Doctorate in Electrical Engineering. So many of these good athletes are also outstanding in the academic field. There is Jay, working for a Ph.D. in a difficult field; Seibert, the 800-meters man in Tokyo, who is a nuclear physicist at Stanford...Spero, the #1 man in sculling, who is Ph.D. in a new kind of physics, at Columbia; a half-dozen fellows on the track team are either teaching, or doing graduate work. This can be done, but it requires a genuine interest in athletics -- not in terms of undergraduate popularity and success, using athletics as a means to an end, but instead, a genuine interest is the end itself.

Through the years, Kiphuth had envisioned the impact that the older mature athlete could make on the sport of swimming. Perhaps it is best he did not live to see his vision come to pass. This new era of sport as mass media entertainment, athletes funded by endorsements, and the loss of academic integrity and responsibility, would have been a "bridge too far" for him.

On March 21, 1922, the *New York Times* featured an article by Kiphuth in favor of adding the 440-yard swim to the collegiate program. He said, "[T]he time seems ripe for the innovation now." His purpose was to override the "scorn" of opponents and to highlight the important role a collegiate distance race would play in developing America's international level competitors. Kiphuth indicated that the present program of 50, 100, 220 freestyle and the 200 freestyle relay and the plunge for distance, tended to discourage middle distance swimming and to hinder the development of international level competitors.

A consultation with L. de B. Handley combined with a survey of Intercollegiate Swimming Association (ISA) league coaches, convinced Kiphuth that the time had come. He petitioned the leadership of the ISA, composed mainly of undergraduate managers, not coaches, to add the 440-yard freestyle and breaststroke and backstroke events, based on the growth of collegiate participants. The usual opposition to change initially clouded the issue with statements that "college youth would be unwilling to practice for such a great distance." However, Kiphuth was not to be denied. On December 6, 1922, he announced to his team that the ISA had held a special meeting. The plunge for distance would no longer be part of the program of events, the 440-yard freestyle would replace the 220-yard freestyle, and that the 220-yard breaststroke and the 150-yard backstroke, as well as a two-day championship meet, were now part of the program. The *Yale Daily News* quoted Kiphuth as saying the above changes "will stimulate interest in the sport." This was a significant step forward for the sport of swimming as the Eastern, Western, and Pacific universities, the AAU, and the International Federation of Swimming would now be conducting similar events and distances.

Whenever controversy or issues arose concerning the proper implementation of rules, Kiphuth was not one to be silent. He learned early that swimmers create the innovations that best test the limits of the rule. He strongly supported Erich Rademacher of Germany, the three Spence brothers of the USA, Sydney Cavill of Australia and others who were experimenting with an over-arm breaststroke (eventually to become the butterfly).

In 1938, letters to Otto Brewitz, a German swim official, and to Max Ritter, a leading AAU official, Kiphuth wrote, "The breaststroke executed in any style is a stroke measured by form, consequently the rules governing the form of the stroke have to be carried out whether they be underwater, on top of the water or the present butterfly (with frog kick) as the stroke has changed considerably."

In the 1950s, Kiphuth struggled at first with the separation of the breaststroke into the two competitive strokes, the butterfly and the breaststroke, swum today in competition. I had been privy to conversations between Phil, Harry, and Bob, where Bob initially took a firm stand that the emerging butterfly was nothing but a double arm freestyle with a dolphin kick. After all in some respects Kiphuth was a traditionalist. While his strongest critics argue, perhaps rightfully, that Kiphuth's acceptance of the new butterfly stroke was a result of butterfly sensation Bill Yorzyk's membership in the YNHSC, in the final analysis public interest, the beauty of the stroke, and the opportunity for more swimmers to compete were certainly major factors that dictated a reversal of his original mind set.

Perhaps one of the most outstanding forecasts Kiphuth made was regarding the 100-yard freestyle. In numerous discussions with Phil Moriarty and Harry Burke he forecast that sometime in the future, due to improved facilities, diet, increase in the number of competitors, etc., a swimmer would go below 40 seconds in the 100 freestyle. While this prediction has not yet come true, Caleb Dressel of Florida went 40.00 at the 2017 men's NCAA Championships, and Michael Chadwick of Missouri went 40.95. In 1956, at the Melbourne Olympics, when the record for the 1500-meter freestyle was 17:00, Kiphuth, in a conversation with Carlile, predicted that the time would eventually drop as low as 15:00. The record now stands at 14:31.02.

In Kiphuth's vision, "There is a technical ideal but so comparatively few people attain this that there would seem to be no limit to the excellence which will be achieved."

Kiphuth, unknown in 1918, and administratively ignored in 1919, had proceeded to grasp the reigns of a fledgling sport. In a period of six years, by utilizing his leadership skills, his flair for showmanship, and his ability to create enthusiasm, he had revolutionized the sport at Yale, impacted the national scene, and become a influential world figure. More importantly, by his consistent ability to grab headlines, he had advanced the cause of collegiate swimming. His quick, critical, and analytical mind had moved swiftly from the provincial domain of the Yale scene to the universal concept of global competition. Yale swimming, like Yale education, was about to become an international household word.

# Kiphuth's Irish Staff

Kiphuth clearly understood that a strong leader hires only extremely competent assistants. In the early years of private institutions, university budgetary considerations were always subject to tuition, fundraising, endowments, and unpredictable tax revenues. The coach never let this inconvenience prevent him from finding highly motivated employees.

To best describe his philosophy for hiring, a few lines from Dr. George Washington Carver's favorite poem written by Edgar A. Guest, Detroit newspaper man and radio host, paints the perfect picture:

*Equipment*
Figure it out for yourself, my lad,
You've all that the greatest of men have had,
Two arms, two hands, two legs, two eyes
And a brain to use if you would be wise.
With this equipment they all began,
So start from the top and say, "I can."

Time and time again Kiphuth utilized the talents of ambitious local high school students or recent graduates to work within the gymnasium. Many of these young men were bright and gifted students but lacked the opportunity and resources for furthering their education. His two earliest protégés went on to become head swimming coaches: Howard Stepp at Princeton beginning in 1928, and Karl Michael at Dartmouth beginning in 1939. Fortunately for Kiphuth, both Harry Burke, whom he hired in 1923, and Phil Moriarty, whom he hired in 1932, remained as faithful assistant coaches throughout his tenure.

## *Harry Burke*

Harry Burke was born on August 26, 1892, in New Haven, Connecticut. According to his application to work at the Payne Whitney, Burke was a three-sport athlete at New Haven's Hillhouse High School, playing football, basketball, and baseball. Upon graduation in 1910, he faced the same three options available to most children of local Irish immigrant

families: to work in the police or fire department or to find employment in one of the manufacturing plants.

Burke began working at the Winchester Arms Factory of New Haven in the fall of 1910. However by 1913, the drudgery of factory work became unbearable. Ten-hour days and four dollars a week no longer appealed to him.

Former Yale swimmer Alan Ford stated it best when he said Burke decided to discover America and a new life for himself by "hopping on and off trains whenever he felt like it." Initial disappointment turned to opportunity for Burke while waiting for his next train. A fellow traveler, rambling off numbers into the millions "one million five hundred thousand and ninety two," attracted his attention. "What are you talking about Buddy?" Burke inquired. When the man replied, "That's the sum of the numbers on the box cars," Burke realized the man was a numerical savant. With Burke as his agent, appearances as a Vaudeville act or at carnivals became a way of life over the next 11 years. In 1923, the act toured New Haven. In attendance was Yale's doctor of psychiatric medicine, Dr. Clement Fry. Burke agreed to Dr. Fry's request to study the savant as long as Burke was allowed to be present. At some point along the way, Kiphuth's friendship with Dr. Fry resulted in the introduction of Burke to Kiphuth.

In the fall of 1923, Kiphuth offered Burke a position as swim instructor. Now, anxious to be off the road and marry his beloved Catherine, Burke readily accepted. This allowed him to fulfill his wish to avoid the fate of his two brothers, local policemen. He became a faithful Kiphuth lieutenant and remained at Yale for 41 years.

From 1923 onward, Burke was in charge of the undergraduate swim program required of all Yale students, and served as supervisor of the intramural swim program. During the Second World War, he conducted all swimming classes for the Armed Services. He coached the Yale freshman team for 16 years from 1948 to 1964, compiling a record of 223 victories with only eight losses. He was a superb tactician and was blessed with an observant eye.

Additional Saturday morning duties required him to supervise the faculty children's swim program. This is where he humorously recalled the discovery of a new and fatal disease he labeled "parentisis." One such example was the faculty lady who removed her son from swim class because she did not want the child to turn into "a good swimmer and have bad marks in school. Subsequently, she enrolled him in horseback-riding classes." Burke opined in what was sometimes mistakenly perceived as grumpy verbiage, "Who was the horse's ass?"

He was a storyteller with few peers. His tales of woe were embellished by his Irish wit and gift of Blarney. These traits endeared him to the entire Yale community.

In 1950, his Yale freshman squad won the National AAU title. Swift recognition and fame followed. In May of 1950, Australia's renowned swim coach Frank Guthrie thanked Burke for responding to a recent letter of inquiry. Guthrie informed Burke that he had taken the liberty of "quoting some of his remarks in *Swim News*, Australia's only swimming paper." And, after mentioning an Australian "thirst for modern swim books," requested Burke publish an Australian edition of his book *Basic Swimming* (1950), co-authored by Kiphuth. Guthrie requested additional information on John Marshall, Dick Thoman, and Jimmy McLane, and questioned whether Burke's freshman squad would enter the summer nationals in Seattle independently or as part of the Yale New Haven Swim Club. And so it was at this point Burke, with the blessing of Kiphuth, entered the realm of international recognition.

### *Phil Moriarty*

Phil Moriarty was born April 12, 1914, also in New Haven. He graduated from Hillhouse High School in 1932. At this time Hillhouse High School was located just across the street from the Payne Whitney Gymnasium. Kiphuth hired high school student Moriarty to work at Yale's Carnegie pool under the supervision of Burke. Immediately, Burke recognized that the Hillhouse team had a future state champion diver in Moriarty who did not disappoint.

Upon Moriarty's graduation in 1932, in order to keep his talented assistant on staff, Kiphuth hired Moriarty for various and sundry duties at the Payne Whitney. When diving coach and assistant swim coach Karl Michael departed Yale in 1939 to take the reins at Dartmouth, Kiphuth appointed the gifted Moriarty as assistant varsity swim coach and head diving coach. In the fall of 1949, Kiphuth suffered his heart attack, and, without hesitation, turned the fate of Yale's varsity over to Moriarty. He was unfazed and led the Yale varsity team to an undefeated season and a second place finish at the NCAAs. When Kiphuth eventually retired in 1959, Moriarty, with the blessing of his mentor, became head coach of swimming and diving. The news release was met with disbelief and even skepticism by a large segment of the swimming family.

Despite the early criticism, Moriarty went on to become one of America's most successful swimming coaches. He mentored some of America's greatest swimmers, including Olympic medalists Don Schollander, Steve Clark, Mike Austin, John Nelson, and Jeff Farrell. His dual meet record was 195-25, with 11 Eastern Intercollegiate Swim League titles and nine Eastern Seaboard titles. Renowned swimmer Steve Clark related, "I was a fidgety little boy, depending on blazing speed and luck. I matured with Phil so that he didn't have to hold my hand and I didn't have to rely on certain superstitious rituals. He let me grow and gave me confidence."

As quoted in the *New York Times*, on August 22, 2012, "He also designed a revolutionary starting block that allowed backstrokers to avoid pushing off a slippery wall. It was successful in the United States, but after three years the international federation refused to sanction it." According to Moriarty, the stumbling block within the U.S. was Max Ritter, a powerful AAU and FINA official.

Moriarty wrote two instructional books on swimming and diving. Unbeknownst to most people, this self-educated man also wrote and published 10 volumes of poetry, donating the proceeds to Yale.

To earn additional income, he spent his summers as pool director of the St. Louis Country Club. Since Moriarty was also recognized as one of America's most knowledgeable and premier diving coaches, in the summer of 1952 future gold medalist David "Skippy" Browning moved to St. Louis so Moriarty could prepare him for the Helsinki Games. In 1956, prior to the Melbourne Games, future gold medalist diver Bob Clotworthy took up residence in New Haven to train with Moriarty. In 1960, Moriarty was Olympic diving coach at the Rome Games. His divers, Gary Tobian, Samuel Hall, Robert Webster, and Paula Jean Meyers-Pope, won two gold and four silver medals.

### *Bobbie Higgins Dawson*

Bobbie Dawson, whose maiden name was Eleanor Higgins, was born in New York City in 1908, the daughter of the New York Giants baseball scout Joseph F. Higgins and his wife Elsie Schuetz. Dawson learned to swim as a three-year old on the shores of her family's cottage in Sea Bright, New Jersey. As a teen she competed for the Women's Swimming Association of New York, coached by L. de B. Handley, and ultimately became an alternate on the 1924 women's Olympic swim team.

Dawson was a graduate of Columbia University and attended Fordham University School of Law for one year. With the onset of the Great Depression, she took a position with the United States Mortgage and Trust Company. There she met her future husband Edwin P. Dawson, a banker's son. An innovator in his own right, Edwin Dawson, assisted by an associate, produced the first practical commercial soda fountain and formed the Liquid Carbonic Co. of New York. A move to New Haven made him the most successful soda fountain salesman in the U.S. By 1938, he had formed his own soda fountain company and continued in the business until New Year's Day 1942, when the government, due to the war effort, cut off his supply of tin and copper. Ed then became a publicist for the Seamless Rubber Company.

At some point during this period, his wife Bobbie Dawson accepted a position as the secretary for Yale's legendary sports publicist Charlie Loftus. As fate is the hunter, Kiphuth, Yale, and the sport of swimming would all be the beneficiaries.

As reported by Bill Ahern of the *New Haven Register*, in his column "Looking 'Em Over: The World of Sport," in the fall of 1946, Bob's "girl Friday" Eileen Wall had just given notice. Kiphuth was talking with a group in the Ray Tompkins House and lamenting about the members of a relay team and the order in which they swam. Mrs. Dawson, as part of that group, had the audacity to dispute his findings. Kiphuth, acknowledged as an unquestioned authority on world swimming, in his gruff and defensive manner, immediately challenged her right "to proclaim it and to verify her facts." With "bull dog spirit" she certified the correct order of each swimmer and, with no loss of bearing, defended her position on the basis that she had swum for none other than the Women's Swimming Association of New York under the renowned Handley.

Kiphuth, never offended by "facts verified" nor "bull dog spirit," wasted no time. He immediately contacted Handley who stated Dawson "had the heart of a thoroughbred." The next morning Loftus, with orders from Kiphuth, notified her that "henceforth you are assigned to Mr. Kiphuth."

This was to be an historic event for both Kiphuth and the sport of swimming. Kiphuth's distaste for the detail of office work dated back to his first two jobs as a clerk at the local power company and at the hardware store of H.E. Koenig. Not intimidated by Kiphuth, and with strong willed determination, Dawson took control of his office; and what was once "a maelstrom of confusion," became efficient, orderly, and a depository of men's collegiate, AAU, and world swimming records.

The wonderful precision of her mind allowed Dawson to multi-task, especially when charged with the operational aspects of national swim meets. A wealth of swimming knowledge, combined with her boundless energy, established her as a force in national and international swimming circles. The AAU "borrowed Mrs. Dawson as secretary for its meets, first at Yale and gradually wherever the meets occurred nationally." Both vibrant and outspoken, she was a perfect match for Kiphuth. "When the bespectacled lady was right she never sidestepped for the man she called her boss." (Bill Ahern, *Bobby Dawson: Life's Swim Over*, New Haven Register). Yet the Kiphuth-Dawson team developed a strong mutual respect.

Poseidon – Kiphuth – had found his Athena, the shrewd companion of heroes, the goddess of wisdom and courage, or perhaps Malory's Lady of the Lake, Viviane, had re-incarnated presenting Neptune his sword of Excalibur. It mattered not. For, as her reputation grew, no one entered the portals of the Payne Whitney without encountering the confident protector, and at times mentor, to the man. She was, without a doubt, the lady behind the throne.

Her wealth of talents was well utilized. She was called on to manage all aspects of Yale's collegiate meets, to take splits of record performances, and to conduct summer long course workouts in Kiphuth's absence. In the words of sports writer Bill Ahern of the *New Haven Register*, "[H]er autobiography…is written in accomplishments and service." He went on to say that "she brought meticulousness to the scene of swimming." Men's records were now "chronicled unhurriedly in a flowing penmanship that somehow denoted authority." Robert M. Whitlow, president of the Eastern College Athletic Conference, in a letter to Dawson dated April 18, 1972, summarized the way so many former Yale swimmers, visiting swimmers, coaches, and officials throughout the world of swimming felt about Dawson: "[She was] one of those truly solid individuals who lent so much of herself for so many swimmers, officials, administrators, spectators, etc.…in the development and promotion of swimming."

When Kiphuth retired in 1959, Dawson's duties remained unchanged. The Men's Olympic Committee to Rome appointed her as an official keeper and statistician of men's records. Serving in this capacity, according to Ahern, she devised "a dexecut - the cross-check method of timing versus judging designations and put the results into the indisputable realm of mathematics."

She accompanied America's teams to the Pan-Am Games in Winnipeg, Manitoba, Canada, and on a European tour to England, Sweden, and Germany. Like her former boss, Kiphuth, decorum was part of her very being. Ahern wrote that Dawson related "with some relish" the success of the American delegation to the international meet in Japan but with "a shudder of distaste bemoans" the behavior of the Yanks who grabbed what was theirs (awards) and stepped off the podium presenting an image of the "ugly American." Bobbie "at a loss to explain this great indifference" noted the two exceptions were Carl Robie and Mike Burton who respectfully bowed to the crowd.

She was not only a confidante to Yale swimmers and many "of the immortals of the sport" but to "even those of lesser abilities" who entered the portals within her domain. Perhaps Yale swimmer Alan Cunningham, a member of the class of 1962, best described the esteem the swimmers had for Dawson when he wrote, "Bobbie Dawson was a sacred treasure."

Perhaps the relationship between Kiphuth and his team of Dawson, Moriarty, and Burke is best epitomized by the words of poet John Donne:

No man is an island,
Entire of itself
Every man is a piece of the continent,
A part of the main.

## KIPHUTH AND *SWIMMING WORLD* MAGAZINE

In the latter days of 1950, Peter Daland, Kiphuth's swimming statistician at that time, cautiously approached his boss with the suggestion that Kiphuth forgo his swimming newsletter to Yale alumni and friends and in its place publish a swimming magazine. Kiphuth wisely pointed out the financial difficulty of such a venture and the fact that many sports publications had failed, including the initial issue of *Sports Illustrated*.

Nonetheless, Kiphuth agreed to underwrite the cost of the venture and to serve as the editor and publisher assigning Daland the task of compiling the statistical data. The first issue of the magazine appeared in January 1951. Understanding the importance of maintaining contact with alumni and friends of Yale swimming, Kiphuth continued to publish his *Yale Swimming News Letter*.

Prior to the summer of 1951, Daland asked Kiphuth if he would allow him to publish a quarterly magazine called *Junior Swimmer*. Kiphuth concurred but made it clear that he (Kiphuth) would continue as editor and publisher of *Swimming World* with all of the financial responsibility. Daland departed Yale's ivy tower in 1956 to accept the dual positions of swimming coach at the Los Angeles Athletic Club and coach of the University of Southern California. Feeling the pressure of multiple duties, Daland approached Al Schoenfield, an advertising executive and enthusiastic swim parent, and offered to sell him *Junior Swimmer*. Under Schoenfield's expertise, and due to the number of age group swimmers in the United States, *Junior Swimmer* became quite popular.

Impressed with Schoenfield's professionalism, journalistic talent, and success with *Junior Swimmer*, Kiphuth realized the importance a professional journalist could play in the future success of *Swimming World* magazine. More importantly, he understood the impact of journalistic exposure for the sport he loved.

Schoenfield was his man and Kiphuth was determined. Kiphuth approached him for the first time at the Detroit Olympic Trials in August of 1960, offering to turn over the reins of *Swimming World* at no cost to Schoenfield. Not discouraged by Schoenfield's refusal, Kiphuth addressed him again at the AAU convention in Las Vegas in December 1960. Once again Schoenfield refused on the basis of his full-time position at his ad agency and his commitment to *Junior Swimmer*. Sensing Schoenfield's increased commitment to and love for swimming, Kiphuth reaffirmed the offer at the NCAA Championships in March 1961. Schoenfield again rejected Kiphuth's initiative.

Schoenfield perhaps miscalculated the depth and nature of Kiphuth's persistent personality. Like most great leaders, when Kiphuth envisioned a course of action, he was not to be denied. And so, at the conclusion of the AAU Championships in April of the same year, Kiphuth phoned Schoenfield and informed him that he was forwarding the magazine to him. Schoenfield continued to insist that he could not take on additional duties. At this point, Kiphuth abandoned the politics of friendly persuasion and hung up the phone. He turned to his secretary Bobbie Dawson and told her to package all pertinent materials and ship them to Schoenfield. Thus, Kiphuth, in his usual manner of one brief phone call, had determined that the future of world publicity for competitive swimming was now in the hands of Al Schoenfield.

As luck would have it, on the day of that historical phone call, this author had just dropped by to see Kiphuth and had entered his secretary's office as she handed over the phone to Kiphuth so he could deliver his ultimatum. At the conclusion of the call, Bobbie Dawson let out a muffled sigh of relief and a slight smile came to her lips. She no longer would have to spend endless hours typing, mimeographing, and mailing *Swimming World* to the subscribers.

Schoenfield summarized the event with the following statement: "I don't believe there were many anecdotes in the transfer except Kiphuth's persistence.... We [Schoenfield and his wife] never wanted to do it and never anticipated that in...1965, to be exact, in March, I would also become ill from trying to do two jobs at once. I had a decision to make. Quit publishing, or quit the ad agency.... We took the plunge, using my profit sharing from 13 years of employment, and the income from selling back to the company our stock in same. For two years we worked like hell trying to make it, and feeding five. The rest I guess is history."

Personal ego never dominated Kiphuth's ability to advance the cause of competitive swimming. His ability to highlight the individual performance of a superior athlete, friend or foe, trumped all other motives. He had carried the financial responsibility of publishing the results of senior swimming for more than 11 years. And, although the magazine, in terms of good business sense, was a failure, Kiphuth had kept the new forum for swimming media alive and functioning until the reins could be turned over to a highly qualified professional.

Kiphuth had recognized that the combination of *Swimming World* and Schoenfield was the perfect storm. The decision proved to be a wise and unselfish contribution to the sport of swimming. Schoenfield revived the financially insecure magazine into a superb medium of communication for the swimming populace. Kiphuth's last issue was March 1961. When he turned over the magazine in April 1961, he reported 1,000 subscribers. By the end of that same year, Schoenfield listed 2,319 subscribers. In 1962, Schoenfield combined *Junior Swimmer* with *Swimming World* and reported a circulation of 3,869. By 1972, the list of subscribers was reported at 21,022. Schoenfield said that he and his wife always spent time with Kiphuth at championships and conventions, and that Kiphuth "always said that he was most pleased that he had given us a 'bankrupt' magazine and that we had done what he had been unable to do."

# The Swimmers Speak

Kiphuth's pool deck image was overpowering. His commands were law, and were not to be questioned. Once he gave the call to order and to take the blocks, no swimmer dared to breach that wall of infallibility. Mr. Yale believed a swimmer must prepare for the "long haul" both in the pool and in life. He knew that insufficient preparation leads to the "torment of defeat."

David Livingston, the captain of the 1934 Yale team, recalls a teammate from Chicago's arrival one day just as practice was ending: "Bob [Kiphuth told [Bob Anderson] to swim 500, and that the team would see him at the afternoon workout. When the team came back for its afternoon practice, they found Anderson still swimming. Anderson, having a guilty conscience, assumed Bob meant lengths when he really meant meters." Anderson never questioned the directive and interpreted the command as a 25,000-meter swim instead of a 500-meter swim.

Often overlooked was Kiphuth's "on-the-job" bliss. Watching him stand at his wooden lectern, eyebrows raised, twirling his pencil between thumb and forefinger, you knew the moment had arrived. He would then bellow, with a good-humored chuckle, that the swimmers should "take it along for 20" – his standard two-thirds of a mile warm up.

Barr Clayson, a Navy swimmer and Brown University graduate, describes how Kiphuth, in a lengthy conversation "probed" and questioned him as to "why" he would choose the path of investment banking, in Kiphuth's eyes not a "noble profession," instead of teaching and coaching. Clayson, so impressed with the "thought process of the man," could now fully appreciate the "absolute love" and the "commitment" Kiphuth had for what he was doing. Clayson went on to say, "I will never forget…the love he had for the life he was leading."

Although Kiphuth was democratic in service to and treatment of his charges, former South African and Canadian swim coach and scientist Cecil Colwin recalled Kiphuth's observation, "Good swimmers are carried on by the momentum of the pack" – an infallible motto of Kiphuth's belief system.

There was a lighter, more mischievous, side to Kiphuth as well. A number of swimmers recall when Bill Early, a member of the class of 1958, arrived late and Kiphuth in booming voice announced "Early is late!" The swimmers had to endure Kiphuth's chuckled oxymoron for the remainder of the session.

As Rex Aubrey, class of 1958, and others recall, there was the "great watermelon battle" by the swimmers, while they were billeted on cots in the rowing tank area. The swimmers believed they had removed all evidence, but, because of darkness, they neglected to remove some marks left on the walls and floor. Kiphuth arrived, let out a blast on his fog horn (his alarm clock), threw on the lights, and issued one and all a mop and bucket. As Kiphuth departed, most ears heard a stifled chuckle.

In the summer of 1960, Allan Cunningham remembers walking into the practice pool at 8:30 a.m. to be greeted by "a huge and colorful oriental-stylized paper fish hanging from the ceiling." And there was "Kippy with his bamboo pole and a shit-eating grin on his honorable face." The Emperor of Japan had just honored Kiphuth with The Order of the Sacred Treasure – Third Class.

According to Tim Jecko, for most of Kiphuth's charges, his very presence was a force; even today, people speak of him as if he were still among them. For scores of those most closely associated with him, he was the single most influential figure in their lives. Jecko also believed, and it definitely was a consensus among many former swimmers, that Kiphuth represented "a larger than life figure that stands as an example of the moral force conspicuously lacking in athletics today." Don Sheff, the great sprinter from the class of 1953, tells how "Kiphuth beamed with the pride of a proud father as he announced to us that he had been informed that the swim team had the second highest scholastic average, bested only by Phi Beta Kappa."

Nevertheless, Jecko recalls the continual dilemma both Kiphuth and his swimmers faced in "how to navigate the treacherous straight through world-class training, scholastic responsibility, and the increasing intrusive attentions of an awestruck public." From the beginning of his career, Jecko observes, "it was obvious that, discreet or not, Kiphuth relished the attention and the 'rush' generated by performance and high achievement." Although Kiphuth enjoyed the attention, his class and sense of professional decorum would never have allowed him to display it outwardly. Don Miller, class of 1957, recalled that in his day "if you did something to draw attention to yourself other than perform, the whole team would have been on your ass with Kiphuth leading the way."

The coach expected his swimmers to comply with the decorum of the era.

As such, a shirt, tie, and coat were mandatory protocol for all swimming trips. Once, as the team was preparing for an away meet at Cornell, a swimmer boarded the bus without his tie. Kiphuth refused to let the bus leave. The issue was only resolved when the bus driver loaned his tie to the offending athlete.

Miller also identified Kiphuth as a "Renaissance man, broad in every aspect, interested and interesting. He just happened to be a swimming coach." He recalls when George Balanchine, the Russian dancer and choreographer who transformed American ballet, was in town for a play. He was a friend of Kiphuth's and brought his male dancers to swim practice, to the fascination of team members. At another point, Miller recalls that, at a time when he considered himself a budding poet, "Bob took me aside after my warm up prior to the Harvard meet and introduced me to one of my great heroes, Archibald MacLeish, who was attending the meet with his wife."

Fletcher Collins, swimming and water polo manager from 1927 to 1928, wrote, "Bob and I as well as other adult un-aquatics, sometimes frequented the steam baths that adjoined the locker-room showers in the old gym. On several occasions, I found him in earnest conversation with Thornton Wilder, class of 1921…all three of us, fresh out of the steam and shower, Hellenic in towels. Kiphuth was always able to contribute to a light but witty discussion of current literary matters, and without trying to show off the extent of his learning."

Bill Osborne, class of 1951, recalled a conversation between Kiphuth and Ted Coe of the Cleveland Museum of Art in 1960, after Kiphuth's speech at the Yale Club of Cleveland. Bill declared that, "Bob had charmed that guy no end." The conversation centered, not on paintings, but on "the history of various collections, who put them together, who sold them, who donated them to museums. Bob was intrigued with the nuts and bolts of how great collections were assembled."

The coach had a tremendous drive for perfection in all things. A number of people recall how this drive could raise the anger level of untold people within his PW. As Phil Prince, class of 1952, remembers, "Bob, annoyed at the lack of thoroughness of the custodial staff, purposely put some dirt in the corner of the lobby." Kiphuth waited, wondering, "how long would it take the custodial staff to respond."

This author recalls an occasion when Kiphuth spared no words about what it now took to change a burned-out light bulb in the pool office. Kiphuth sarcastically roared, "It takes a damn work order to change a simple light bulb. Change it yourself and the union will file a grievance." But as Navy ROTC swimmer John McGill pointed out in 2015, "I was in New Haven several years ago with one of my sons, and I took him to PW. I was shocked, not so much by the many changes, but by the seedy condition of the place." A point I can verify as well.

The Payne Whitney was never the same once Kiphuth left. Coach Cozza recalls that, even in his retirement years, Kiphuth "ran the PW like a drill sergeant. He kept the place spotless. I think some people were somewhat afraid of him and in awe, but they had nothing but deep respect for him."

One legendary mode of conduct reported by many witnesses, including myself, was that when Kiphuth wanted use of the elevator he would hold the button down, with its incessant ringing, until the operator arrived with the elevator. Kiphuth would then make no comment, but just board the elevator. Was this his signal to let the operator know it was Kiphuth? Or was it just his usual "there are bridges to cross and time is of the essence?"

McGill, remembers "he could make you feel like a million bucks and he could also make you cringe." Kiphuth could be a "curmudgeon, a martinet, a bully, or all three in any given day." He was an "elitist and a snob" when it came to the Ivies and Yale. Kiphuth "had an opinion about almost everything, and I found him to be right most of the time." He was "a thinker and a genius, 50 years ahead of his time. I owe Kiphuth a great deal" for he shared this knowledge with "anyone wanting to learn."

George Breen, America's great distance ace in the 1950s, who was a member of Kiphuth's 1955 Japan swimming delegation, recalled how Kiphuth drove over from New Haven on May 16, 1956, for his inauguration into the Cortland University Hall of Fame: "I was so honored that he would drive over." Kiphuth had both dinner and lunch with Breen's parents and tells how they always "raved (about) how he treated them so special and the (entertaining) stories he told." His parents felt so honored that "a person of his stature" would dine with them "and say such nice things about their son."

Breen worked out with the Yale team between the NCAAs and the AAUs in 1956, as his coach Doc Councilman returned to Cortland. "I never trained there at any other time...as Doc would not allow it."

Breen recalls at the Osaka dual meet, in August of 1955, as he stood next to Kiphuth, the Flying Fish Furuhashi "walked out from an overhang unannounced...the crowd of 25,000 in recognition gave him a standing ovation." Kiphuth turned to Breen and said: "Now that is greatness."

Simon Epstein, M.D., pulled no punches. "Saying positive things was not really part of Bob's personality...He always did what he wanted to do without much thought as to its effect on a situation." Epstein told how Kiphuth corralled Epstein's future wife "to time all the elements of the dive and was very specific about what he wanted." Task completed, Kiphuth reclaimed the stopwatch and recording sheet and with "no thanks, no nothing," walked off. But, Epstein goes on to say that his experience as manager was "probably my most important experience [at Yale]. It was all worthwhile."

Kiphuth held a strong view on the importance of a person's origins. Jecko and Hanley recalled a quote by Kiphuth about an ex-swimmer who had been adopted into a wealthy family: "The boy doesn't know where he is from, who his parents are. Imagine how god-damn awful that must be, not knowing who you are. The riches don't mean a shit."

To quote J. B. Holloway, B.A., 1943, M.D., 1945, "Bob was the most memorable person I knew in the entire seven years I spent in New Haven. He had more to do with my learning self-discipline and tenacity than anybody in my life. My [Yale] 'Y' [hangs] beside my degrees…and means more than they."

## Man of Criticism

Rarely does a man reach administrative levels of an organization without finding himself the subject of controversy and criticism. Kiphuth was no exception to this rule. By the fall of 1918, Kiphuth, certainly because of his own interest, but also partly at the advice of Louis de Breda Handley, began his first of many trips from New Haven to New York. The purpose was to become a known and active participant in the AAU political arena. This was a time when few if any coaches were either interested in or accepted by the "amateurs" who controlled the reins of the aquatic sport. These "amateurs" were not athletes themselves, but rather were educated, wealthy, and influential people of society who had the time and interest to govern the sport.

Because of his positive personal image and because of the prestige associated with his position at Yale, Kiphuth soon won acceptance to this elite group in charge of amateur swimming. Both critics and advocates alike agree that these factors played an important role in his appointments. And yet, there were other, more subtle factors, as well. Kiphuth's success with the Yale team, mastery of the sport of swimming, his willingness to travel anywhere, anytime, even at his own expense, his leadership expertise, and his intelligence all contributed to his appointments and his ability to maintain a leadership role in national and international swimming.

His power grew over the next 20 years as a member or chairman of the National Olympic Committee, the National AAU Swimming Committee, and the NCAA Rules Committee. Then with his subsequent assignments as America's coach on foreign trips, strong criticism of the AAU and of Kiphuth erupted among both NCAA and AAU coaches.

Kiphuth made 33 foreign trips from 1921 to 1964. Three of the trips (1923, 1925, and 1957) were personal study tours. Five of the trips were arranged between Yale and a foreign team exclusively. This fact was true of his trips to Hawaii in 1921 and 1930, the trip to Cuba in 1946 (arranged by Chip Lazo, the father of a Yale swimmer), and the trips to Bermuda and Mexico in 1951. Nine other foreign trips to Germany, Iceland, Israel, and South Africa, were in response to a request to the U.S. State Department by the U.S. Army. A trip to Germany in 1938 was at a direct request of German officials, certainly influenced by his relationships with Avery Brundage, Max Ritter, and German athletic authorities. Four trips to the Olympics as coach, and four other trips were by virtue of his service as a FINA official at the 1924, 1952, 1956, and 1960 Olympic Games. Another trip to the 1964 Olympiad was as a guest of the Japanese Swim Federation. Six of the remaining trips were the Japanese-American dual meets held from 1931 to 1955. He was at his professional height – busy, in-demand, and exerting a tremendous influence on international swimming and amateur sports during this time.

As if controversy over his foreign assignments was not enough, Kiphuth's Olympic appointments were also the subject of further criticism. His appointment as Olympic coach on four occasions raised questions as to why the honor could not go to other deserving coaches. In 1952, many of Kiphuth's critics, as well as his close friends, agreed that the honor of Olympic Coach should be awarded to Mann of Michigan. Karl Michael, the Dartmouth coach and former Yale assistant, admitted to Kiphuth that even he had voted for a change. West Point coach Gordon Chalmers wrote a letter to Kiphuth complimenting him on his accomplishments, but stating that the time had come for other deserving coaches to have the honor. It was the first Olympics Kiphuth had not coached since 1928. True to his nature, the coach accepted the judgment in his typical gracious fashion, and moved forward, strengthening his role as America's international voice in swimming.

The annual Yale Swimming Carnival became the third most controversial issue. By 1923, Kiphuth changed the status quo of what had been an intramural meet by inviting nationally known swimmers and initiating world record performances. With the opening of the Payne Whitney facility in 1932, the Yale Carnival attracted national and international headlines for swimming and Yale. Critics immediately murmured that the changes were instituted as a mechanism to set "odd records," that it was used as a recruiting measure, and that the relay records were the result of the swimmers prematurely leaving the blocks.

However, Gordon Chalmers, the national backstroke champion and 1932 Olympian, who was also the former athletic director at Indiana State, stressed the fact that "only qualified officials were used," and that Kiphuth spent a lot of time "perfecting relay take-offs." He also said that Kiphuth had developed a technique of "framing the incoming swimmer between the thumb and forefinger of each hand in order to prevent [premature relay starts]."

Initially, the NCAA, FINA, and the AAU recognized five types of record performances: American noteworthy (for records set for distances not normally swum in competition), American citizen (for fastest times ever swum by an American citizen), American (fastest time ever swum within the Continental United States), intercollegiate (for fastest times by a college athlete in collegiate competition), and world records. What critics called the "odd" relay records were all bona fide record distances found in FINA, AAU, and NCAA handbooks. The fact that these events were not usually swum in dual or championship meets was more a by-product of such consideration as lack of manpower, time requirements, and the priority of freestyle swimming. On the other hand, Kiphuth had large teams, which gave him the needed manpower, and by 1932, he had the finest facility in America. In addition to the so-called "odd" distances, Kiphuth's swimmers continued attacking records in the normal dual meet events as well. This wholesale assault on American, American noteworthy, NCAA, AAU, and world records afforded Kiphuth the opportunity to achieve his two objectives: favorable publicity for Yale and competitive swimming, and the opportunity for his mermen to earn major "Y's" – the criteria for which was nothing less than a world record. In line with his philosophy of athletics, Kiphuth would utilize the hard work and determination of other swimmers, gifted or non-gifted, giving them the opportunity to swim on a world-record relay team, thus earning the coveted major "Y." This allowed more than just a gifted few to experience success.

A fourth controversy was Yale's fantastic dual meet record. Critics contended Kiphuth maintained his record by refusing to swim the outstanding Western teams of his era. This was an unjust criticism. As Yale extended its success, it became the team to beat. To fit every ambitious team into Yale's schedule would have been a physical impossibility. Most travel was done by train, and distance was an issue. Yale normally had a schedule of 11 teams which it swam each year and Kiphuth, in line with his sense of fair play, did not drop a school unless it was mutually agreed upon.

On the other hand, there did exist administrative considerations such as the approval of the Board of Athletic Control, finances, scholastic considerations such as time away from class, and Yale's two-week January reading period in preparation for exams. Historically, the Great Depression, World War II and its aftermath, restrictions imposed by the Ivy League, Kiphuth's appointment as athletic director, his heart attack, and of course the issues of different academic standards with respect to entrance requirements and scholarship aid, all played significant roles in the dual meet record.

Perhaps as Yale's tremendous dual meet record continued to grow and Kiphuth's retirement approached, one can only speculate that some effort was no doubt made for its protection. But the fact remains that Yale's basic policy with respect to scheduling dual meets remained consistent throughout the years.

Further controversy surrounded the eligibility of Bill Yorzyk to represent YNHSC in AAU competition. The rules at the time required a swimmer to swim unattached for a year and a day before representing a new club. Furthermore, a strict residency requirement was in effect. This allowed a swimmer to represent a club only in the state in which the swimmer resided. Yorzyk transferred to YNHSC in 1954, and listed his weekend residence as the address of Bobbie Dawson, Kiphuth's secretary, in what appeared to circumvent the residency requirement. Mike Peppe requested confirmation of residency by the AAU. When Yorzck confirmed his dates of residency in a letter dated May 26, 1955, to both the AAU and Mike Peppe, he was exonerated and his membership with YNHSC continued.

There was also no doubt that the issue of private colleges vs. land grant colleges, with the perception of Ivy League snobbery, played a significant role in the relationships among coaches. And Kiphuth very proudly, as noted by many, wore the Ivy mantle on his sleeve.

It would have been difficult not to be envious of Kiphuth's perceived role as the leader of the powerful political wing of the AAU, and of the fact that he had the finest facility in the country. This jealousy among the coaches of the early era may well have been a key issue in much of the criticism about Kiphuth, his program, and his international appointments. Kiphuth never denied, and was even outspoken about, the advantage provided by his facility. Mike Peppe and other prominent coaches, like brothers Willis Casey of North Carolina State University and Ralph Casey of the University of North Carolina, complained in writing to the NCAA about Kiphuth's open-door policy for summer training. Rather than taking advantage of the generous policy, these coaches considered it to be an unfair recruiting advantage. Kiphuth, always the consummate professional, apparently refrained from engaging in the controversy, as there exists no correspondence from him that criticizes other coaches or programs.

With the University of Michigan's hiring of Mann in 1925, and the Ohio State University's hiring of Mike Peppe in 1931, three powerful swimming dynasties were now in play. Michigan, Yale, and Ohio State reigned supreme, dominating the NCAA Championships for 23 years from 1937 to 1959. From the very beginning there existed an intense and competitive rivalry among all three collegiate institutions and coaches.

There remains no question, from all evidence gathered, that Mann wanted to be the Yale coach. Impatience on his part, by signing a three-year contract with the Duluth Boat Club, had sealed his fate. The fact that Kiphuth, an aquatic neophyte, had providentially ascended to the helm, remained a determining force in the competitive relationship. Yet, the professional and dynamic Mann, each time he took center stage, did so with pride and respect. And Kiphuth as always, kept his head above the fray, for Yale was his kingdom.

Once Mann secured his position at Michigan, the rivalry intensified, but to the credit of both coaches, professional disagreement on the proper training regime for swimmers was confined to the competitive waters of the pool. They met on six occasions, with Yale winning in 1928 (39 to 23), 1930 (42 to 18), and 1942 (59 to 16). Michigan returned the favor in 1938 (41 to 34), 1939 (53 to 22), and 1940 (46 to 29).

In 1943, Mike Peppe reached the pinnacle of national recognition when his OSU team won both the Big 10 and NCAA meets. In total, Peppe won 12 Big 10 and 11 NCAA titles. Yale defeated Ohio State in two dual meets by wide margins in 1940 (55 to 20) and 1941 (51 ½ to 23 ½). These were the only two times the teams met in dual meet competition. Peppe, without remorse, took pride in, and bragged about, his ability to recruit and his stable of outstanding divers. On both the professional and diplomatic levels there did exist a strong divide. While Kiphuth wrapped himself in Ivy decorum, Peppe never hesitated to challenge the status quo at every level. Their relationship remained cordial and professional but always extremely competitive on all fronts.

# Farewell to Team Yale: 1954-1959

The next six seasons, 1954-1959, marked Kiphuth's final years at the helm. During this time, Yale won an additional 83 dual meets, six EISL titles, five AAU titles and four second place finishes in the NCAA meet. All told, Kiphuth ran his dual meet total to an unprecedented 183 victories prior to his mandatory retirement in July of 1959.

During this final six-year period, Yale maintained a predominant position in the EISL team and individual championships. The stiffest competition came from Hal Ulen's great Harvard teams. The most highly contested competition between the two Ivy's was the 1955 dual meet at Harvard.

In recalling that meet, Kiphuth stated that a "great" Harvard team took full advantage of a "complacent" Yale team. After the conclusion of the 440-yard freestyle, the "outlook looked dim." Yale would need enough points in the final two individual events, the three-meter diving and the 200-yard breaststroke, in order to take advantage of Yale's great sprint quartet Kerry Donovan, Rex Aubrey, Dave Armstrong, and Sandy Gideonse in the 400-yard freestyle relay. After a back-room consultation with his son Delaney, Yale's athletic director, Kiphuth recalled "we both stiffened our upper lips, put on our best face and prepared to congratulate Hal and his Harvard team." Returning to the pool area, Kiphuth realized that a superb effort on the part of divers John Whitfield and Jack Erickson, soon followed by Bill Fleming's effort in the 200-yard breaststroke, gave Yale 11 points and set the stage for what turned out to be a 44 to 40 Yale victory, cemented by the final relay.

Sandy Gideonse held a different view of the close meet with Harvard. He wrote that because of the wealth of talent at Yale, "[Kiphuth] likes to give everyone a chance to swim and that means we aren't as sharp as we might be when we get to a tough dual meet and have to swim several times. It almost cost us the Harvard meet last year. I was really dragging by the time that one was over."

A third place finish at the NCAA Championships at Syracuse in 1954 was followed by second place finishes each of the next four years, 1955 to 1958. Although Ohio State won a decisive victory in 1955, the 1956 meet went to Ohio State by only 14 points. The Buckeyes won in

*Farewell to Team Yale: 1954-1959*

### The Omnibus Encounter

In 1955, Yale, the first university to have any of its competitive meets broadcast, became the first university to have its team appear on television. Under the direction of Bill Suchman, and following the script by Andy Lewis, the *Omnibus* show, a production of the Ford Foundation Television Workshop, featured Kiphuth, Yale swimming, the girls from Stan Tinkham's Walter Reed Swim Club, and Esther Williams. The central theme of the show was to present an accurate portrayal of the history of swimming. *Omnibus*, with Alistair Cooke as the host, was a Sunday afternoon program that presented famous people of the day as well as science, arts, Shakespearian plays, and the works of more recent playwrights. Famous actors, singers, and dancers of that era were also featured. On November 3, 1955, L. Thomas Linden of the *Harvard Crimson* wrote an article about the event, titled "Swim Star Over New Haven" in the "Egg In Your Beer" column.

Don Miller, class of 1957, recalled that, "In exchange for the use of our facility and our team personnel (and for special camera shots during the program), Ford built an underwater window in the side of the pool."

In a more humorous light, Miller remembered Esther Williams's refusal to rehearse "until she got a new blade for her razor." Kiphuth, forgetting he "was wired for sound," went off on a tirade about women in general and Esther in particular." Hearing the "technicians, who were set up in the pool office laughing like hell," Kiphuth realized his tirade had been recorded. Kiphuth, an entertainer at heart, was "both upset and pleased."

John Phair, class of 1956, recalled in an email how Bob and the director were looking for something to fill the hour long show. They came up with the idea of the epic poem *Horatius at the Bridge* by Thomas Babington Macaulay. Phair was elected to play Horatius and swim the length of the exhibition pool, dressed in armor. He was not happy about being chosen, but Harry Burke told him that "if it would benefit Yale swimming Bob would stand on his head nude on New Haven Green, so grin and bear it."

Jerry Dolbey, class of 1959, remembered Kiphuth's encounter with six-feet, six-inch Ben Gage, Williams' husband. Ben, used to getting his own way, had the audacity to take out a cigar. "Kiphuth walked up to him, poked him in the belly (about eye level for Kiphuth), leaned his head back and said in a booming voice 'Nobody smokes in my gym.' Ben was all over himself trying to find a place for that cigar."

1956 with a dominant diving performance, taking first through fourth place on both the one- and three-meter boards, for 38 points. In 1957, despite Michigan's 23 diving points, Kiphuth's Bulldogs almost secured the championship. Yale earned four gold medals: a triple by Jecko who won the 100- and 200-yard butterfly, and the 200-yard individual medley, and the 400-yard freestyle relay of Hibbard, Cornwell, Armstrong, and Aubrey. However, the title again slipped from his grasp, 69 to 61, when, in the final event, the 400 medley team of Dolby, Hardin, Clinton, and Aubrey was disqualified in their gallant attempt to close the gap on Michigan. At the 1958 NCAA Championships at Michigan, the home team again secured victory, 72 to 63, by virtue of its superior diving ability.

In his annual letter to the alumni, Kiphuth expressed the following rationale with respect to diving:

> It is interesting to note here that Michigan scored 16 points in the dive and Ohio State 21, while Yale and Michigan State, although second and third, had no divers at all. Of course, this is nothing new in the NCAA Championships, for Yale has scored very seldom in diving through the years, but Michigan and, particularly, Ohio State have taken the lion's share of the 44-point total in the two diving competitions. I do not mean to suggest that this is an unfair advantage, because diving is an integral part of the swimming program, but I do want to again call to mind Yale's great strength in the swimming events and its lack of power in diving.... All in all, the National Collegiate Championships, conducted in the new pool at the University of Michigan, were an outstanding success, and Yale again proved itself a worthy competitor.

Although the Elis did not win another NCAA crown during Kiphuth's final six years, Yale not only remained a swimming power but crowned 13 individual NCAA champions. In Kiphuth's final season at the helm, 1959, Yale finished fourth behind Michigan, Ohio State, and Indiana.

Kiphuth certainly must have been disappointed in his final season. But, in comments to the alumni he congratulated the team, expressed his sincere thanks to his two capable assistants, Phil Moriarty and Harry Burke, and continued on to say:

> The years 1917-1959 have been filled with excitement, pleasure, thrills galore and deep satisfaction. Successful swimming seasons all, and yet enough disappointment to give proper balance to what constitutes the proper measure of a sound sports program. I can only say, again and again, what a privilege and honor it has been to be associated with this

great institution these past 45 years and particularly with Yale Swimming for 42 years.

Kiphuth's five AAU titles over those six years were the result of indoor titles in 1954, 1955, and 1957, and two consecutive outdoor victories in 1955 and 1956. Kiphuth had not lost his flare or appreciation for record attempts. Prior to the commencement of the 1954 AAU meet, Kiphuth secured AAU sanctions for record attempts by Dick Cleveland and Yoshi Oyakawa, both of Ohio State. Cleveland successfully lowered the world and American records of Yale's Alan Ford in the 100-meter freestyle, while his teammate erased the world standard of Gilbert Bozon of France in the 100-meter backstroke.

The 1958 AAU National indoor meet in New Haven witnessed the team title going to the University of Southern California's freshman team. Kiphuth's former assistant Peter Daland, with a squad of only five swimmers that included Australian imports Murray Rose and Jon Henricks, turned the trick and won the praise of his ex-boss who wrote:

> At the Indoor AAUs a great freshman team from the University of Southern California defeated the Yale New Haven Swim Club by one point for the championship. The Yale team did exceeding well, but in faltering in the freestyle relay (one of the few times in Yale history that this has happened), a great USC freshman team was able, by superhuman swimming on the second day of the meet, to climax their efforts with a team victory. This performance was a great inspiration to everyone who was at the meet, and compared with that of the great Yale freshman team (class of 1953), who turned this trick for the first time in the 1950 AAU meet.

Daland and his strong Southern California team returned to Yale the following year to repeat as champions, overpowering second place New Haven, 62 to 33. Daland's team had been primed and ready, as they had been barred from the NCAA Championships due to football violations that caused sanctions to be imposed against all USC athletic teams.

On June 30, 1959, Kiphuth's long-time, capable assistant, Phil Moriarty, took the reins of Yale's collegiate program with the request that Kiphuth continue the Yale New Haven Swim Club. Kiphuth accepted Yale's mandatory retirement policy with grace and dignity. To him, it was a matter of protocol not to be challenged. Kiphuth was not prone for an inactive retirement. On the contrary, per his usual approach to imminent and predictable events, he looked not to the past, but to what role awaited him now.

# The Final Yale Years

The next eight years prior to his death on January 7, 1967, would be most active ones. The University honored him with the following Emeritus titles: Professor, Director of the Gym, and Head Coach of Swimming. In addition, Yale bestowed on him the title of lecturer and requested he carry on as head of the physical education department on a year-to-year basis. He also accepted the responsibility of coaching a team of Naval ROTC officers and enlisted men assigned to the Yale Naval ROTC unit.

## *Kiphuth's NROTC Team: 1959-1960*

In a letter to Clayson, as quoted in Jeff Farrell's book, *My Olympic Experience*, Kiphuth wrote about how the NROTC team came to be: "The substance of my conversation (with a naval officer at the AAU convention in 1958) was that anyone they had would be more than welcome (to train at Yale)…that we had been doing this sort of thing since 1930, as a labor of love…and we would be very glad to do this for the Navy."

As stated in that letter, Kiphuth did offer the Yale facilities and his services, for free of course, to train any Navy swimmer with aspirations for membership on America's 1959 Pan American or 1960 Olympic teams. The offer was not without precedent. In 1956, Kiphuth accommodated a similar request by the U.S. Air Force. This author trained at Yale in the summer of 1956, and in looking at the photos and newspaper clippings, the members of that first group were U.S. Air Force 2nd Lieutenant John Hoaglund and Lieutenants Charles Baldwin, Jim McCarthy, and Clarence Burnett, as well as West Point Cadet Don Kutyna. With Kiphuth's coaching offer on the table, the Navy re-assigned any qualified swimmer, whether an officer or enlisted man, to Yale to serve in its NROTC program. Three of the most outstanding initial assignees in 1959 were Dave McIntyre from North Carolina State University, John McGill from Syracuse University, and Jeff Farrell from the University of Oklahoma. For Kiphuth a dream had come true. He now had mature, post-college athletes, with the ability to achieve beyond their college years.

John McGill, a former All-American swimmer at Syracuse University, clearly remembers entering the World of Kiphuth. He relates, "In the fall of 1958, I was a young ensign serving on a Navy ship on the West Coast… [when] a fellow officer and former UCLA long jumper informed me that the military services were providing training opportunities for qualified athletes and handed me the necessary paper work." After applying for, and being accepted into, a special sports program for naval personnel in January of 1959, McGill was re-assigned to the Naval ROTC unit at Yale.

When he reported to the exhibition pool and met both Phil Moriarty and Kiphuth, it became very clear to McGill that Kiphuth remained "a factotum extraordinaire" within the Payne Whitney. Handed a swimsuit and told to exhibit his talent, he realized that Navy acceptance was subject to Kiphuth's personal selection.

Immediately thrown into the afternoon and morning workouts, no grace period allowed, he met some of the Navy swimmers. Part of the initial group consisted of "Telfair Mahaffy and Walter Rose (UNC); Dave M$^c$Intyre (NC State); Farrell (OU) and Rodney Ruffle, a recent high school graduate and the least experienced and accomplished of the group, with Farrell and McIntyre at the other end of the spectrum. The rest of us ranged somewhere in between." At the end of May 1959, Jerry Dolby and Tim Jecko, recent Yale graduates and now commissioned officers, joined the group.

McGill continued, "Things happened fast and in a few days I found myself sharing an apartment with Jeff, [Telfair Mahaffy], and Dave; and training more intensely than I ever had in high school or college. Although it was not obvious to me at the time, a grand adventure had begun." According to McGill, Kiphuth's workouts were "state of the art." First and foremost, every swimmer had to undergo physiological measurement and "a chart was kept as to how many sit-ups, push-ups, and pull-ups he could do. Kiphuth tested how far and how high we could jump and how powerful our grip was with either hand. The morning workout was all pulley weights, low-weight, high-repetition to develop strength and endurance." Kiphuth's highly respected dry land and medicine ball workout dominated the afternoon session. In between the two daily workouts, "we were encouraged to do some swimming."

McGill, new to the kingdom, tried to school the master, Kiphuth, that conventional wisdom of that era dictated, "alternate days of hard work and rest allowed the body a chance to recover." Kiphuth, ignoring the affront, laughed and said "young as you are you have plenty of time for rest," and that was the end of that.

McGill recalls that at the conclusion of the six weeks, all athletes were tested again. Each participant's test score improved by a factor of 10 or more. "After three of these dry land adventures, every part of your body improved; arms, legs, shoulders and, most importantly, our core."

In 1960, many coaches still believed that 1000 to 1500 yards a day of swimming was sufficient. But McGill points out that Kiphuth's sprinters and middle distance swimmers were "doing four-to six-times that." The workouts were "eight to ten times as much as I had done in college with most of it being state-of-the-art interval training. No longer would I or my teammates be undertrained."

Disappointed in his progress, McGill decided to shave his body hair prior to the 1960 AAU championship meet at Yale. For swimmers to shave their body hair, although an accepted practice now, was a new, and many times rejected, innovation at the time. Unable up to this point to capitalize on the new workload, the moment of truth came when he set the national 200 IM record at the 1960 Indoor AAU Championships. McGill, who this author swam against in college, credited Kiphuth's program of dry land training and "several thousand yards of swimming, kicking, pulling, and interval training and repeats each day," as responsible for his and other swimmers' "dramatic" improvement.

In evaluating Kiphuth's effectiveness and the success of his athletes, McGill cites Farrell's career as a "window" into how Kiphuth produced the virtual perfect storm. "We brought to the program all of our past – good and bad. We couldn't change that." He added that combining the totality of the program with the talent and commitment of the athlete produced "world record performances." In addition, he credits the "environment that fostered success; training with swimmers used to success; and the final element – individual commitment and the subsets of heart and determination – at which Jeff excelled." It was a most successful two years. Prior to arriving at Yale, Farrell had trained under two of America's finest coaches – Mann and Sakamoto. Now, exposed to Kiphuth's muscle and mileage regime, Farrell, by February of 1960, began his onslaught on American, national, and international records.

As Farrell recalls in his book, "I had achieved success in college, but not like this. The reason was I had never worked my body to this extent, had never taken on a workload of training like I was doing now. In the past, I had undertrained. And now my muscles were reaching strength levels they had not known. Kiphuth's experience and regime were giving me almost unbelievable results."

**1959 U.S. Navy Swimmers**

L-R: Barr Clayson; John McGill; Harry Burke; Walter Rose; David McIntyre; Telfair Mahaffy; Jeff Farrell.

## The End of an Era

When the NCAA college coaches drew up plans for the development of a Swimming Hall of Fame in the early 1960s, Kiphuth served in the capacity of Charter Vice President. According to Buck Dawson, the Executive Director, Kiphuth "had tremendous ideas about what a hall of fame could and should be and about honorees and what they should represent." Kiphuth believed this institution could best serve the interest of swimming as a depository of historical records. According to his son DeLaney, Kiphuth accepted with "reservation the idea of glorifying people for doing what they loved to do." And yet, Kiphuth personally nominated Mann's protégé and World War I Congressional Medal of Honor awardee, Tedford Cann.

Even in retirement, Kiphuth continued to serve on various local, state, national and international committees of which he was a member. These included the National Art Museum of Sport, the Board of Park Commissioners for New Haven, the Board of Trustees at the Hotchkiss School, and the Boy Scouts of America, among others.

On January 7, 1967, many former Yale swim captains returned to watch Yale defeat Army in a dual meet. According to Kiphuth's son Delaney, "it was a special moment in time for [Kiphuth]. Two of Kiphuth's greatest prodigies, Alan Ford and Steve Clark, were being honored for their recent induction into the International Swimming Hall of Fame." This gave Kiphuth the opportunity to have discourse about the present, to reminisce about the past, and to speculate as to the future of Yale swimming.

At the conclusion of the meet, a payback for the previous year's loss to the Cadets, Kiphuth personally congratulated West Point coach Jack Ryan and his team on their excellent performance. In turn, he lauded coach Moriarty and the Yale team for their victory. After enjoying a victory meal at Mory's with the former team members, he proceeded to his home in Hamden, where he was stricken with a heart attack. He died that evening at Yale-New Haven Hospital. Kiphuth was 76 years old.

The swimming world, the university, his friends, and his former swimmers greeted the news with shock and dismay. Yale and the Kiphuth family received testimonials from all over the world. It would be impossible to replicate them all.

Perhaps *New Haven Register* reporter Bill Ahern stated it best: "There will be no phase of his life which will not mourn his death." Ahern went on to write: "In swimming, he was the widest known; in physical education, he was the authority of his generation; in politics, he was the toast of kingdoms and republics; in the arts, he was a self-taught expert."

Kiphuth died as he had lived, a physical and mental giant among men. His personal image and magnificent intellect had cultivated the elite of Yale's administrative elements including the presidents. His enthusiasm for the sport and his ability to relate to his athletes won for him not only a devoted alumni, but large and dedicated teams. True, he inherited success, but in turn, he built that success into international recognition for American swimming and Yale. He offered use of the Payne Whitney pools and his time and effort to anyone wishing to take advantage of the opportunity. He parlayed regional success into international fame. And, although this resulted in many personal honors, Kiphuth never failed to accept them in the name of his beloved Yale.

His legacy contained few if any monetary allotments. Kiphuth had never labored for material rewards. To Yale and swimming he left the labors of a lifetime, represented in part by the mementos of years of service, Yale's rich and colorful swimming history, and the intangible product of his "Cathedral of Sweat," the Payne Whitney Gymnasium.

There exists little question that Kiphuth was one of the visionaries of the sport. By sheer force of his personal image, the prestige of his position with Yale, and the dedication of his efforts, he became one of the most powerful administrative forces in swimming.

According to the internationally famous Australian coach Forbes Carlile, "We (coaches) can only be judged in relation to our time." In looking back at coaches of the past, one must be careful not to subject them to analysis by employing present day knowledge as the tool for evaluation. On the other hand, one must be careful not to disguise their programs, unjustly giving them credit for conducting modern day workouts. Swimming, like all sports, underwent and is undergoing a continual evolution.

Kiphuth was a man of high moral and ethical standards, but that he was subject to human error, all agree. According to colleagues, his greatest error was the result of his greatest strength. He just never could comprehend the eight-hour workday.

His dedication to the task of raising the standards and status of competitive swimming is revealed in the fruits of his labor. Kiphuth saw a real need for developing America's international program of swimming. He had the facility, the interest, and the ability to devote the time. Success and criticism went hand-in-hand.

An innovator in his own right, Kiphuth never failed to recognize the innovations of others nor the importance of the psychologist and physiologist to swimming. His ability as an administrator is evident from his long years of service to Yale and swimming. He proved once again that self-education is one of the purest forms of intellectual genius. His early years, as well as his twilight years, were characterized by his vigorous, energetic activity, and practical impatience. Yet, God had endowed him with a rich, analytic imagination and a constructive creativeness. Experience prepared him with superior leadership skills. With only a high school diploma as a credential, he braved what appeared to be an impregnable fortress of the intellectual giant, making his impact on Yale and swimming total and complete.

On February 25, 1967, with permission from the Whitney family, the Payne Whitney Exhibition Pool was rededicated as the "Kiphuth Exhibition Pool." The Yale Swimming Association further honored Kiphuth by development of a Kiphuth Trophy Room on the second floor of the Gymnasium. In honor of his co-founding and serving as the first chairman of the Council for National Cooperation in Aquatics, the CNCA established the Kiphuth Undergraduate Scholarship and the Research and Graduate Study Grant. His obituary, written by sports writer Bill Ahern of the *New Haven Register,* perhaps summarized it best: "He was the authority that put the sport on its feet and took it from the drabness of the underwater plunge to the excitement of freestyle and butterfly strokes. It was no miracle. Nor was the transformation born overnight. It was his revolutionary thinking, political maneuvering, iron will, and persuasion which brought the sport to the peak which it enjoys today."

I still look back on and cherish the four years from 1960 to 1964. Teaching only a few miles from Yale, I occasionally visited Kiphuth at PW, usually in the fall and spring. He saw my passion for coaching and I, for the first time, in brief but meaningful conversations with him, began to understand the underlying root of the passion that drove him. The culture of his childhood had left an indelible mark on the very essence of his being. He firmly believed that the virtues of honesty, integrity, and fair play, combined with hard work, marked the most honest path to success. His message, that one should pursue a life of service, rather than the almighty dollar, never changed.

He understood fully the words of Thomas Gray:

> The boast of heraldry, the pomp of pow'r
> And all that beauty, all that wealth e'er gave

> Awaits alike the' inevitable hour.
> The paths of glory lead but to the grave.

I grew to know him better, but even then I could not "crack" his inner shell. Like the character Buck in Jack London's *The Call of the Wild*, he possessed an instinct, primordial in nature, to be the leader of the pack. And I began to see that as in Frost's poem *The Road Not Taken*, Kiphuth "took the one less traveled by," and that road "made all the difference."

Even now, each time the Heavens roar with thunder, I hear Bob's call:

"Mount the blocks!"

But to quote *The Raven*:

"Nevermore."

## Afterward

## My Journey to the Castle within the Kingdom (Bob and Me)

At the height of the Great Depression on January 4, 1936, I was born in Waterbury, Connecticut. By the turn of the 20th Century, Waterbury and the surrounding Naugatuck Valley had become a giant industrial complex. Waterbury became known as the "Brass City," because of the quality and durability of its brass products. The major manufacturing companies were American Brass, Chase Brass and Copper, and Scovill Manufacturing. Because of the manufacture of bullet casings, buttons for military uniforms, and other war products, the above companies employed over 10,000 workers during World War II.

Out of necessity, my dad became a machinist at age 14. My mother, trained as a teacher, was not allowed to teach once she married. By 1936, my dad was working for the WPA (Works Progress Administration) collecting $5 a week and a bag of groceries, provided he signed a few additional work sheets for non-existent workers so the politically powerful elements of Waterbury society could prosper.

In 1938, as the tumultuous clouds of war threatened, my family moved to Jamestown, Rhode Island, when my dad accepted a guaranteed lifetime position as a machinist at the Naval Torpedo Station. My parents, two sisters, and I survived the devastating hurricane of 1938. The Great New England Hurricane, also known as the Long Island Express, with its storm surge of up to 15 feet remains fixed in my mind. I watched the waters of the Narragansett Bay reach my doorstep. Because of the effects of the hurricane, my family moved from Jamestown to Newport. I became a self-taught swimmer when, as Longfellow stated, "The heart of the great ocean [sent] a thrilling pulse through me."

The war years in Newport, with the influx of all of the military branches, were exciting to a child of my age. The Navy, Coast Guard, Marines, and Army units were constantly on display, and I often visited their barracks, joined in their training parades, and reveled in my family's open-door policy of free transportation and room and board to any military

## Afterward - My Journey to the Castle within the Kingdom (Bob and Me)

personnel. In spite of gas rationing (an "A" decal in the car window – three gallons a week), and a rationed food and meat purchase policy (at times overcome by my mother's secret signal to let the butcher know the fleet was in) the service personnel's home away from home remained intact. One of our guests, a semi-pro boxer, would smuggle sugar and butter from the ship with a wink from the debarking officer.

But in 1945, the government's promise of a lifetime position was no longer a reality and, with the offer of Oak Ridge or Los Alamos as an alternative, neither a friendly option to New Englanders, my family moved back to Waterbury. As a result, I joined the YMCA. While taking the mandatory swim classes, the instructor, an ex-marine, directed me to the volunteer swim coach, Tip Turley. As a nine-year old fifth grader, I had my first exposure to swim competition in the Y's 20-yard oval pool. The training was minuscule; meets were mostly 20-yard races of the three strokes and a freestyle relay, with a championship meet to conclude the season. My dream remained as Masefield wrote:

> I must go down to the seas again, for the call of the running tide
> Is a wild call and a clear call that may not be denied;

After four Y seasons and a gold medal in the breaststroke, high school beckoned. At age 13 and just four feet, 11 inches, and 97 pounds, I entered a new world of competition. The volunteer coach was Jim Farrar, an ex-swimmer, multi-sport athlete in high school, and an ex-Navy swim instructor, who was now employed by the United States Rubber Company. His background was solid, as he swam under the legendary Coach Alex "Gimbo" Sullivan at Naugatuck High School. He coached many former collegiate champions, mostly Michigan graduates, at the Navy's Great Lakes Center and later in Florida during World War II. He is now enshrined in the International Swimming Hall of Fame.

In 1947, two years prior to my attendance, Jim had approached the Principal of Sacred Heart High School, the Rev. John Dial, with the promise of a state championship team in three years. The high school lacked any athletic facilities. However, with the rental of a 20-yard by 17-foot pool from 7:00 to 9:00 p.m. for workouts, Jim won four straight state titles, two New England titles, and a runner-up finish at the Eastern Championships by 1953.

My first exposure to the Payne Whitney pool and Yale swimming was on February 11, 1950, at the 18th Annual Yale Carnival. In complete awe of the whole spectacle, I swam the first leg on a second place high school 300 medley relay team. Kiphuth, still recovering from his heart attack, remained in Florida.

In April 1950, while watching Yale's freshman squad create history by winning the AAU Championship, I saw Kiphuth for the first time. I was fascinated as he unobtrusively disappeared from the pool deck, reappearing in an upper level alcove in order to have a clear view of each championship final.

In the fall of 1951, my coach introduced me to Kiphuth. As we entered the throne room of his Castle (the exhibition pool), the coach extended an arm of friendship, but he had a twinkle in his eye. Then without warning, he gave a deep prolonged and resonant command "swimmers to the blocks!" The workout began and I, frightened but resolute, had entered for the first time the world that belonged to RJHK.

Terrified and under extreme pressure from Kiphuth's retort of, "Who is that in lane one?" I never swam so fast in my life.

I spent the summer of 1952 training on my own in Smith Pond at the YMCA Camp Mataucha in Watertown, Connecticut. Being naive, I decided to enter the National AAU Championships in Newark, New Jersey. In need of an AAU card, I approached the local AAU official, a man of dubious reputation, who convinced me that I should represent his Libra AA Track Club, as it would give me improved status in the eyes of the AAU officials in Newark.

Kiphuth, returning from the Games in Finland and in need of a backstroker, learned of my plight (a swimmer in a track suit) from the chairman of the AAU registration committee in New Haven. He called me at the YMCA camp where I worked and invited me to represent the Yale New Haven Swim Club (YNHSC). I roomed with Yale's "three M's" – Jimmy McLane, Wayne Moore, and John Marshall at the AAU Championships. From that moment onward, Kiphuth became Bob, my mentor.

I continued to represent the Club in indoor and outdoor AAU Championships for seven years, through the summer of 1958. My lifeguard position, 50 miles from Yale during the summers of 1953 and 1954, required a self-imposed regimen of individual lake training. During the summers of 1955, 1956, and 1958, a different lifeguard position 20 miles from Yale allowed me to commute daily to Yale for training. My affiliation with the YNHSC resulted in my being a member of seven national championship teams.

In the 1953 outdoor meet, I finished sixth in the evening final of the 200-meter backstroke, the first time I had ever swum the event. In 1955, at the Los Angeles meet, I finished eighth in the qualifying rounds of the 100 backstroke. At the time, the LA Coliseum pool only had seven lanes. But, thanks to my three great teammates, Dean Hardin, Bill Yorzyk and Sandy Gideonse, our 400 medley team set a meet and American record. During the summers of 1953 and 1954, under the banner of the YNHSC, I won both the annual Bridgeport (two mile) and New Haven (three mile) harbor swims on consecutive days. I established a new record for Bridgeport of 39 minutes, 30 seconds. At the 1956 Olympic Trials in Detroit, I finished 14th in the 100-meter backstroke. I spent the summer of 1957 at ROTC camp, Ft. Bragg, North Carolina. My final meet was the 1958 Outdoor AAU Championships.

My competitive career had drawn to a close. My only regret is that I had never been able to take advantage of Kiphuth's dry land program.

In the fall of 1958, I entered graduate school at Indiana University. Bob wrote to me on a number of occasions requesting information concerning my field of study (history) and the exact topic of my Civil War thesis. He sent his best regards to Indiana University's new swimming coach, James "Doc" Counsilman, and was particularly interested to know how Olympian George Breen was doing, and did I have an insider's view of the "flap" that occurred over whether the judging was biased in the dual meet between Indiana and Ohio State? In return, he kept me abreast of Yale and eastern collegiate swimming.

To my surprise, he called me in the spring of 1959 and asked if I wanted to compete in the Nationals in Daytona Beach. I had to decline such a generous offer as I was concentrating on a strong academic schedule that would allow me to complete my degree by August 1959. After a six-month tour of Europe, I reported to Ft. Benning, Georgia, for active duty in February of 1960. In August of 1960, I returned to teach and coach in Connecticut.

When Kiphuth returned from the 1960 Rome Olympics and opened the door of Yale's indoor 50-meter Olympic pool to any swimmer, male or female (for the first time), interested in training, I was coaching in Connecticut. Beginning the following summer, in 1961, and for the next three summers, I would bring swimmers to Bob's evening workouts to supplement early morning lake training. Bob, as usual, conducted all workouts. Surprisingly, on one occasion, he turned and offered to let me run the workout for my swimmers. It was not until later that I fully realized the extent of this compliment. Bob rarely, if ever, gave a direct compliment to an individual for work well done. The reward should be the work itself. I had been an assistant coach and then head coach at a Connecticut high school, and the team had been very successful. Each of those four years our team, without a pool, won the Yale Carnival scholastic 220-yard freestyle (for high school swimmers), improving by more than six seconds the record that had stood since 1937.

At the end of June 1964, I departed for California. I had accepted an offer from Peter Daland at the Los Angeles Athletic Club.

The competitive relationship between Bob and me lasted seven years, (1952-1958); the professional bond formed during the period of 1960-1964; and after my departure to Los Angeles in 1964, a personal relationship continued until his passing in January 1967. Each phase of our relationship competitive, professional, and personal opened the lens of observation to the strengths and weaknesses of Robert J.H. Kiphuth, the Renaissance Man.

In June 1966, I brought my soon-to-be-bride to meet Bob. Pre-warned by "tales" I had told and my sister's depiction of the man, my future bride questioned in pure innocence, "Should I wear gloves?" As we entered the portals of Payne Whitney, his warm and gracious welcome did not disappoint. But, with a raised eyebrow and perhaps a twinkle in his eye, came the words, "Robbing the cradle are you, Peter?"

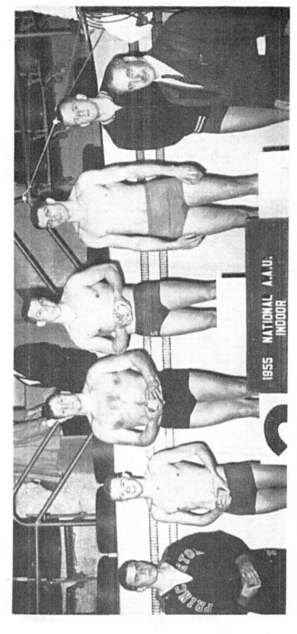

1955 Finalists—400 Medley Relay, Left to Right—John Swabey (Princeton); Peter Kennedy (N.H.S.C.); George Pappas (N.Y.A.C.); Robert Mattson (No. Carolina State); Kerry Donovan (N.H.S.C.); Richard Baker (Univ. North Carolina); Philip Harburger, Chairman, NCAA Records Committee.

# Works Cited

Portions of this book are based upon Peter Kennedy's Ph.D. dissertation: *The Life And Professional Contributions of Robert John Herman Kiphuth To Yale and Competitive Swimming*. The Ohio State University, 1973.

Colwin, Cecil. "Inside Swimming." *International Swimmer*, Jan. 1971, pp. 5–6.

Lovett, Rev. Sydney. Personal interview. 20 Dec. 1972.

Keller, Deane. Personal interview. 20 Dec. 1972.

Knowles, John. "How to Make Champions." *Saturday Evening Post*, 3 Mar. 1956.

Gallagher, J. Roswell, M.D. Personal interview. 20 Dec. 1972.

Michael, Karl. Personal interview. 28 Dec. 1972.

Keller, Deane. Letter to Peter Kennedy. 17 Oct. 1972.

Lovett, Rev. Sydney. Letter to Peter Kennedy. 7 Nov. 1972.

Michael, Karl. Letter to Peter Kennedy. 17 Feb. 1972.

Gallagher, J. Roswell, M.D. Letter to Peter Kennedy. 5 Dec. 1972.

Steadman, Richard "Dick". Personal interview. 8 Apr. 1972.

McGill, John. "New Pool and Ex-President." Message to Peter Kennedy. 24 May 2015. E-mail.

McGill, John. "Body Shaving." Message to Swimming-lore E-mail Group. 3 Feb. 2016. E-mail.

McGill, John. "Going Below 50 Seconds." Message to Peter Kennedy. 24 July 2015. E-mail.

Esselstyn, Caldwell B., Jr., M.D. "Olympic Reflections 50 Years Later." *Dr Esselstyns Prevent Reverse Heart Disease Program*. http://www.dresselstyn.com/site/study-13/.

Brown, Gwyneth King. Letter to Peter Kennedy. 15 Nov. 1972.

Jecko, Tim, John Hanley, and Jeff Farrell. "Kiphuth: A Mighty Fortress." 2002. Book Proposal.

Wright, Alfred. "Yale Churns On at the Water Works." *Sports Illustrated*, 23 Jan. 1956.

Ryan, Jack. Personal interview. 23 Mar. 1972.

# WORKS CITED

Carlile, Forbes. Personal interview. 8 Apr. 1972.

Carlile, Forbes. "A History of Australian Swimming Training." *Swimming Science Bulletin*. Ed. Brent S. Rushall. Swimming Science Journal, 31 Oct. 2004.

Smith, Red. *New York Herald Tribune*, June 1959.

Warner, Chuck. "ISHOF'S Poseidon: More Than A Trophy." *Swimming World*, Aug. 2017, pp. 28–29.

Niawa, Jiro (Japanese Consulate, New York, New York). Telephone interview. 24 July 1973.

"Orders And Medals Of Japan: Highest Honors For Meritorious Service." *Japan*, 1971, p. 27.

"Kiphuth Honored By Japan at Yale." *New York Times*, 28 Feb. 1953, p. 11.

Daland, Peter. Personal interview. 16 Aug. 1972.

Kiphuth, Delaney. Letter to Peter Kennedy. 14 Jan. 1972.

Kiphuth, Delaney. Personal interview. 24 Nov. 1972.

Kiphuth, Delaney. Personal interview. 28 July 1973.

Tonawanda City Directory, Lockport, New York: Robert Brothers, 1913, p. 109.

Gangwish, Meta. Letter to Peter Kennedy. 14 Jan. 1972.

Gangwish, Meta. Personal interview. 16 Jan. 1973.

MacTaggart, Ryrie E. *A Labor History of Buffalo (1846-1917): Containing an Introduction*. 1940.

"YMCA of the Tonawandas, One Thousand Strong." Rand Company, 1906, pp. 1-15.

Downes, Virginia. Letter to Peter Kennedy. 29 Nov. 1972. (Librarian, National Council of YMCAs).

Pierson, George Wilson. *Yale: College, 1871-1937: Vol. 1-2*. New Haven: Yale UP, 1952.

Kiphuth, Robert J. H. "Introduction." *National YMCA Aquatic Program*, vol. 1, Association Press, 1948, p. 7.

*Twentieth Century Club Gymnasium from 1905 to 1915*. Buffalo: Twentieth Century Club, 1915, p. 3-4.

Buffalo Public Library. "Clubs, Associations...of Buffalo Scrapbook," vol. 7, p. 190, 198, 222-23.

# WORKS CITED

"New Gymnasium Instructor." *Yale Daily News*, 13 Oct. 1914, p. 1.

Kistler, George. "Historical Sketch of Intercollegiate Swimming Association." *Intercollegiate Swimming Guide*, 1915, pp. 39–44.

"Swimming In America - 100 Years Ago." *ISHOF.org*, International Swimming Hall of Fame, www.ishof.org/assets/1916-one-hundred-years-ago-in-swimming.pdf.

"Penn Biographies - George Kistler 1864-1942." *Archives.upenn.edu*, University of Pennsylvania, www.archives.upenn.edu/people/1800s/kistler_george.html.

"Ogden Mills Reid." *The National Cyclopaedia of American Biography*, James T. White & Company, 1947, pp. 34–35.

Robert Nelson Corwin Papers, Yale University Athletic Association archives, Yale University Library.

Menke, Frank G. *Encyclopedia of Sports*, 4th rev. ed., A.S. Barnes & Co., 1969, p. 897.

"Matt Mann - Honor Coach." *International Swimming Hall of Fame - The First 100 Honorees* 1966-1970, 1971, p. 75.

"Successful Swimming Year Ends With Banquet To-Night." *Yale Daily News*, 12 Apr. 1918, p. 1.

Kelley, Brooks Mather. *Yale: A History*. Yale University Press, 1974.

Candee, Marjoriee Dent. "Kiphuth, Robert John Herman." *Current Biography, 1957, p. 303.*

Kennedy, Ed. Personal interview. 23 Mar. 1972.

"Holc York Sees Summer Work for Hockeymen." *Yale Daily News*, 29 May 1937, p. 4.

"Bob Kiphuth, Yale's Body-Builder." *The Literary Digest*, 3 Feb. 1934, p. 28.

Carlile, Forbes. *Forbes Carlile on Swimming*. Pelham Books, 1971.

Geigengack, Robert. Personal interview. 27 Dec. 1972.

Dawson, Buck. Personal interview. 9 Apr. 1972.

Oppenheim, Francois. *The History of Swimming*. Swimming World Publishers, 1970.

Counsilman, James E. *The Science of Swimming*. Prentice Hall Inc., 1968, p. 202.

# WORKS CITED

Kiphuth, Robert J. H. *Swimming*. A.S. Barnes & Co., 1942, p 106.

"Navy Challenges Yale to Prove Its Tank Superiority." *New York Times*, 22 Mar. 1922, p. 11.

"Yale Decisively proves Superiority Over Navy Swimmers in Challenge Meet." *New York Times*, 2 Apr. 1922, p. 26.

"Yale Lends Coach to Princeton to Train Swimmers for Meet of the Two Schools." *New York Times*, 4 Mar. 1928, p. 1.

"Yale Swim Coaches Drill Princeton Men: Plan Advanced To Make System Permanent." *New York Times*, 6 Mar. 1928, p. 24.

Moriarty, Phil. Personal interview. 26 Nov. 1971.

Moriarty, Phil. Personal interview. 28 July 1972.

Moriarty, Phil. Personal interview. 17 May 1973.

Moriarty, Phil. Personal interview. 10 July 1973.

Moriarty, Phil. Personal interview. 28 July 1973.

Smith, R. Jackson. Personal interview. 24 July 1973.

Burke, Harry. Personal interview. 27 Dec. 1972.

Kiphuth, Robert J. H. "The Payne Whitney Gymnasium of Yale University." *Research Quarterly*, Mar. 1932, pp. 134–137.

Kiphuth, Robert J. H. "Pool Features." *Yale Daily News*, 10 Dec. 1932, p. 7.

Deegan, William. Yale Swimming 1899-1948. Payne Whitney Gymnasium, Yale University. (unpublished manuscript.)

Effrat, Louis. "Michigan Defeats Yale Swimmers: Wolverines Take Final Event to Win Exciting Meet at New Haven by 41-34." *New York Times*, 17 Feb. 1938.

"Michigan Crushes Yale's Natators." *New York Times*, 12 Feb. 1939.

"Michigan Swimmers Defeat Yale." *New York Times*, 20 Jan. 1940.

Sedgwick, Hubert. "Yale Supremacy in Swimming the Result of Intensive Study." *Boston Evening Transcript*, 7 Jan. 1924. (found in the General Athletic File 1906-25, Archives, Yale University Library).

Treadway, Ken. Letter to Jeff Farrell. 18 Dec. 1999.

Hainsworth, Harry. Personal interview. 17 Feb. 1972.

Kiphuth, Robert J. H. Letter to Peter Kennedy. 17 July 1964.

# WORKS CITED

Kiphuth, Robert J. H. Letter to Peter Kennedy. 20 July 1964.

Farrell, Jeff. *My Olympic Story: Rome, 1960*. Vintage Team Press, 2014.

"Our Four Years With Bob." Yale Class of 1953, undated.

Brown, Gwyneth King. Letter to Peter Kennedy. 15 Nov. 1972.

Munhall, Edgar. Personal interview. 23 Dec. 1972.

Glidden, Germain G. "Robert J. H. Kiphuth." *News From The National Art Museum of Sport, Inc.*, Mar. 1967.

*Yale Alumni Magazine*, Jan. 1951.

*President's Report, 1940*. Yale University, pp. 2-3.

Peters, Dick. Message to Jeff Farrell. 3 Apr. 2000. E-mail.

"Yale Swim Team Routs Ohio State." *New York Times*, 16 Feb. 1941.

"Michigan Outscores Yale, 61 – 58, For Eighth Straight Swim Crown." *New York Times*, 30 Mar. 1941.

"Natatutorees." *Time*, 6 Apr. 1942, p. 58.

Knowles, John. "How to Make Champions." *Saturday Evening Post*, 3 Mar. 1956, p. 91.

McLane, Jim. Telephone interview (recorded). 5 May 2016.

Puffenberger, Jen Moore. Message to Peter Kennedy. 12 Apr. 2016. E-mail.

Puffenberger, Jen Moore, Coliene Moore, and Wayne Moore Family. *Remembering Wayne Moore*.

Sheff, Don. Message to Peter Kennedy. 9 May 2016. E-mail.

Kiphuth, Robert J. H. "Gentlemen." *Yale Swimming News Letter*, June 1951, p. 1.

Murphy, Morgan. "John Marshall." *Ballarat Swimming Club*, www.ballaratswimmingclub.org.au/uploads/2/0/1/4/20147399/johnmarshall.pdf.

"How Fast Can A Man Swim?" *Life*, 7 May 1951, p. 60.

Sheehan, Joseph M. "Yale Dethrones Ohio State; Oyakawa Swims To Second Mark." *New York Times*, 29 Mar. 1953.

Sheehan, Joseph M. "M'Lane Captures 1500 Meter Swim." *New York Times*, 27 Mar. 1953.

# WORKS CITED

Parsons, Peter. "Commander Chick Parsons and the Japanese." *US-Japan Dialogue on POWs*, US-Japan Dialogue on POWs, www.us-japandialogueon-pows.org/Parsons.htm.

Parsons, Peter. Message to Peter Kennedy. 14 June 2015. E-mail.

Parsons, Peter. Message to Peter Kennedy. 13 June 2015. E-mail.

Parsons, Peter. Message to Peter Kennedy. 12 Nov. 2015. E-mail.

"Japanese Mermen Set For Trip To U.S." *New York Times*, 8 Aug. 1949.

Holway, John B. "Japan Beats Us In Baseball; That's The Good News." *The Baseball Guru*, baseballguru.com/jholway/analysisjholway62.htm.

Buege, Bob. "Global World Series: 1955-57." *Sabr.org*, Society for American Baseball Research, sabr.org/research/global-world-series-1955-57.

"Marshall Swim Victor." *New York Times*, 5 Aug. 1951.

Hodak, George A. "1936 Olympic Games - Berlin." *An Olympian's Oral History*, May 1988, library.la84.org/6oic/OralHistory/OHCummings Critchell.pdf. Amateur Athletic Foundation of Los Angeles.

Marvin, Carolyn. "Avery Brundage and American Participation in the 1936 Olympic Games." *Journal of American Studies*, 1982, pp. 81–106. dx.doi.org/10.1017/S002187580000949X.

Kiphuth, Robert J. H. Letter to AAU Foreign Relations Committee. (Date unavailable, but most likely November 1938.)

Kennedy, Doug, "Kiphuth Swimming Champions' Coach Has Own Pool Mark," *New York Tribune*, 4 Feb. 1949, p. 26.

D'Eliscu, Francois, "Bob Kiphuth and His Yale Mermen Leave for the Mainland Today." Unidentified newspaper clipping (likely *Honolulu Advertiser*), 25 Jul. 1930. (1930 Meiji-Yale Dual Meet Scrapbook found at Yale.)

Kiphuth, Robert J. H. "Japan Extends Challenge to American Swimming— Failure of United States to Retain Olympic Swimming Championship due to Economic Conditions." *Yale Daily News*, 15 Dec. 1932, p. 3.

Kiphuth, Robert J. H. "Japan Challenges America in the Water." *Literary Digest*, 12 May 1934, p. 24.

"Japan's Powerful Swimming Organization." *Japan Advertiser*, 11 Aug. 1934.

"Bob Kiphuth: Yale's Body Builder," *The Literary Digest*, 3 Feb. 1934, p. 28.

# WORKS CITED

Fishkind, Silas B. "Kiphuth Yale's Successful Coach." *New York Times*, 6 Mar. 1931.

Kiphuth, Robert J. H. "Furuhashi, World's Champion." *Official Program of the 3rd Keo Nakama Swimming Meet July 5-8*, 1950.

Kiphuth, Robert J. H. Letter to Peter Kennedy. 15 July 1964.

"Yale Coach Would Add 440-Yard Swim." *New York Times*, 21 Mar. 1922, p. 23.

Kiphuth, Robert J. H. "The Old Order Changeth in Collegiate Swimming." *Yale Daily News*, 6 Dec. 1922, p. 1.

Kiphuth, Robert J. H. Letter to Max Ritter. 15 June 1938.

Kiphuth, Robert J. H. Letter to Otto Brewitz. 29 May 1938.

"Record Breakers...ISHOF Speaks With Alan Ford." *Swimming World*, 27 July 2014, www.swimmingworldmagazine.com/news/record-breakers-ishof-speaks-with-alan-ford/.

Guthrie, Frank. Letter to Harry Burke. 19 May 1950.

"Ex-Yale Swim Coach Harry M. Burke Dies." Unknown newspaper, 12 Sep. 1978.

"Funeral Set Friday For Harry M. Burke." *New Haven Register*, 14 Sep. 1978.

Listsky, Frank. "Phil Moriarty, 98, Coach Of Olympians in the Pool." *New York Times*, 22 Aug. 2012.

Moriarty, Phil, Jr. Message to Peter Kennedy. 7 Oct. 2015. E-mail.

Moriarty, Phil, Jr. Message to Peter Kennedy. 14 June 2015. E-mail.

Ahern, Bill. "Looking 'Em Over: The World of Sport." *New Haven Register*.

Ahern, Bill. "Bobby Dawson: Life's Swim Over." *New Haven Register*.

Dawson, Bobbie. Personal interview. 26 Nov. 1971.

Dawson, Bobbie. Personal interview. 5 Aug. 1973.

Cunningham, Allan S. Message to Yale Swimming Lore. 14 June 2015. E-mail.

Schoenfield, Al. Letter to Peter Kennedy. 8 Oct. 1972.

Aubrey, Rex. Message to Peter Kennedy et. al. 23 Feb. 2015. E-mail.

McGill, John. Message to Peter Kennedy. 24 May 2015. E-mail.

Breen, George. Message to Peter Kennedy. 11 Apr. 2017. E-mail.

Chalmers, Gordon. Personal interview. 16 Oct. 1972.

# WORKS CITED

Peppe, Mike. Personal interview. 14 Aug. 1973.

Kennedy, Ed. Personal interview. 23 Mar. 1972.

"Swim Coach Complains; Wants Others Besides Kiphuth to Be Sent on Trips Abroad." *New York Times*, 31 July 1938.

Kiphuth, Robert J. H. "Kiphuth's Comments." *Yale Swimming News Letter*, Summer 1953, p. 2.

"Bob and Yale Honored by 'Omnibus.'" *Yale Swimming News Letter*, Fall 1955, p. 1.

Linden, L. Thomas. "Egg In Your Beer." Harvard Crimson, 3 Nov. 1955.

Dolbey, Jerry. Message to Peter Kennedy. E-mail.

Phair, John Philip. Message to Peter Kennedy. 11 Mar. 2017. E-mail.

Kiphuth, Robert J. H. "Comments from Bob." *Yale Swimming News Letter*, Spring 1958, p. 1.

McGill, John. Message to Peter Kennedy. 24 July 2015. E-mail.

Schoenfield, Albert. "Bob Kiphuth: The Beginning and the End of Swimming's Greatest Era." *Swimming World – Junior Swimmer*, Feb. 1967.

Kiphuth, Robert J. H. "Kiphuth's Comments." *Yale Swimming News Letter*, Summer 1953, p. 2.

Handley, L. de B. "Intercollegiate Swimming Association Review of Season, 1920-21." *Intercollegiate Swimming Guide*. American Sports Publishing Co. 1921, p. 11.

"The Swimming Team's Summer Trip." *Yale Alumni Weekly*, 14 Oct. 1921.

"Eli Swimmers Win at Brighton Beach." *New York Times*, 26 June 1921.

Checkoway, Julie. *The Three-Year Swim Club*. Abacus, 2016.

"Kiphuth Will Coach American Swimmers; Yale Man to Be Both Mentor and Manager of Team Going to Japan." *New York Times*, 26 May 1931.

"Noted Coaches Praise Kiphuth for Victories." *Yale Daily News*, 14 Mar. 1936, p. 6.

"Swim Coach Complains; Wants Others Besides Kiphuth to Be Sent on Trips Abroad." *New York Times*, 31 July 1938.

Hetzler, Peter. "Manager's Report on the Yale Swimming Season, 1948-1949." Manuscript located at Payne Whitney Gymnasium, Yale University.

# WORKS CITED

Jamerson, Richard Elmer. *The Administration of Intercollegiate Swimming in the United States.* Dissertation. Teachers College, Columbia University, 1949.

Saltonstall, Nathaniel. "Manager's Report – Swimming History of the 1950-51 Season." Manuscript located at Payne Whitney Gymnasium, Yale University.

Steele, Leonard E. "Manager's Report – Swimming History of the 1951-52 Season." Manuscript located at Payne Whitney Gymnasium, Yale University.

Randle, John. Personal interview. Jan. 1972. (Assistant librarian, YMCA Historical Library.)

"Kiphuth Beaten Only Six Times." *Yale Daily News*, 14 Mar. 1936, p. 5.

"Water Polo and Swimmer Candidates Won 6 Straight Titles." *Yale Daily News*, 15 Nov. 1917.

"Max Schwartz Retires." *Yale Daily News*, 19 Oct. 1917, p. 2.

"1890—Robert (Bob) Kiphuth—1967." *Amateur Athlete*, Feb. 1967, p. 9.

Daily, George. "Eastern Intercollegiate Swimming Season 1917-18." *Official Swimming Guide 1918-1919.* Thomas E. Wilson & Co., 1920, pp. 65-67.

Kiphuth, Robert J. H. "The Swimming Team's Transcontinental-Hawaiian Trip." *Yale Daily News*, 29 Sept. 1921, p. 7.

"Transcontinental –Hawaii Trip of the Yale Swimming Team." *Intercollegiate Swimming Guide*, American Sports Publishing Co., 1921, pp. 17-19.

"Grudge Fight." *Time*, 28 Feb. 1938, p. 25.

Pratt, C. Dudley. "The Development of Intercollegiate Swimming." *The Book of Athletics*, 1922, pp. 437-38.

Photos Courtesy of Yale University Library Manuscripts and Archives, the International Swimming Hall of Fame, and Peter Kennedy's personal files.

## ABOUT THE AUTHOR

Pete Kennedy was born in Waterbury, Connecticut, January 4, 1936. He began his college education at the University of Notre Dame, and received his A.B. from Niagara University in 1958. He received an M.A. from Indiana University in 1959, and a C.A.S. degree from Fairfield University (Connecticut) in 1962. He earned his Ph.D. from The Ohio State University in 1973. He had a distinguished coaching career at the age-group, high school, and college level for 35 years. He lives in Iowa City, Iowa, with his wife Barbara. He has four children and 13 grandchildren.